Digitalization of the Industry in a Brand New Normal

Tuna Tetik, Ömer Vatanartıran, Hasan Kemal Suher
(Eds.)

Digitalization of the Industry in a Brand New Normal

Media and Art

PETER LANG

Bibliographic Information published by the Deutsche Nationalbibliothek
The Deutsche Nationalbibliothek lists this publication in the Deutsche Nationalbibliografie; detailed bibliographic data is available online at http://dnb.d-nb.de.

Library of Congress Cataloging-in-Publication Data
A CIP catalog record for this book has been applied for at the Library of Congress.

Book Cover by Dilay Özgüven Tetik

Funded by Bahçeşehir University

ISBN 978-3-631-88849-0 (Print)
E-ISBN 978-3-631-89430-9 (E-PDF)
E-ISBN 978-3-631-89431-6 (EPUB)
DOI 10.3726/b20450

Peter Lang – Berlin · Bern · Bruxelles · New York · Oxford · Warszawa · Wien

This publication has been peer reviewed.

www.peterlang.com

To all who courageously question and embrace the new.

Acknowledgements

At first, we are glad to present our gratitude to Şafak Şahin for *Foreword.*

Şafak Şahin, Ph.D.
Assist. Prof. at Bahçeşehir University
Director of BAUKEM
Bahçeşehir University Center of Creative Industries

We are pleased to thank our authors for their comprehensive studies in their *Chapters* and contributors by respecting their university affiliations.

Bülent Sezgin, Ph.D.
Assoc. Prof. at Bahçeşehir University

Çisil Sohodol, Ph.D.
Prof. at Bahçeşehir University

Ece Arıhan, Ph.D.
Inst. at Bahçeşehir University

Dilay Özgüven Tetik, Ph.D.
Grad from Bahçeşehir University

Hakan Erkılıç, Ph.D.
Assoc. Prof. at Mersin University

Hasan Kemal Suher, Ph.D.
Prof. at Bahçeşehir University

Hüseyin Kutay Tinç, Ph.D.
Res. Assist. at İstanbul Technical University

İdil Karademirlidağ Suher, Ph.D.
Prof. at Bahçeşehir University

İsmet Aydın, Ph.D. (c)
Inst. at Bahçeşehir University

Murat Durusoy, Ph.D. (c)
Inst. at Bahçeşehir University

Nilüfer Geysi, Ph.D.
Res. Assist. at Bahçeşehir University

Nisa Yıldırım, Ph.D.
Assist. Prof at İstanbul Gelişim University

Ömer Vatanartıran, Ph.D.
Assist. Prof. at Bahçeşehir University

Özgecan Karadağlı Kuntz, Ph.D.
Assist. Prof. at Bahçeşehir University

Servet Can Dönmez, Ph.D. (c)
Res. Assist. at Mersin University

Sırrı Serhat Serter, Ph.D.
Assoc. Prof. at Anadolu University

Tolga Ovatman, Ph.D.
Assoc. Prof. at İstanbul Technical University

Tuna Tetik, Ph.D.
Assist. Prof. at Bahçeşehir University

Volkan Hacıtahiroğulları, M.Sc.
Res. Assist. at Bahçeşehir University

We would also like to thank Dilay Özgüven Tetik for her extraordinary work on our book's cover.

Tuna Tetik
Ömer Vatanartıran
Hasan Kemal Suher

Editors
Digitalization of the Industry in a Brand New Normal: Media and Art

Tuna Tetik and Ömer Vatanartıran

Preface

Digitalization of the Industry in a Brand New Normal: Media and Art addresses digitalization's transformative effects on the creative industries, highlighting media and art. The book approaches the term, "*the brand new normal*," as the digitalization itself. The chapters are collected from the scholars at Bahçeşehir University Conservatory and the Faculty of Communication with several guest authors. The book is the second partnership of two faculties, which could also be considered as the new collaboration after the book titled *Transformation of the Industry in a Brand New Normal: Media, Music, and Performing Arts* (Tetik, Sezgin, and Vatanartıran, 2022). The collaboration of two faculties brings broad and new perspectives to gain an understanding of the transformative effects of digitalization on several fields from communication to creative industries, and from digital streaming platforms to art in digital. For that matter, the book traces the relation of digitalization to media in general, cinema, theatre, music, and creative industries.

Chapters are centered on many debates and fields of digitalization in media and art, including the market dynamics of NFT (Non-Fungible Token), the current scene of the VR (Virtual Reality) technology, digital video games, digitalization of festivals and digital participation in art events, film language's transformation in the digital streaming platforms, animation productions for digital and creative industries, social media and crises communication, digital self-presentation, the relation of theatre plays to digital platforms, audience development and musical developments in the digital world.

The term, the brand new normal, becomes the digitalization itself.

Undoubtedly, the world is becoming more and more digital in each new day. Moreover, our lives have become more dependent on digital devices, opportunities, and industries. Even this could be argued that digitalization has affected our lives as well as a variety of industries. This contemporary digital techno-culture causes many new debates and recent arguments in the academic field, in which many scholars attempt to bring the field new perspectives. Not only devices and ways of production have become digital, but also exhibition and distribution of the content have moved into digital spaces. These constant, unstoppable, and rapid developments with the help of digital technologies have brought several novelties and a new terminology to the field. That is why consumers, subscribers, users, researchers, scholars, content creators, artists, and producers have struggled to adapt themselves to the recent novelties in the field. Therefore, *Digitalization of the Industry in a Brand New Normal: Media and Art* investigates both advantages and disadvantages of digitalization in specified industries and explores the main changes in the content from the conventional era to the digital one.

This book focuses explicitly on the mutual relationship of media and art in order to develop new debate opportunities on the changing paradigms of arts and humanities, communication, and media theories. It could contribute to the multidisciplinary fields to provide insight to investigate digitalization's effects on creative industries.

In the Foreword, Şafak Şahin evaluates the relation of digitalization to cultural and creative industries regarding media and art through the panorama of the field. Şahin directs and manages a center of creative industries, and his ideas and comments on the scene are comprehensive in the Foreword. In the first chapter, Tuna Tetik proposes a reconsideration of the popular cinema and the subscription video-on-demand platforms' strategies on the content in Turkey through the filmography of Cem Yılmaz. The chapter particularly aims to highlight the popular figures' of Turkish Cinema's connection to the digital. In the second chapter, Nisa Yıldırım focuses on the recent theatre play adaptations in digital. Her chapter showcases that one of the opportunities of digital platforms is the increased visibility of theatre texts in digital adaptations. Dilay Özgüven Tetik examines a unique concept that she calls "reality in quality" through the third chapter, in which Özgüven Tetik analyzes the relation of a fictional reality show in a Turkish original series to the one of the most everlasting Turkish reality shows on broadcast. In the fourth chapter, Ece Arıhan aims to trace the transformation of a popular American animated series on a global SVODs from the perspective of gender theories.

In their chapter, Hakan Erkılıç and Servet Can Dönmez explore the relationship between film language and VR (Virtual Reality) technologies, focusing on the influence of VR on narrative, filmmaking, editing, and production. Besides, the chapter provides to clarify the high-tech-based terminology with many contemporary examples. Sırrı Serhat Serter explains transformation of film festivals into digital and hybrid in his chapter, in which Serter categorizes the characteristics of online events in the digital era.

In the seventh chapter, Volkan Hacıtahiroğulları, Hüseyin Kutay Tinç, and Tolga Ovatman present a significant research on the coloration between player/ user reviews and achievements and player engagement based on Western action role-playing games. In his chapter, Murat Durusoy exhibits and questions contemporary debates on the NTF (Non-Fungible Token) technologies, blockchain system, and digital art and security that include recent researches and reports. In the ninth chapter, Çisil Sohodol, İdil Karademirlidağ Suher, and Nilüfer Geysi propose to examine how Turkish PR practitioners evaluate social media in terms of its threats and opportunities for crisis communication and its effects on the crisis consulting process. The chapter's study is constructed by significant in-depth interviews, conducted with twenty senior PR practitioners from agencies that are members of the Turkish Public Relations Association (TUHID) and the Communication Consultancies Association of Turkey (IDA).

Ömer Vatanartıran examines the changes in ways of self-presentation through the debates on influencership in the digital era. Besides, his chapter includes several arguments on artistic freedom, political correctness, and market demands of the influencers. In the eleventh chapter, Bülent Sezgin aims to discover the transformation of theatricality from live performance to the digitalized stage. In his chapter, Sezgin explores how the digital era transforms the theater stage and artistic performances. İsmet Aydın focuses on crucial aspects of the Turkish music ecosystem within changing musical culture regarding new music trends in the digitalized world. In the thirteenth chapter, Özgecan Karadağlı Kuntz analyzes audience development and digital transformation in classical music with a comprehensive literature review and arguments.

Through the thirteen chapters, *Digitalization of the Industry in a Brand New Normal: Media and Art* centers on contemporary issues on digitalization's transformative effects on filmmaking, film language, and narrative, adaptation ways of theatre texts to digital, VR and NFT technologies, online festivals and events, social media, digital self-presentation, new music trends, player experience and engagement in video games. Therefore, the book proposes to broaden new perspectives on the creative industries, particularly media and art.

Contents

Şafak Şahin

Foreword

On Creative Industries…

It is an undeniable fact that cultural and creative industries have become more attractive, important, and effective not only in developed but also in developing countries in various ways. The creative industries of an economy, the capacity of a society for innovation, and the entrepreneurial zeal of the citizenry are the true triple helix of the social and economic development. It has become "conventional wisdom" that innovation "requires a form of intensive collaboration that goes well beyond the kind of joint ventures and project partnerships we have seen in the past" (Agtmael & Bakker, 2016).

Although cultural and creative industries are at the top of the industries that contain the most areas that continue their way from digitalization, it is also the industry that accepts digitalization the fastest and most often. It incorporates creators who continue their way with classical methods in many different fields from theater to performing arts, from painting to ceramics, etc. However, as can be seen from the working topics in this book, digitized creative works and the rapid rise of creators have been embraced with a synergistic approach. It is obvious when it comes to the digitalization of creative industries; it is obvious that the first areas that come to mind and carry the flag are games, animation, and film-production. Of course, visual design, music, and advertising follow the others as fast digitalizing areas. In the study edited by Massi, Vecco, and Lin (2020), this reality is explained by the title "digital transformation in the cultural and creative industries" by analyzing different aspects. Due to this undeniable fact, two more essential issues grow and come into prominence: sustainable projects in creative industries, and creative entrepreneurship. Also, United Nations celebrated 2021 as the International Year of Creative Economy for Sustainable Development (UNCTAD, 2021).

It is necessary to share with the readers of this book that there is an evidence that proves all these chronological developments, mentioned above, have come to life. This is a brief summary of a youth project implemented by BAUKEM, of which I am the director as the author of this Foreword, in cooperation with the Ministry of Culture and Tourism of Turkey. D-Art House BAU (2022) is a training program for young entrepreneurs who have ideas possible to realize.

During the phase of the call, it is noticed that all the young applicants have creative ideas that can be realized and these ideas generally had the potential to affect or change the World in a positive way as UNCTAD declared about the creativity of sustainability. Another aspect of this Project is that young entrepreneurs are highly motivated to develop art-related digital business models. The fresh art-based innovative ideas are related to very wide range of various issues such as; children, artists, elder people, audiences, art-lovers, LGBT+, animals, and more. This situation can be considered as an indicator of transformation in creative industries in the close future.

As mentioned in the Global Report of UNESCO (Ochai, 2022), "bilateral and multilateral cooperation in the digital and technological fields should include the creative and cultural industries, as these are critical to the digital economy. Similarly, international agreements in the field of culture should have clear outputs related to digital competency development -especially for women, young people and disadvantaged groups." Probably without any information about this declaration, it is understood that young creative brains have also started to think about these issues by integrating digital features.

According to all facts mentioned above, it is seen that all the authors of this book have studied the digital aspects of their specific fields, and also explain the different effects of this digital transformation in the light of technical, theoretical, and social basics. Although each study looks just related to its own field, it can be easily created links between new issues such as NFT, AI, Meta, social media, disruptive technologies, etc. Especially the implementation of these new concepts in the art-based fields can be linked and mind-opening to researchers and academics. Evaluated from all these perspectives, I believe that this book will be a very useful resource for those who will study the effects, contributions, and consequences of digitalization in the creative industries. In particular, it is very important that the different sub-branches of the creative industries are interconnected not only to stimulate the economy but also to contribute to a sustainable world. In this respect, it is obvious that such publications will provide positive benefits to both academia and creative industries in the near future.

References

Agtmael, A., & Bakker, B. (2016). *The smartest places on earth: Why rustbelts are the emerging hotspots of global innovation.* New York: PublicAffairs.

D-Art House BAU. (2022). Meet D-Art House. Retrieved from https://bau.edu.tr/haber/17573-d-art-house-ile-tanisin [Accessed on Sept., 17. 2022].

Massi, M., Vecco, M., & Lin, Y. (2020). *Digital transformation in the cultural and creative industries: Production, consumption and entrepreneurship in the digital and sharing economy*. New York: Routledge.

Ochai, O. (2022). UNESCO Report. Reshaping Policies for Creativity: Addressing Culture as Global Public Good. [Online report]. Retrieved from https://www.unesco.org/reports/reshaping-creativity/2022/en/download-report [Accessed on Sept., 15. 2022].

UNCTAD. (2021). International Year of Creative Economy for Sustainable Development, 2021. Retrieved from https://unctad.org/topic/trade-analysis/creative-economy-programme/2021-year-of-the-creative-economy [Accessed on Sept., 15. 2022].

Tuna Tetik

Turkish Cinema Goes to Digital? Reviewing the Popular Cinema in Turkey on the Filmography of Cem Yılmaz from the Beginning to Netflix

Abstract: This chapter proposes to review the condition of popular cinema in Turkey through one of the most prominent figures, Cem Yılmaz, whose filmography includes commercially successful mainstream comedies, mostly genre parodies, both made for cinema and digital. The majority of Cem Yılmaz movies have become box office winners, which have gathered genre and parody filmmaking together. Cem Yılmaz is known for his stand-up shows and commercially successful movies from the beginning of the 2000s. In 2022, he made an original comedy series aired on Netflix titled *The Life and Movies of Erşan Kuneri* (Cem Yılmaz, 2022-), based on the character called Erşan Kuneri, who had his first appearance in Cem Yılmaz's first box office winner movie, *G.O.R.A.: A Space Movie* (Ömer Faruk Sorak, 2004). *G.O.R.A.* becomes the first installment of a trilogy followed by *A.R.O.G* (Ali Taner Baltacı and Cem Yılmaz, 2008) and *Arif V 216* (Kıvanç Baruönü, 2018). After the appearance of the character, Erşan Kuneri, in a short flashback scene (*G.O.R.A.*, 2004), Erşan Kuneri has a more extensive sequence in *Arif V 216* (2018). Those movies reached significant box office records that marked them in Turkish Cinema. The last return of the character, Erşan Kuneri, is on Netflix in 2022 with a Turkish original series, which is also the first series of Cem Yılmaz in any medium.

The study aims to showcase the current scene in popular Turkish Cinema after the encounter of both national and global video-on-demand services, BluTV, puhutv, Netflix, Exxen, GAIN, Amazon Prime Video, and Disney+, in the market. The first director chairs of Turkish original series and movies on SVODs have mostly given internationally award-winning independent art-house movie directors. However, the release of *T.L.M.E.K* (2022-) on Netflix highlights that the prominent figures of popular Turkish Cinema have started to land on digital. Therefore, the study attempts to bring a new perspective on the current state of Turkish Cinema through popular cinema's one of the most well-known names, Cem Yılmaz, his filmography's characteristics, and *T.L.M.E.K*'s (2022-) way of storytelling.

Keywords: Cem Yılmaz, Turkish Cinema, Popular Cinema, Mainstream, Box Office, Netflix

Introduction

Turkish Cinema and television industry have been in an adaptation process to the encounter of the digital streaming platforms (VODs), BluTV, puhutv, Netflix,

Exxen, GAIN, and Disney+, in the market since the second half of the 2010s. The reaction of the Turkish productions to this encounter is still in progress. From 2015 (the launch of the first Turkish SVODs, BluTV) to 2022 (the present), the Turkish industry has experienced several changes for many reasons, including COVID-19-related occasions. Before mentioning the transfer of Turkish artists, directors, producers, and creators to the VOD services, an understanding of the Turkish Cinema and television industry's dynamics is necessary. Comedy, as a genre, which was also one of the dominant genres of Yeşilçam[1], has been the dominant genre for Turkish productions at Turkey's box office between 2000 and 2021 (Arslan, 2022, p. 461). Besides, Turkish productions in the market have held the high ground that 142 of 220 movies have been Turkish productions in the top ten list of the box office Turkey for twenty-two years (ibid.).

Currently, *Recep İvedik 5* (Togan Gökbakar, 2017), *Recep İvedik 4* (Togan Gökbakar, 2014), *Düğün Dernek* (Selçuk Aydemir, 2013), *Fetih 1453* (Faruk Aksoy, 2012), *Müslüm* (Ketche and Can Ulkay, 2018), *Düğün Dernek 2: Sünnet* (Selçuk Aydemir, 2015), *Ayla* (Can Ulkay, 2017), *Bergen* (Mehmet Binay and Caner Alper, 2022), *7. Koğuştaki Mucize* (Mehmet Ada Öztekin, 2019), and *Aile Arasında* (Ozan Açıktan, 2017) constitute the top 10 list at the box office among both national and foreign productions[2] in Turkey. The total of the movies are mainstream examples, which could be regarded as a crucial part of the popular cinema in Turkey. As it is seen, half of the list consists of comedy movies, including sequels. *Müslüm* (2018) and *Bergen* (2022) are based on the lives and dramatic journeys of two iconic Turkish arabesque singers, whereas the genre of *Fetih 1453* (2012) could be defined as a historical epic. *7. Koğuştaki Mucize*[3] (2019) is a drama, which is a Korean adaptation of a movie[4] with the same title. The data provides to understand the dominance of Turkish comedy movies in the market. Several figures are prominent in Turkish comedies both for cinema and television, including Cem Yılmaz, Şahan Gökbakar, Yılmaz Erdoğan, Ata Demirel, and Ahmet Kural and Murat Cemcir. Şahan Gökbakar is the writer and the actor of the title role of the *Recep İvedik* franchise, currently including six movies that have achieved to reach over 30 million spectator[5] record in total at the box office. *Recep İvedik 5* (2017) is still the leader of the box office, with the 7.4 million spectator record in the theatrical releasing period.

However, *Recep İvedik 7* has been announced as a Turkish Disney+ original movie in-production. Gökbakar (2022) shares the news with a video, in which Gökbakar (2022) describes that "even though Disney is one of the global and major studios, covering many superheroes, there are not any Turkish superheroes on the platform." He continues that "thus, Recep İvedik would be a perfect fit, which audience knows the character's superpower when Gökbakar implies 'farting' with his gestures (Gökbakar, [Tweet video], 2022).

The transfer of the character, Recep İvedik, from bigger screens to the digital platform is an indicator to showcase the current condition of the popular cinema in Turkey. National and global VOD services have produced many Turkish originals[6], including series, movies, and documentaries, for a couple of years. Sarı and Sancaklı (2020, p. 245) mention that "it is necessary to carry out, more specifically, local works to be able to exist in such a [Turkey] market and to carry out long-term productions for global brands."

The first years of national and global VOD platforms' choices have been new generation Turkish directors, who have international and national award-winning independent art-house movies, for the initial original works. BluTV's, as a national (Turkish) SVODs, first original series, *Masum* (*Innocent*, 2017), was directed by Seren Yüce, who is an award-winning art-house movie director whose filmography includes *Çoğunluk* (*Majority*, 2010) and *Rüzgarda Salınan Nilüfer* (2016). *Çoğunluk* (2010) was awarded the Best Debut Film for Luigi De Laurentiis Award at Venice Film Festival (2010), when the movie won many other awards, such as three Golden Oranges at Antalya Golden Orange Film Festival (2010), two Gateway awards at Bombay International Film Festival (2010), and four awards at Turkish Film Critics Association Awards (2010). After BluTV's *Masum* (*Innocent*, 2017), Yüce has become the co-director of Netflix's Turkish original series titled *Kulüp* (*The Club*, 2021-2022).

Likewise, Tolga Karaçelik is regarded as a talented independent art-house movie director whose filmography consists of international award-winning movies, covering *Gişe Memuru* (2010), *Sarmaşık* (*Ivy*, 2015), and *Kelebekler* (*Butterflies*, 2018). When *Sarmaşık* (*Ivy*, 2015) achieved to earn several winnings at Turkey's one of the prestigious film festivals, including Adana Film Festival (2015), Ankara International Film Festival (2016), and Antalya Golden Orange Film Festival (2015), the movie was nominated for the Grand Jury Prize at Sundance Film Festival (2015). Karaçelik's following movie, *Kelebekler* (*Butterflies*, 2018) achieved to win Grand Jury Prize at Sundance Film Festival (2018). After that, he directed a mini-series titled *Bartu Ben* (*I, Bartu*, 2018) for BluTV, and an original series, *Yakamoz S-245* (2022) for Netflix. These examples could be varied with Can Evrenol, the director of the first Turkish Netflix original series called *Hakan: Muhafız* (*The Protector*, 2018-2020), Onur Saylak, the director of the original series, *Şahsiyet* (*Personality*, 2018) for puhutv[7], and *Uysallar* (*Wild Abandon*, 2022) for Netflix. The point is that both Netflix and Turkish VOD services' first choices for the director chair have been internationally award-winning independent Turkish directors for the Turkish (local and national) original content. Popular figures, such as Cem Yılmaz, Yılmaz Erdoğan, and Şahan Gökbakar, of the market had stayed behind when the topic became producing only for digital in the mid-2010s.

However, Yılmaz Erdoğan's *Organize İşler: Sazan Sarmalı* (*Money Trap*, 2019) created a conflict that when the movie was still released in the theaters, it was also aired on Netflix. According to the news by Mehmet Çalışkan at HaberTürk (2019), *Organize İşler: Sazan Sarmalı* (*Money Trap*, 2019) started the theatrical release on February 1, 2019, however the movie was aired on Netflix during the second week of the theatrical release. Even over 2.5 million spectators have watched even the movie in only fifteen days (ibid.).

The beginning of 2019 became a stage for the conflict between producers/directors and movie theatres (Mars Ent. Group) on revenue-sharing, also known as "the popcorn crises" in Turkey. The regulations on movie theatres with eleven changes passed on January 30, 2019. Yazıcı (2020) underlines that "as a result of the failure of reconciliation of cinema enterprises and local production companies, new regulations prepared by the Ministry of Culture and Tourism were enacted." Yazıcı (2020) makes a study titled "*Transforming Cinema Sector and Changing Audience Habits: Evaluation of Law 7163*" and he states that in the study, "the regulations of the Law Amending the Law No. 7163 on "evaluation and Classification of Cinema Films and their Support" which were published in the Official Gazette on 30 January 2019 were examined from the perspective of cinema enterprises." The date, January 30, 2019, was crucial because it indicates the time before the *Organize İşler: Sazan Sarmalı*'s (*Money Trap*, 2019) theatrical release. According to Çalışkan's news (2019), "after the agreement between BKM [Yılmaz Erdoğan] and Netflix, the new cinema law was enacted. *Money Trap* was screened in movie theaters when the problem of campaign tickets was eliminated with the enactment of the law."

The beginning of 2019 witnessed this crisis for the market in Turkey when the ending of 2019 experienced the inception of the major pandemic called COVID-19 that has also affected global cinema. After the silent year for movie theatres, 2020, which has been seriously affected by COVID-19, Yılmaz Erdoğan's (as the writer, not the director) three movies have aired on Netflix, including *Sen Hiç Ateş Böcegi Gördün Mü?* (*Have You Ever Seen Fireflies?*, Andaç Haznedaroglu, 2021), *Kin* (*Grudge*, Türkan Derya, 2021), and *Aşkın Kıyameti* (*Doom of Love*, Hilal Saral, 2022). Therefore, the first encounter of the popular cinema's prominent figures (in other words, box office winners) to an SVODs became Yılmaz Erdoğan. As mentioned above, Şahan Gökbakar's *Recep İvedik 7* is still waiting for Disney+, which could also be regarded as a massive change in the popular cinema of Turkey for questioning do prominent figures start to leave the movie theaters for digital.

This chapter seeks to broaden an understanding of popular Turkish Cinema's prominent figures' (big names) reaction to digital streaming services, VOD, SVOD, AVOD, and TVOD, over Cem Yılmaz's filmography's position in Turkish Cinema, and the meaning of Cem Yılmaz's first original series', *The Life and Movies of Erşan Kuneri* (2022-), release on Netflix. Along with Yılmaz Erdoğan and Şahan Gökbakar, Cem Yılmaz is a prominent figure in the popular cinema of Turkey who is a cartoonist-based comedian, mostly known for his stand-ups and box-office winner mainstream comedies. Currently, Yılmaz has over 15.9 million followers on Twitter[8], while he follows only 257 accounts. Örsler and Kennedy-Karpat (2020, p. 38) mention that "a true multimedia impresario, Yılmaz has also built a successful filmmaking career as a producer, screenwriter, director, and a star." They continue that "no portrait of Turkish popular culture in the twenty-first century would be complete without Cem Yılmaz, though Yılmaz himself would not be who nor where he is in the media pantheon without the waves of production and stardom that set up the media landscape before his arrival" (ibid.). Cem Yılmaz wrote twenty comedy movies in the years between 1998 and 2000, in which he played the leading roles, whereas he directed some of them. Even though he is a mainstream figure in the market, his filmography could be defined as quite divergent when his all works are counted. This chapter's one of the initial objectives is to showcase the popular cinema's current condition in Turkey by scanning Cem Yılmaz's filmography and his latest work, a Turkish Netflix original series titled *The Life and Movies of Erşan Kuneri* (2022-).

The Place of Cem Yılmaz's Filmography in Turkish Cinema and the Next Step to Digital

Cem Yılmaz started his carrier as a stand-up comedian and a caricaturist. In 1998, he had his first role in a feature-length movie titled *Her Şey Çok Güzel Olacak* (*Everything's Gonna Be Great,* Ömer Vargı, 1998), in which he shared the leading role with a well-known Turkish singer Mazhar Alanson. Besides, Cem Yılmaz was the co-writer of the movie with Hakan Kahsun and Ömer Vargı. Significantly, he became famous in Turkey with three stand-up shows, including *Millennium* (1999), *Bir Tat Bir Doku* (1999), and *CMYLMZ* (2001-2007).

As mentioned in the previous subchapter, Yılmaz Erdoğan could also be regarded as one of the prominent figures in the popular cinema of Turkey. Cem Yılmaz has a special guest role in *Vizontele* (Yılmaz Erdoğan and Ömer Faruk Sorak, 2001). *Vizontele* has been released in the movie theatres for forty-nine weeks and achieved to reach 3.3 million spectators. Following that *Vizontele*'s director, Ömer Faruk Sorak, the production company BKM, and Cem Yılmaz came together for a Turkish space adventure parody called *G.O.R.A.: A Space Movie*[9] (Ömer Faruk Sorak, 2004).

The production and the release of the movie were also an adventure. Barış Ergin at BeyazPerde (2004) states that when the production company called TürkFilm, which was the owner of the movie's rights, was seized by TMSF[10], the movie was left half-completed in the post-production process. With the involvement of the Vice Prime Minister in the issue, the rights of *G.O.R.A.* (2004) were transferred to BKM productions. According to Ergin (2004), Cem Yılmaz (as the writer and the leading actor) and Ömer Faruk Sorak (as the director) mentioned that $2 million was given to the production company to complete the post-production process, mostly for special effects, after the conflicts on the movie rights has been solved. Eventually, *G.O.R.A.* was released in theatres on November 12, 2004. Gönül Dönmez-Colin (2014, p. 8) underlines that "the pseudo science fiction, *G.O.R.A.* (Cem Yılmaz, 2004), a parody of *Matrix*, *Fifth Element* and several other similar films, had record earnings of $30 million worldwide." *G.O.R.A.* could be described as a space adventure science fiction parody in which the main character, Arif Işık (Cem Yılmaz), takes a journey to return to the world from the fictional planet called G.O.R.A. after being abducted by a group of aliens.

Even though science fiction is still not a dominant genre in Turkish Cinema, there is a history of unofficial adaptations, pastiches, and parodies. One of the globally well-known Turkish science fiction movies is *Dünyayı Kurtaran Adam* (*The Man Who Saved the World*, Çetin İnanç, 1982). In his book titled "*The Hollywood Meme: Transnational Adaptations in World Cinema*," Iain Robert Smith (2017) analyzes *The Man Who Saved the World*'s (1982) relation to the 1970s Hollywood blockbusters' influence on transnational cinema examples. Smith (2017, p. 68) states that "...*Dünyayı Kurtaran Adam* may initially seem a strange choice in my analysis of transnational adaptation since the film is not itself a remake or a parody, nor does it use the plot or characters from any prior cultural texts." In this respect, the main difference between *The Man Who Saved the World* (1982) and *G.O.R.A.* (2004) is that whereas *G.O.R.A.* (2004) embraces itself as a genre parody, *The Man Who Saved the World* was not a parody, even it has become a cult movie.

In *G.O.R.A.* (2004), Cem Yılmaz played the leading role with secondary and minor roles, such as the villain of the movie named Commander Logar, a Turkish erotic film producer called Erşan Kuneri[11], and Kubar. The movie could also be regarded as a standard "what if" story that questions what if a Turkish man, who is a practical person[12], finds himself in outer space, what he is going to do for his return.

> Similar to globally recognizable Hollywood comedians like Mel Brooks and Mike Myers, Yılmaz commonly portrays more than one character in the same film: protagonists, antagonists, and some supporting roles. The first and still the biggest of Yılmaz's films is *G.O.R.A.: Bir Uzay Filmi* [*G.O.R.A.: A Space Movie*] (2004), a genre parody targeting *Star Wars* (Dir. George Lucas, 1977), *The Matrix* (Dir. The Wachowskis, 1999) and other science fiction touchstones.... (Örsler & Kennedy-Karpat, 2020, p. 40)

After the theatrical release, *G.O.R.A.* (2004) achieved considerable commercial success with over 4 million spectators[13] at the box office. Despite the commercial success of *G.O.R.A.* (2004), Cem Yılmaz's following movie became a road movie titled *Hokkabaz* (*The Magician*, Ali Taner Baltacı and Cem Yılmaz, 2006) instead of the sequel of *G.O.R.A.* (2004). Even though the movie got good reviews from critics, the movie was left behind *G.O.R.A.* (2004) at the box office with 1.7 million[14] spectators. Then, an inevitable sequel of *G.O.R.A.* (2004) called *A.R.O.G* (Ali Taner Baltacı and Cem Yılmaz, 2008) was released on December 5, 2008.

The character, Arif Işık (Cem Yılmaz), is sent 1 million years back in *A.R.O.G* (2008) after his arrival to the world at the ending of *G.O.R.A.* (2004). At this time, the character's main conflict is to civilize the people to invent a time machine to return back to his time. Several characters from *G.O.R.A.* (2004) also appeared in *A.R.O.G* (2008), such as Arif Işık's wife Ceku (Özge Özberk), Commander Logar (Cem Yılmaz), and Tihulu (Muhittin Korkmaz). *A.R.O.G* (2008) is an obvious example of a mainstream movie (*G.O.R.A.*) sequel. Besides, some actors had different roles in *A.R.O.G* (2008) from *G.O.R.A.* (2004), such as Ozan Güven (as Taso) and Özkan Uğur (as Dimi). *A.R.O.G* (2008) became the second highest-grossing movie in 2008 at the box office. Significantly, 2008 is the year when the first *Recep İvedik* movie was released, and it achieved to be the box office leader in Turkey with its 4.3 million[15] spectator record.

In 2010, Cem Yılmaz's following movie called *Yahşi Batı* (*The Ottoman Cowboys*, Ömer Faruk Sorak, 2010) was released that the movie is disconnected from *G.O.R.A.* (2004) and *A.R.O.G* (2008), expect from several Easter eggs and cross-references in dialogs. *Yahşi Batı* (2010) is a Western parody, in which two Ottoman lieutenants take a journey in the Wild West to accomplish a state mission. Yılmaz shared the screen with Ozan Güven and Özkan Uğur again in *Yahşi Batı* (2010). The movie reached 2.3 million[16] spectators at the box office, which made the movie the fourth highest-grossing movie in 2010. Four years after, Yılmaz directed a comedy movie, which has many nostalgic elements from Yeşilçam, titled *Pek Yakında* (Cem Yılmaz, *Coming Soon*, 2014). Conventionally,

Cem Yılmaz played the leading role in the movie, which cast includes similar faces from Cem Yılmaz's filmography, such as Ozan Güven and Özkan Uğur. Different from *G.O.R.A.* (2004), *A.R.O.G* (2008), and *Yahşi Batı* (2010), defining *Pek Yakında* (2014) as a genre parody would not be accurate. These three, *G.O.R.A.*, *A.R.O.G*, and *Yahşi Batı*, challenge characters with huge conflicts, such as an inter-planet adventure, "time travel staff," and an intercontinental-long journey, whereas *Pek Yakında* (2014) tells the story of a character Zafer Yıldız (Cem Yılmaz), whose main motivation is achieving something real by making a movie to prove himself to his wife. Therefore, *Pek Yakında* (2014) and *Hokkabaz* (2006) have more common elements in the narrative.

After *Pek Yakında* (2014), Cem Yılmaz returned to the genre parody with *Ali Baba ve 7 Cüceler* (Cem Yılmaz, *Ali Baba and the Seven Dwarfs*, 2015), which has many similar generic elements to well-known survival-themed movies, such as *The Running Man* (Paul Michael Glaser, 1987) and *Hunger Games* (Gary Ross, 2012). Cem Yılmaz played the leading role, Ali Şenay who finds himself with his workmate in a manhunt in Bulgaria.

However, the total box office records of *Pek Yakında* (1.8 million spectators) and *Ali Baba ve 7 Cüceler* (2.1 million spectators) fell behind *G.O.R.A.* (4 million spectators) at the box office. That signals the return of the character Arif Işık (Cem Yılmaz). Örsler and Kennedy-Karpat (2020, p. 41) also mention that "this decline in [box office] performance indicates a need for innovation in the form, and a full decade after *A.R.O.G*, Cem Yılmaz dialed down his reliance on Hollywood to find different sources of intertextual meaning for *Arif V 216*." In 2018, another *G.O.R.A.* (2004) sequel titled *Arif V 216* (Kıvanç Baruönü) was released in theatres. *G.O.R.A.* (2004), *A.R.O.G* (2008), and *Arif V 216* (2018) constitute a trilogy that Örsler and Kennedy-Karpat (2020) call that "Arif Trilogy." In the movie, Arif and his robot friend 216 (Ozan Güven)[17] travel to 1969 with a time machine. Similar to *Pek Yakında* (2014), *Arif V 216* (2018) has many moments to show Cem Yılmaz's adore to Yeşilçam, or in other words, the good old days with parodic, referential, and pastiche elements. Örsler and Kennedy-Karpat[18] (2020, p. 43) indicate that "*Arif V 216*'s vision of twenty-first-century Turkey argues that hate, egoism, and asperity have displaced the kindness and community-building spirit of the 1960s and 1970s..." *Arif V 216* (2018) could be also regarded as "a genre-savvy parody," which could be regarded as "Cem Yılmaz's trademark" (Örsler and Kennedy-Karpat, 2020, p. 4). With *Arif V 216* (2018), Cem Yılmaz returned to his box-office winner performance. *Arif V 216* (2018) reached 4.9 million spectators in twenty weeks that made the movie second highest-grossing movie[19] in 2018 at the box office.

Importantly, Cem Yılmaz's position in Turkish Cinema is not only all about commercial success, box office achievements, and generic characteristics of the movies but also his acting choices and performances in non-Cem Yılmaz productions. He played leading and supporting roles in some Turkish and foreign movies, which are critically acclaimed and/or commercially successful, including *Organize İşler* (Yılmaz Erdoğan, *Magic Carpet Ride*, 2005), *Av Mevsimi* (Yavuz Turgul, *Hunting Season*, 2010), *Magnifica Presenza*, (Ferzan Özpetek, *A Magnificent Haunting*, 2012), *The Water Diviner* (Russell Crowe, 2014), and *İftarlık Gazoz* (Yüksel Aksu, *61 Days*, 2016).

Besides, Cem Yılmaz tried to experiment with making "double-featurettes," including two middle-length movies in one feature-length film with *Karakomik Filmler* (*ComiDark Films*, Cem Yılmaz, 2019) and the sequel (Cem Yılmaz, 2020). Both double-featurettes, *Karakomik Filmler* (700K spectators in eight weeks) and *Karakomik Filmler 2* (440K spectators in seven weeks), became crucial box office flops in Cem Yılmaz's filmography. This commercial failure could be explained with several reasons, such as the quality of the content, the structure of the movies as double-featurettes, releasing time of the sequel during COVID-19, and many other causes.

Nevertheless, Cem Yılmaz is a prominent figure of the popular cinema in Turkey, especially for the commercial potential of any work. Even Cem Yılmaz released his stand-up show titled "*CM101MMXI Fundamentals*" (2013) in movie theatres, which reached 3.8 million spectators that led the production to be the second position in the list of 2013's the highest grossing movies at the box office. However, seven years after the theatrical release of "*CM101MMXI Fundamentals*," Cem Yılmaz's choice for the latest stand-up show to release the production is digital. *Cem Yılmaz: Diamond Elite Platinum Plus* was aired on Netflix on the last day of 2021. That choice also foreshadows the relationship between Cem Yılmaz and Netflix. Shortly after, Cem Yılmaz's first comedy series called *The Life and Movies of Erşan Kuneri* (Cem Yılmaz, 2022-) was aired on Netflix, including eight episodes in one season. The series is based on the adventures and ambitions of the character named Erşan Kuneri, which first appeared in *G.O.R.A.* (2004), then *Arif V 216* (2018). Therefore, "Arif Trilogy" becomes "Arif Universe" with a spin-off comedy series on a global SVODs, Netflix.

From Bigger Screens to Netflix: *The Life and Movies of Erşan Kuneri* (2022-)

The Life and Movies of Erşan Kuneri[20] (Cem Yılmaz, 2022-) is Cem Yılmaz's latest work on Netflix, which is also his first series in any medium. Before *T.L.M.E.K*, he appeared in a few television series as a one-episode guest star (in other words, a cameo), such as *Canım Ailem* (2008-2010), *Avrupa Yakası* (*The European Side*, 2004-2009), and *Fi*[21] (*Phi*, 2017-2018).

T.L.M.E.K centers on the story of Erşan Kuneri (Cem Yılmaz) firstly appeared in a flashback scene in *G.O.R.A.* (2004). In one hundred and thirty-five-second-long flashback, Kuneri is portrayed as a Turkish erotic film producer in 1980. In Turkish Cinema history, the years between 1974 and 1979 are marked as an erotic (also defined as sex films) movie period (Scognamillo and Demirhan, 2000, p. 141). According to them (2000, p. 163), the story in many movies was just a tool to logicize to combine several sex and nudity-included scenes. While some movies' sex and nudity-included scenes were dominant during that period, some movies were regarded as erotic comedies in a short cycle. One of the prominent actors in these erotic comedies is Aydemir Akbaş. The logic of narrated and hastily displayed events is not essential in these movies. The important thing is that Aydemir Akbaş plays the leading role, displays his little jokes and gestures, and makes love uniquely (Scognamillo and Demirhan, 2000, p. 169). This period could be explored for industry-related reasons, the spread of television, the sociological and economic condition of the country, and many other causes. Arslan (2011, p. 20) indicates "...the rising popularity of 16 mm sex films aimed at a young male group of spectators primarily from migrant families in the cities." One way or the other, these movies are part of Turkish Cinema history. According to Arslan (2011, p. 101), "these sex films maintained Yeşilçam's filmmaking patterns and filmic texts."

Erşan Kuneri is also a fictional figure, a character who has a part in this history. In the flashback scene of *G.O.R.A.* (2004), Erşan Kuneri auditions for the male-casting of a new sex film when his friend, Bob Marley Faruk (Rasim Öztekin), pitches him a Turkish science fiction movie idea. At the end of the scene, the police arrests Erşan Kuneri for illegal tobacco trade on September 12, 1980, the date of the 1980 military coup. Fourteen years after the character's first appearance, Erşan Kuneri appears within a more extensive sequence. In *Arif V 216* (2018), Erşan Kuneri is represented as a music club owner, film lover, and music producer in the late-1960s. In *Arif V 216*'s Erşan Kuneri sequence, two Cem Yılmaz depictions, Arif Işık and Erşan Kuneri, come together. The movie becomes the last movie installment in the "Arif Trilogy."

A spin-off series based on Erşan Kuneri aired as a Netflix original in 2022. Obviously, Cem Yılmaz played the title role with many other roles. The narrative structure of each episode consists of two main parts, including one opening act, in which Erşan Kuneri and his film crew attempt to make a particular genre film, and an approximately twenty-five-minute-long movie that the characters made. As mentioned in the previous subchapter, one of Cem Yılmaz films' characteristics is being a genre parody. In *T.L.M.E.K* (2022-), Erşan Kuneri and his crew make seven different movies in different genres, such as a period action film, a horror movie, a country drama, a melodrama, a detective drama, and a superhero movie. Like Cem Yılmaz, Erşan Kuneri plays the leading role in each episode's movie part.

One of the statements of the study is that "Arif Trilogy" becomes "Arif Universe" within *T.L.M.E.K* (2022-). Because *T.L.M.E.K* is not only a spin-off series but also a connecting narrative of Cem Yılmaz's filmography. Even though there is no generic or narrative bond between "Arif Trilogy" and *Pek Yakında* (2014), *T.L.M.E.K* (2022-) links the two in a contemporary way. The character, Ahben Soner (Zafer Algöz), is portrayed as a retired Yeşilçam director who teams up with Zafer Yıldız (Cem Yılmaz) to make a movie, which announces his "magnificent" return to Turkish Cinema with a science fiction movie called *Şahikalar* in *Pek Yakında* (2014). Like Erşan Kuneri's friend Bob Marley Faruk's ambition to the science fiction genre in *G.O.R.A.* (2004), Ahben Soner has a dream project in the science fiction genre in *Pek Yakında* (2014). The character, Ahben Soner, appears as a young and ambitious concept artist who tries to convince Erşan Kuneri and his film crew of his futuristic production design templates in *T.L.M.E.K* (2022-).

The appearance of Ahben Soner in *T.L.M.E.K* (2022-) is notable because it is the point that gathers *G.O.R.A.* (2004), *A.R.O.G* (2008), *Pek Yakında* (2014), *Arif V 216* (2018), and *T.L.M.E.K* (2022-) together into the "Arif Universe." Although Arif Işık and Ahben Soner do not come together in any productions, Arif Işık's friend, Bob Marley Faruk, knows Erşan Kuneri who knows Ahben Soner in the "Arif Universe."

As stated before, genre parody is significant for Cem Yılmaz's movies. Even his filmography includes two double-featurette movies, respecting thriller and science fiction genres. Making a comedy series on an SVODs, Netflix, gives him opportunities to play various genres through eight episodes. That is why Cem Yılmaz's Netflix series consists of Erşan Kuneri's seven different movies, including *Dry Murad*, *The Midwife's Hunt*, *Cooperative Kemal*, *Bad Stuff*, *Faqbadi*, *Er-man*, and *Couldn't Get Enough*. Precisely, all of them are genre parodies, even though Erşan Kuneri and his film crew's purpose is not to make a parody. Thus, this could be stated that Cem Yılmaz's narrative style in these movies makes the movies parodies, whereas Erşan Kuneri intends to make a genre film, including some erotic plots rooted from his erotic film producer background.

Conclusion

From 1998 to 2020, Cem Yılmaz movies[22] reached over 24 million spectators[23] at the box office. *T.L.M.E.K* (2022-) could be seen as a turning point in Cem Yılmaz's filmography that could also be regarded as his determination for digital. As underlined many times in the study, even though his filmography consists of box office-winning productions, his last two movies, *ComiDark Films* (2019) and the sequel (2020), were mentioned as box office flops with 1.1 million spectators[24] in total. The Netflix original, *T.L.M.E.K* (2022-), is Cem Yılmaz's first production after the box office failures. Despite many possible speculative readings for the medium-changer data at the box office, in fact, Cem Yılmaz's releasing place is changed from movie theatres to digital.

Melisa Eyiakkan and Elif Obdan at Netflix (2022) announce that "Cem Yılmaz signs a multi-project deal with Netflix." The press statement also declares *T.L.M.E.K* (2022-) as "the most viewed local show on Netflix in Turkey in its first month" (ibid.). When the second season of *T.L.M.E.K* (2022-) is announced and planned to be released in 2023, the details of the deal between Cem Yılmaz and Netflix are shared that "Cem Yılmaz and Netflix have also settled for a multi-project deal including multi-format content with 6 series, films and stand up shows in total" (ibid.). Interestingly, the deal includes a Netflix original Turkish movie titled *Do Not Disturb* (in pre-production), which is based on the story of the character called Ayzek firstly appeared in one of the double-featurettes in *ComiDark Films* (2019). *Do Not Disturb* can open a new dimension in "Arif Universe" or other projects in Cem Yılmaz's filmography with transmedia cross-overs, such as the character Ahben Soner. Therefore, especially with Ahben Soner as an example, this could be mentioned that narratives and characters in his filmography overflow from movie theatres to digital.

Likewise, Şahan Gökbakar[25] is an up-front figure in popular cinema whose trademark character Recep İvedik is waiting to be presented on Disney+ within the sixth sequel. The character Recep İvedik was firstly appeared in a sketch show titled *Dikkat Şahan Çıkabilir* (2005-2006), then the character was transferred to the cinema in 2008.

As observed, the launch of national VODs and operations of global SVODs in the market are worth to be examined to gain an understanding of Turkish Cinema's current scene. At first, independent art-house movie directors have begun to work with these digital platforms, then the prominent figures of popular cinema started to be on digital. That is why the transition of Yılmaz Erdoğan, Şahan Gökbakar, and Cem Yılmaz[26] from movie theatres to digital should be marked to comprehend popular cinema in Turkey, especially in the 2020s. This could also be stated that the competition between the popular cinema's figures in Turkey is moving from the box office records to viewing rates.

Filmography

Açıktan, O. (2017). *Aile Arasında.* [Motion picture]. Turkey: BKM Film Productions.

Aksoy, F. (2012). *Fetih 1453.* [Motion picture]. Turkey: Aksoy Film Production.

Aksu, Y. (2016). *İftarlık Gazoz* [*61 Days*]. [Motion picture]. Turkey: NuLook Productions.

Atabey Özbek, J., & Algül, H. (2004-2009). *Avrupa Yakası* [*The European side*]. ATV. [Television series]. Turkey: Plato Film Productions.

Aydemir, S. (2013). *Düğün Dernek.* [Motion picture]. Turkey: BKM Film Productions.

Aydemir, S. (2015). *Düğün Dernek 2: Sünnet.* [Motion picture]. Turkey: BKM Film Productions.

Baltacı, T. A., & Yılmaz, C. (2008). *A.R.O.G.* [Motion picture]. Turkey: CMYLMZ Fikir Sanat Productions.

Baruönü, K. (2018). *Arif V 216.* [Motion picture]. Turkey: CMYLMZ Fikir Sanat Productions and NuLook Productions.

Baykal, M. (2017-2018). *Fi* [*Phi*]. [puhutv original series]. Turkey: Ay (Yapım) Film Productions.

Besson, L. (1997). *The fifth element.* [Motion picture]. France: Gaumont.

Binay, M., & Alper, C. (2022). *Bergen.* [Motion picture]. Turkey: Orchestra Content.

Celen, S. (2008-2010). *Canım Ailem.* ATV. [Television series]. Turkey: TMC Productions.

Crowe, R. (2014). *The water diviner.* [Motion picture]. Australia and United States: RatPac Entertainment and Seven Network Australia.

Erdoğan, Y., & Sorak, F. Ö. (2001). *Vizontele.* [Motion picture]. Turkey: BKM Film Productions.

Erdoğan, Y. (2005). *Organize İşler* [*Magic carpet ride*]. [Motion picture]. Turkey: BKM Film Productions.

Erdoğan, Y. (2019). *Organize İşler: Sazan Sarmalı* [*Money trap*]. [Motion picture]. Turkey: BKM Film Productions.

Evrenol, C., Aral, U., Tiryaki, G., Alptekin, B., & Uyanık, G. (2018-2020). *Hakan: Muhafız* [*The Protector*]. [Netflix original series]. Turkey: O3 Media.

Derya, T. (2021). *Kin* [*Grudge*]. [Motion picture]. Turkey: BKM Film Productions.

Glaser, M. P. (1987). *The running man.* [Motion picture]. United States: Braveworld Productions and Taft Entertainment.

Gökbakar, T. (2014). *Recep İvedik 4.* [Motion picture]. Turkey: Çamaşırhane Film Productions.

Gökbakar, T. (2017). *Recep İvedik 5.* [Motion picture]. Turkey: Çamaşırhane Film Productions.

Gökbakar, T. (n.d.). *Recep İvedik 7.* [Motion picture]. Turkey: Çamaşırhane Film Productions.

Haznedaroglu, A. (2021). *Sen Hiç Ateş Böcegi Gördün Mü? [Have you ever seen fireflies?]*. [Motion picture]. Turkey: BKM Film Productions.

İnanç, Ç. (1982). *Dünyayı Kurtaran Adam [The man who saved the world]*. [Motion picture]. Turkey: Anıt Film Productions.

Karaçelik, T. (2010). *Gişe Memuru.* [Motion picture]. Turkey: Karaçelik Film Productions and BKM Film Productions.

Karaçelik, T. (2015). *Sarmaşık [Ivy]*. [Motion picture]. Turkey: Karaçelik Film Productions.

Karaçelik, T. (2018). *Kelebekler [Butterflies]*. [Motion picture]. Turkey: Karaçelik Film Productions.

Karaçelik, T. (2018). *Bartu Ben [I, Bartu]*. [Blutv original series]. Turkey: Karaçelik Film Productions and BKM Film Productions.

Karaçelik, T., & Aral, U. (2022). *Yakamoz S-245.* [Netflix original series]. Turkey: OGM Pictures.

Ketche, & Ulkay, C. (2018). *Müslüm.* [Motion picture]. Turkey: Dijital Sanatlar [Digital Arts].

Lee, H.-K. (2013). *7-beon-bang-ui seon-mul.* [Motion picture]. South Korea: Fineworks/CL Entertainment.

Lucas, G. (1977). *Star Wars: Episode IV-A new hope.* [Motion picture]. United States: Lucas Film.

Mestçi, A. (2005-2006). *Dikkat Şahan Çıkabilir.* TV8 & ATV. [Television show]. Turkey: Dada Film.

Özpetek, F. (2012). *Magnifica Presenza [Magnificent presence* a.k.a. *A magnificent haunting]*. [Motion picture]. Italy: Fandango, Faros Film, and Rai Cinema.

Öztekin, A. M. (2019). *7. Koğuştaki Mucize.* [Motion picture]. Turkey: O3 Media.

Ross, G. (2012). *Hunger games.* [Motion picture]. United States: Lionsgate and Color Force.

Saral, H. (2022). *Aşkın Kıyameti [Doom of love]*. [Motion picture]. Turkey: BKM Film Productions.

Saylak, O. (2018). *Şahsiyet* [*Personality*]. [puhutv original series]. Turkey: Ay (Yapım) Film Productions.

Saylak, O. (2022). *Uysallar* [*Wild abandon*]. [Netflix original series]. Turkey: Ay (Yapım) Film Productions.

Sorak, F. Ö. (2004). *G.O.R.A.: A space movie.* [Motion picture]. Turkey: BKM Film Productions & Böcek Productions.

Sorak, F. Ö. (2010). *Yahşi Batı* [*The Ottoman Cowboys*]. [Motion picture]. Turkey: Böcek Productions and Fida Film.

Turgul, Y. (2010). *Av Mevsimi* [*Haunting season*]. [Motion picture]. Turkey: Fida Film and ProFilm.

Yılmaz, C. (2022-). *The life and movies of Erşan Kuneri.* [Netflix original series]. Turkey: CMYLMZ Fikir Sanat Productions.

Yılmaz, C. (2014). *Pek Yakında* [*Coming soon*]. [Motion picture]. Turkey: NuLook Productions and CMYLMZ Fikir Sanat Productions.

Yılmaz, C. (2015). *Ali Baba ve 7 Cüceler* [*Ali Baba and the seven dwarfs*]. [Motion picture]. Turkey: NuLook Productions and CMYLMZ Fikir Sanat Productions.

Yılmaz, C. (2019). *Karakomik Filmler* [*ComiDark Films*]. [Double featurettes]. Turkey: CMYLMZ Fikir Sanat Productions.

Yılmaz, C. (2020). *Karakomik Filmler 2* [*ComiDark Films 2*]. [Double featurettes]. Turkey: CMYLMZ Fikir Sanat Productions.

Yılmaz, C. (n.d.). *Do not disturb.* [Motion picture]. Turkey: CMYLMZ Fikir Sanat Productions.

Yüce, S. (2010). *Çoğunluk* [*Majority*]. [Motion picture]. Turkey: Yeni Sinemacılar [New Filmmakers].

Yüce, S. (2016). *Rüzgarda Salınan Nilüfer* [Motion picture]. Turkey: Motiva Film and Yeni Sinemacılar [New Filmmakers].

Yüce, S. (2017). *Masum* [*Innocent*]. [BluTV original series]. Turkey: D Productions.

Yüce, S., & Tan, G. Z. (2021-2022). *Kulüp* [*The Club*]. [Netflix original series]. Turkey: O3 Media.

The Wachowskis. (1999). *The Matrix.* [Motion picture]. United States: Warner Bros.

Ulkay, C. (2017). *Ayla.* [Motion picture]. Turkey: Dijital Sanatlar [Digital Arts].

Vargı, Ö. (1998). *Her Şey Çok Güzel Olacak* [*Everything's Gonna be great*]. [Motion picture]. Turkey: Filma-Cass.

Notes

1 According to Arslan (2011, p. 17), "instead of postulating Yeşilçam as a category of a culture industry of popular filmmaking, Yeşilçam is the name given to the filmmaking practice in Turkey roughly between 1950 and 1990."
2 Data in the top ten list was formed by both national and foreign productions, which have been released in Turkey since 1989. The data was retrieved from boxofficeturkey.com [Accessed on Sept., 25. 2022].
3 Internationally known as *Miracle in Cell No. 7* (2019).
4 *7-beon-bang-ui seon-mul* (Hwan-kyung Lee, 2013).
5 Data was retrieved from boxofficeturkey.com [Accessed on Sept., 25. 2022].
6 These productions are local for global brands. Some productions, which Turkish platforms have produced, are described as national productions in this study.
7 The only Turkish AVOD service.
8 Retrieved from https://twitter.com/CMYLMZ [Accessed on Sept., 25. 2022].
9 Here after, *G.O.R.A.*
10 Savings Deposit Insurance Fund of Turkey.
11 A character in a flashback.
12 With the character's, Arif Işık (Cem Yılmaz), definition for himself in *G.O.R.A.* (2004).
13 Retrieved from https://boxofficeturkiye.com/film/g-o-r-a--2004171 [Accessed on Sept., 1. 2022].
14 Data was retrieved from https://boxofficeturkiye.com/film/hokkabaz--2006190 [Accessed on Sept., 25. 2022].
15 Data was retrieved from https://boxofficeturkiye.com/yillik/2008/tum-filmler [Accessed on Sept., 25. 2022].
16 Data was retrieved from https://boxofficeturkiye.com/yillik/2010 [Accessed on Sept., 25. 2022].
17 The first appearance of the character 216 (Ozan Güven) is in *G.O.R.A.* (2004) as a fellow (in other words, a sidekick) of Arif Işık (Cem Yılmaz).
18 Örsler and Kennedy-Karpat's (2020) article titled "*Cem Yılmaz and Genre Parody in Turkish National Cinema*" is a comprehensive study to investigate Cem Yılmaz filmography's characteristics, conventions, roots, and inspirations while questioning their relation to "mid-twentieth-century Yeşilçam and to the *meddah* storytelling tradition."
19 Data was retrieved from https://boxofficeturkiye.com/yillik/2018/tum-filmler [Accessed on Sept., 25. 2022].
20 Here after, *T.L.M.E.K.*
21 On the Season 1, Episode 4 (2017).
22 Films, in which Cem Yılmaz is at least the leading role and writer, were counted.

23 Data was retrieved from boxofficeturkey.com [Accessed on Sept., 29. 2022].
24 Data was retrieved from boxofficeturkey.com [Accessed on Sept., 29. 2022].
25 Both play the leading roles and write the scripts in their movies.
26 As the focus of the study.

References

Arslan, S. (2011). *Cinema in Turkey: A new critical history*. Oxford: Oxford University Press.

Arslan, S. (2022). *Türkiye'de sinemanın tarihi: Başlangıçtan günümüze* [*Cinema's history in Turkey: From the beginning to the present*]. İstanbul: Kronik Book Publishing.

Çalışkan, M. (February 19, 2019). Why Money Trap is on Netflix?. *HaberTürk*. Retrieved from https://www.haberturk.com/organize-isler-sazan-sarmali-neden-netflix-te-de-var- 2375164 [Accessed on Sept., 20. 2022].

Dönmez-Coin, G. (2014). *The Routledge dictionary of Turkish Cinema*. London and New York: Routledge.

Ergin, B. (May 4, 2004). Ve G.O.R.A. Esaretten Kurtuldu!!! [And G.O.R.A. Freed from Captivity!!!]. *BeyazPerde*. Retrieved from https://www.beyazperde.com/haberler/filmler/haberler-4751/ [Accessed on Sept., 3. 2022].

Eyiakkan, M., & Obdan, E. (July 5, 2022). Cem Yılmaz Signs a Multi-Project Deal with Netflix. [Press statement]. *Netflix*. Retrieved from https://about.netflix.com/en/news/cem-yilmaz-signs-a-multi-project-deal-with-netflix [Accessed on Sept., 17. 2022].

Gökbakar, Ş. [sgokbakar]. (June 7, 2022, 06:06 P.M.). Recep İvedik 7 on Disney+. [Tweet video].

Örsler, M. M., & Kennedy-Karpat, C. (2020). Cem Yılmaz and genre parody in Turkish national cinema. *Journal of Popular Film and Television*, *48*(1): 38–48. DOI: 10.1080/01956051.2019.1657060

Sarı, Ü., & Sancaklı, P. (2020). The effect of globalizaton on digital platforms' promotion of content: The Netflix example. *Erciyes İletişim Dergisi* [*Communication Journal of Erciyes*], *7*(1): 243–260.

Scognamillo, G., & Demirhan, M. (2000). *Erotik Türk sineması* [*Erotic Turkish cinema*]. Turkey: Kabancı Publishing.

Smith, R. I. (2017). *The Hollywood meme: Transnational adaptations in world cinema*. Edinburg University Press.

Yazıcı, F. (2020). Transforming cinema sector and changing audience habits: Evaluation of law 7163. *International Journal of Society Researches*, *15*(22): 1435–1459.

Nisa Yıldırım

Stage to Digital Screen: Theatre Play Adaptations in Turkish Streaming Services

Abstract: With the launch of streaming services in the last decade, the television industry has begun to deal with the hunger for content more than ever. As the original screenplays could not satisfy the demand in this turmoil, adaptations from different art forms continue to be a lifesaver for the creators. Even though literature has still been the greatest source for adaptations since the beginning of cinema and television, classical and modern theatre plays are also being preferred as an alternative. Different from a literature text which offers freedom to the writer to use descriptions to implant all details to the narrative, being based on stage with limited visualization makes dialog the main element for the transfer of the whole text of a theatre play. On the other hand, a stage-to-screen adaptation allows the play text to transcend the boundaries of time and space. In 2021, Turkish streaming service GAIN released two mini-series adapted from theatre plays. The first one, *Metot* (*Method*, Serkan Keskin, 2021), which focuses on the relentless competition of four white-collar workers in a job interview, was adapted with high level of fidelity to the main text, and thus suits Geoffrey Wagner's "transposition" model. While the other series *Hamlet* (Kaan Müjdeci, 2021) with its extremely local evil uncle who corrupts the town, appears as a different example, and suits Wagner's "commentary" model by retelling Shakespeare's original text with codes of eastern culture in 21st century. In conclusion, it's possible to argue that, regardless of their model, adaptations give theatre plays new spirits to survive forever in our digital libraries.

Keywords: Streaming Services, Series, Turkish Series, Adaptation, Theatre Play

Introduction

Adaptation can be defined as transferring the text of an art work into a new medium. As an alternative to literature texts, theatre play has been the art form which nurtures cinema since the silent film era. If we exclude Shakespeare and Chekov plays, it not easy to find globally popular examples, if they do not have a stage-to-screen adaptation such as *Cat on a Hot Tin Roof* (1958), *Who's Afraid of Virginia Woolf?* (1966), *Amadeus* (1984), *Driving Miss Daisy* (1989), *A Few Good Men* (1992), *The Crucible* (1996), *Closer* (2004) or *Carnage* (2011). Today, theatre has still been regarded as high art while cinema and television stand for the source of entertainment for masses. Stage-to-screen adaptations are reaching millions of audience with their dubbed or subtitled versions all over the world.

Adaptations allow play texts to go beyond the borders of their motherland. In addition to cinema, television had also knocked on the door of theatre too. However, television had adopted a different strategy and broadcast theatre plays live as "television plays" in its early era. Although these plays do not have all the proper features that a television production should have, they can be defined as adaptation, because they are transferred from stage to the screen, and have the touch of a television director (Kale, 2019, p. 128).

In Turkey, first television broadcast was occurred in the evening of January 31, 1968 by the official channel of the state named TRT [Turkish Radio and Television Corporation]. One week later, first drama was broadcast which was a theatre play of İbrahim Şinasi named *Şair Evlenmesi* (*The Marriage of Poet*) performed live in the television studio (Kale, 2019, p. 127). Then, it was followed by plays like Oktay Rıfat's *Yağmur Sıkıntısı* (*Boredom of Rain*), Reşat Nuri Gültekin's *Hülleci* (*Fake Husband*), Ahmet Kutsi Tecer's *Köşebaşı* (*Corner*), Melih Cevdet Anday's *Mikado'nun Çöpleri* (*Rods of Mikado*), and Nezihe Araz's *Çorak Toprak* (*Bitter Earth*). According to Kale (2019, p. 129), "from 1971, Turkish television audience has met with foreign-sourced drama series and feature films, mostly US productions." In the monopoly era of TRT which lasts more than twenty years until the establishment of private television channels, literature adaptations appear as the main source of fiction beside exported content. During this era, theatre play adaptations were also adapted as television drama in TRT. One of the most popular one of these adaptations was Haldun Taner's *Keşanlı Ali Destanı* (*Legend of Ali from Keşan*) released as a miniseries in 1988, and re-adapted again as series with the same name by a private channel named Kanal D in 2011. In addition to television content, theatre plays have also been adapted as movies in Turkey. The most popular stage to screen movies are Güner Sümer's *Bozuk Düzen* (*Corrupt Order*) in 1966, Aziz Nesin's *Yaşar Ne Yaşar Ne Yaşamaz* (*Yaşar, Neither He Lives nor He Doesn't*) in 1974, Vasıf Öngören's *Asiye Nasıl Kurtulur?* (*How can Asiye be Saved?*) in 1973 and 1986, Sadık Şendil's *Kanlı* Nigar (*Bloddy Nigar*) in 1981, Ferhan Şensoy's *Pardon* (*Sorry*) from the play named *Çok Tuhaf Soruşturma* (*Very Weird Investigation*) in 2005. In the theatre play adaptations in Turkish, only one movie appears as a unique example by having a foreign writer. Experienced director Metin Erksan intended to try a totally different adaptation in 1977, and makes *The Angel of Vengeance - The Female Hamlet*. With its female protagonist, this movie appears as one of the most extra ordinary movies of Turkish cinema history.

When the history of Turkish television is evaluated, a coincidence appears in 2017, one year later than the launch of first Turkish streaming services. Two local services BluTV and puhutv were introduced to the audience in the same year with Netflix TR. The arrival of these services, highly welcomed with audience in Turkey who demand diversity and expect to meet extraordinary narratives which are not on television. One year later than its launch, BluTV has released its first original series named *Masum* (*Innocent*, 2017) which is also an adaptation from the theater play named *Bayrak* (*Flag*) written by Berkun Oya. Similar as the first drama of TRT, first content of the first streaming services of Turkey had been a stage-to-screen adaptation.

In terms of cinema, two examples of adaptations appear in the last decade. The movie *Tatlım Tatlım* (*My Sweetheart*, 2017) adapted from the play *Haybeden Gerçeküstü Aşk* (*Surreal Love for Nothing*) written by Yılmaz Erdoğan in 2007. And the play named *Sen Hiç Ateş Böceği Gördün Mü?* (*Have You Ever Seen a Firefly?*, 2021) also written by Yılmaz Erdoğan in 1999, was adapted into a movie with the same name in 2021.

In the last month of 2020, GAIN TV was launched as the third streaming service of Turkey, and followed by the fourth one Exxen one month later in 2021. With the addition of Disney Plus as the third global streaming service in 2022, to the list already including Netflix TR and Amazon Prime Video, Turkish television industry has begun to search for new narratives to satisfy the 'niche' audience of these services. Being subscription based makes these services compete among each other first to attract then to protect their subscribers. As a result, content creators apply to the adaptations of literature and theatre plays for their relatively "new" narratives.

From Stage to Digital Screen

The play named *The Grönholm Method* which is written by Catalan playwright Jordi Galceran in 2003, has begun to be performed in Turkey by name of *Metot* (*Method*) in 2013. After BluTV's *Masum* (*Innocent*), GAIN TV released the second stage-to-screen adaptation in online series with *Metot* (*Method*) in 2021 as a mini-series with four episodes, adapted by Ali Onur S.

The play is about three employee candidates Merve (Şebnem Hassanisoughi), Engin (Mustafa Kırantepe), and Kadir (Sarp Aydınoğlu) who attend to a job interview and manipulated by human resources manager Ferhat (Serkan Keskin) pretending to be a candidate to discover their "real" faces while competing. The office is the only location in the play where these four people have to stay together even if the tension among them rises. The adapted version of the play also takes place in a single location. Director of the series is actor Serkan Keskin who is also in the cast of the series as the protagonist. When the visual aesthetic of the series is considered it is possible to argue that, *Metot* promise audience a television play with dynamic camera moves. When camera cannot leave the room, the text had to be "translated to new medium with adequate lighting and medium or panning shots alternating with close-ups" (Zatlin, 2005, p. 169). Audience of television has been familiar with single location dramas, especially since the golden era of sitcom genre being shot in production set with particular spaces (Zatlin, 2005, p. 170). If the set does not change, lack of visual depiction makes dialogue become the main source of the narrative. During a play, theatre audience mainly concentrate on the "actor" and stage decor functions as a secondary element to transfer the text (Davies, 1994, p. 8). In the series, the office's function is nothing more than convincing the audience that the characters are there for a job interview. In stage-to-screen adaptations, "directors often take advantage of the shot/counter-shot to develop a complex economy of the gaze" (Hatchuel, 2004, p. 51). Here, function of the director cannot go beyond deciding when to focus on whom, and controlling acting performances. Original text of the play generates the screenplay of the series with no interference. As a result, *Metot*'s fidelity to the original text makes the series suit the Wagner's (1975, p. 222) "transposition" model.

Fidelity to the text constitutes the starting point of debates on adaptations, and the classification in adaptation models is made on the basis of originality in the new text. According to Leitch (2007, p. 128), considering fidelity in adaptation can be explained with financial priorities rather than aesthetic concerns, because a popular text already has a potential on reaching the audience. Undoubtedly that, Shakespeare is the writer who provided the greatest source to stage-to-screen adaptations. Even though, his texts are very well-known by the audience all over the world, his retold texts can be seen in very authentic forms in non-English movies. Ko (2020, p. 82) questions the intercultural adaptations of Shakespeare in terms of cultural hegemony of West in his article "*Intercultural Intermediality: The Unspoken Text in Intercultural Film Adaptations of Shakespeare*," and he asks that "is Shakespeare just another global brand, indistinguishable from iPhones and Big Macs, that sustains Western cultural and economic dominance" or is it possible to create a resistance against hegemony of West by referring, even "exploiting Shakespeare as raw material" for adaptations?. According to Davies (1994, p. 3), theatre is "ephemeral" and a play text should be relevant to the era it is performed, and "reflect the hopes, fears, anger and current concerns of the societies from which these productions spring." Hutcheon (2006, p. 176) rejects the idea that adaptation has a "vampiric" impact which exploits the original text. She even underline that, an adaptation gives text a chance to live longer.

Wagner's three models on adaptation also involves "commentary" and "analogy" models. GAIN TV has released second stage-to-screen adaptation series *Hamlet* a few months after *Metot*. On the contrary of *Metot*, *Hamlet* suits the commentary model of Wagner (1975) by referring to the original text of Shakespeare only while structuring the baseline of the plot. With its rewritten dialogues and rearrangements in time and space, the series tells the tragedy of a non-royal family living in modern era, surrounded by social and political corruption. Director and writer of the series is Kaan Müjdeci who is known with arthouse movies, prefers a female Hamlet from a lower class family, with a father who is the head of the gang ruling the transportation system in Büyükada (Big Island).

Island as Elsinore Castle

Islands of İstanbul known as Princes' Islands is off the south coast of İstanbul in Marmara Sea. Consisting of nine islands, the largest of this archipelago is Büyükada (Big Island). In the Byzantine Period, as well as the priests and high-ranking spiritual leaders, exiled members of the dynasty settled on the islands (Ertin, 2022, p. 827). One of the most well-known names exiled to the island in the recent past is Lev Trotsky who was a political exile from the Soviet Union and stayed in Büyükada between 1929 and 1933. He depicted Büyükada as "an island of peace and indifference" in his writings in the last era of his exile (North, 2019). Although the islands conquered by Turks in 1453, the real settlement on the island had begun after the Tanzimat period, and the main value of the islands was realized in 1846 with the start of the ferry transportation (Ertin, 2022, p. 829). In the middle of the 19th century, the prosperous social life of the island was impacted by the Ottoman intellectuals and writers who visit the islands, in addition to the non-Muslim summer residences (Ertin, 2022, pp. 835–836). Today the social life in the island is mostly dominated by both domestic and foreign tourists, especially at the weekends and in summer season. Transportation in the islands has been carried out by phaetons until 2020. Kaan Müjdeci's *Hamlet* is based on a true story and the pilot episode begins with the prologue below:

> **Prologue:** The phaetons, which have been used as a means of transportation in the Islands since the past, turn into a means of income with the influx of tourists in the 2000s. In the absence of adequate supervision, the phaeton riders bring horses to the island illegally and make more tours to earn more. Horses that are not well taken care of get worse and worse. Animal rights activists react to the situation and create public opinion for the phaetons to be lifted. On the other hand, a fight for rent begins. Due to a plague in horses in 2019, 81 horses were culled in one night. This event marks the beginning of the end of the phaeton kingdom. Shortly after the incident, the municipality paid compensation to the owners of the phaetons and ended the phaetons kingdom on the island.

King Hamlet appears as the gang leader Ahmet Kesmeci (Mustafa Alabora) who is the head of transportation system in the island. Even though his wealth makes his brother envious, he is not a rich man, as spoken in the series he only "works for the rich men." He lives in the isolated area of the island in a non-luxury detached house with his wife Nazan (Hatice Aslan) and her nineteen years old daughter Hazar (Elit İşcan) as their only child. On the contrary of the play, audience witness the murder in the beginning of the story. Ahmet's brother Kadir (Erdal Beşikçioğlu) hits Ahmet from behind with a stick while he was watching the horses' burial over the cliff, and makes him fall and die. Kadir as Cladius, manages to cover up his crime and organizes a funeral for his brother. However, Hazar as the young Hamlet does not believe that her father had fallen by mistake and begins to suspect of Kadir. While Hazar looks for ways to reveal the truth, Kadir tries to cope with his regret of his sin. In the series, dialogues are written relevant with the daily language of the folks living in the island. However, monologues as head voices are occasionally used only for Hazar and Kadir, referring to the original text of Shakespeare. Kadir talks to himself at the barn and says:

> **Kadir:** The smell of your crime is everywhere. Brother killer… I can't pray. Aren't the rains enough to wash it and launder it like snow? What's the point of forgiveness if it's not going to stand up to sin? What's the point of prayer if it won't stand against sin? God forgive my sin. What's the point of prayer if it doesn't lift us up when we fall? God help me forgive my sin.

As Davies underlines (1994, p. 184), "a Shakespearean film cannot satisfactorily remain confined to the theatre stage. Neither can it abandon that intrinsic theatricality which beats in the heart of Shakespearean drama." Monologues of Hazar and Kadir makes the audience remember what she/he watching during the series. However, a movie differs from a theatre play with by leaning on the visual narration, and action comes before words. Gestures, body language, even silence can take the place of dialogue. As a result, in stage-to-screen adaptations, only limited part of the play text is involved in the screenplay. Most of the Shakespeare adaptations "use only 25–30% of the source text" (Zatlin, 2005, p. 178). The director of the adaptation has responsibility of visualization with the appropriate using of space which fill the missing parts of the text left for the imagination of the audience (Lind, 2016, p. 83).

In Turkish culture, ghost is not a familiar phenomenon. In Müjdeci's version, ghost of father Hamlet is replaced with a blind horse which Hazar sees in her dreams. When Hazar feels stuck in her suspicions, she visits an old clairvoyant named Amelia (Çiğdem Selışık Onat) who is one of the Greek residents of the island. This old woman takes care of Hazar and let her sleep in her house where

Hazar finds the answers told by the blind horse speaking in her father's voice, addressing his murderer and wants her to take his revenge.

After the funeral of Ahmet Kesmeci, Kadir used to visit Nazan who appears as Gertrude. Even though her interest on Kadir is ambivalent in the early days after the funeral, she begins to take care of herself, by examining her appearance looking in the mirror when she is alone. And her intention about Kadir reveals when she steals her daughter's lace knickers. The sexual tension between Nazan and Kadir is shown with close-ups on Kadir focused on Nazan when she is preparing meal. Soon after, their affair begins and they marry in Islamic way which is defined as "imam marriage" being directed by a hodja, and does not substitute an official marriage.

Hazar has a boyfriend named Öner (Ahmet Rıfat Şungar), who is a very naive man and loves her. However, Hazar begins to behave aggressively at him when Öner does not share her suspicion about Kadir. Öner who takes the place of Ophelia in the series, is the younger son of an old man named Abdullah (Cihat Tamer) who worked for years for Ahmet Kesmeci. After the death of the man he serves dies, he begins to work with the murderer, as Polonius. Abdullah's elder son Serkan (Murat Kılıç) who works with him in the bard used to warn Öner to quit his affair with Hazar, as Laertes who warn Ophelia.

After the marriage of Kadir and Nazan, Hazar makes a plan with Amelia's nephew Nuh (Emrullah Çakay) which would require police investigation in the end. Nuh ties her hands and takes her in the woods where she hides as if she was kidnapped and left there. After looking for hours, Kadir and others finds her with bruises on her body. She says that she does not remember who kidnapped her. In the following days, she begins to behave weird as if she has psychological disorders. She searches a crime-reality show on the internet and apply to it anonymously. Hazar's plan takes the place of the play written by Hamlet to be performed by travelling actors who visit Elsinore.

The show Hazar applies is inspired by a Turkish television show named *Müge Anlı ile Tatlı Sert* which has been broadcast live since 2008, in weekdays from 10:00 to 13:00, and receives very high rating results for years. The show in the series is *Nagehan Tan ile Adalet* (Justice with Nagehan Tan), hosted by a female host who has a similar profile with Müge Anlı, the host of the original program. In *Müge Anlı ile Tatlı Sert,* unsolved cases on murders and missing people are being investigated. Participants of the program including the victims and probable criminals who come up against in the studio, provoke each other frequently. The rising tension which guarantees the rating, blends the real with fiction. As a result, the format of the program can be defined as infotainment, due to both serving information and entertainment (Tetik and Özgüven, 2021, p. 147). The series criticizes *Müge Anlı ile Tatlı Sert* with its replica *Nagehan Tan ile Adalet* for being manipulative on audience, thus on society.

Media Industry as the Fountain for Corruption

Nagehan Tan (Şebnem Bozoklu) is introduced for the first time in the fourth episode, as a woman having sadomasochistic character who arrives at the woods at night with her car alone, wearing a fur jacket on her naked body and meet there two black men. In next scene, she lays alone in her bed in the morning with bruises on her skin. Then she leaves her house with her wolf looking dog and arrives at the television channel. In the meeting with program crew, the reporter Kerem (Serdar Orçin) who previously visited the Island to collect information about Hazar's unsolved abduction case, informs others about the rating potential of the case by giving the details about an accidentally died father, and an uncle who marries his recently died brother's wife. Nagehan admits to use the case on the program with the title "*Mysterious Murder on the Island*."

Kerem visits the police center in the Island, and gives bribe to the Commissar to force Kadir and others to admit to attend the program. Commissar's oppresses on Kadir works and he meets with Kerem to sign a non-disclosure agreement. Kerem talks to Kadir and tells him that they believe that all of them are innocent and they will not be harmed after the program finished. Kadir, Nazan, Serkan and Öner attend the program for the first time, and Nagehan accuses Kadir and Nazan for their marriage seeming unethical. However, Nazan defines her decision as "normal" in the program and they all reject the accuses of the host both for the mysterious murder and unsolved abduction. In the following days, the program crew feels pressure to find a criminal to present to audience, and watches the records of police interrogation with Öner which should be kept by police and not shared. They learn that Öner has killed the puppy he adopted for Hazar after Hazar rejected his present. Program crew agrees upon labeling Öner as a potential killer in the program. They even use social media to provoke audience with hashtags of #killerÖner. After attending the program once more and accused by Nagehan for being the probable murderer, Öner commits a suicide and dies. He hangs himself to the ladder of an empty pool and when the rope broke, he falls down to the water with rotten plants in the ground of the pool, resembling the death of Ophelia. Öner's death makes the public opinion change; people begin to blame Nagehan for being the cause of the death of an innocent young man. In the following program Nagehan makes an explanation to the audience at the beginning of the program, sitting at her chair surrounded by flowers. She rejects these accusations and makes a speech by mentioning her confidence on the success of the program. She talks about the great support of officials due to her support to law and order. At that moment, a huge flower is brought to the studio and given to her. She announces that the flower is from Turkish Ministry of Interior. The orchestra of the program begins to play a well-known Turkish song named Sen Ağlama (*Don't Cry*) and Nagehan breaks into tears.

The program quits the case of Hazar after Öner's death. However, Hazar who has an affair with Kerem for a while, convinces him to continue the case. Kerem who is manipulated by Hazar, insists Nagehan to open the case once more by provoking her. Nagehan confesses about her fear after Öner's death.

Kerem: You gotta attack fearlessly. You know wolves bite when they are scared.
Nagehan: I did bite, the child died.
Kerem: Then bite again. You'll see that your clapping will multiply.
Nagehan: I'm making a show, huh? I'm scared that someone from above will call. We are fiction. Find the woman, find the man, find the subject, have a meeting… The budget is passed. We got the rating of the program, this is my job.

The argument finishes with Nagehan's approval on continuing the case. Kerem talks to Kadir again and convinces him to attend the program for the last time. Before the program, Hazar decides to take her own revenge. She uses the poison she got from Amelia, and secretly puts it in the meatballs her mother prepared for Kadir. In the evening, she takes the basket with poisoned meatballs in it and visits the barn to find Kadir. However, she cannot find Kadir in the barn, gives the meal to Abdullah to be taken by Kadir. After Hazar leaves the barn, Abdullah open the basket and begins to eat meatballs. Soon after, he is found dead in the barn by Kadir. Kadir finds out Hazar's plan to kill himself. Abdullah's son Serkan falls in great depression after losing his father and brother in short-time. Kadir talks to Serkan and tells him that Hazar is the murderer of Abdullah. Serkan decides to kill Hazar, and begins to wonder around Hazar's house. Next day, Kadir, Nazan and Serkan attend Nagehan's program. However, Hazar is in the studio too as the audience behind the camera. Nagehan calls Hazar to come near her and asks her questions. Hazar tells that Kadir is the one who kidnapped her and he is also the murderer of her father. When Kadir starts to shout and reject her accusation, she leaves the studio. A few seconds later, she returns and stabs Kadir from his neck and kills him. At that moment, Serkan takes of his gun and shoots first Nazan, then Hazar. Nagehan runs away, but Serkan catches her in the corridor and kills her too. Security guard shoots Serkan. He is wounded but manages to run. Hazar who is also wounded, finds Serkan. They climb on the roof of the television channel while chasing each other. Serkan finds out that he is out of bullet. They begin to fight. At the end, Hazar manages to stab Serkan deadly, but Serkan chokes her before he dies due to loss of blood. Hamlet and Laertes of the series lose their lives on the roof with landscape of İstanbul. As Lan (2007, p. 115) underlines, in a stage-to-screen adaptation of Shakespeare, the final can be visualized, on the contrary of vocalized final of the play. However, Müjdeci prefers to make audience hear Hazar's head voice for the last time with the monologue below:

> **Hazar:** Farewell, I'm dying. And you are the dumb spectators of this play, who shudder and turn pale at the sight of this. If I had some time, I'd say… Whatever it is, I'm leaving now, but you're still here.

Hazar's words for the "dump spectators" who have to live and witness the corruption reminds us the "indifference" in Trotsky's words for the definition of life on the Island. Final scene closes with the horse corpses in the sea, and seagulls flying in the sky over the İstanbul. The corruption is visualized in the last frames opening from the roof of a media building functioning as the fountain for the corruption among society.

Conclusion

Turkish audience who is familiar with literature and theatre play adaptations since the early era of TRT, met with new stage-to-screen adaptations released by streaming services in last five years. GAIN TV's two adaptation series appear as examples of two different adaptation models. Adapted from a contemporary text, *Metot* remained faithful to the original text and transferred it to the screen without any interruption in dialogues or any changes in terms of time and space. The other series, *Hamlet*, takes a classical text as the core of its narrative, and transmits it as a modern tale through a different culture in today's İstanbul. As Ko mentions (2020, pp. 81–82), in intercultural adaptations of Shakespeare plays "additional meanings and nuances" are derived from "cultural power dynamic between the source and the adaptation." In GAIN's recently adapted *Hamlet*, these nuances reflecting the Turkish culture are very clear, while it preserves it Shakespearean tone in a harmony. When *Metot* and *Hamlet* are compared, it can be seen that fidelity to the original text also limits its visualized version in terms of cinematic aesthetic. A commentary adaptation as *Hamlet*, whose director's own vision enriches the text, can be interpreted as giving an old text new flesh and blood instead of replicating it as a mummy. In conclusion, it can be argued that, regardless of their models, streaming services' stage-to-screen adaptations give theatre plays new spirits to survive forever in our digital libraries.

References

Davies, A. (1994). *Filming Shakespeare's plays: The adaptations of Laurence Olivier, Orson Welles, Peter Brook, Akira Kurosawa*. New York: Cambridge University Press.

Ertin, G. (2022). Tarihte İstanbul adaları (İlkçağdan-1923'e kadar) [İstanbul Islands in the history (From Antiquity to 1923)]. *Journal of Social, Humanities and Administrative Sciences*, *5*(6): 825–841.

Hatchuel, S. (2004). *Shakespeare: From stage to screen*. New York: Cambridge University Press.

Hutcheon, L. (2006). *A theory of adaptation*. New York: Routledge.

Kale, F. (2019). TRT yerli edebiyat uyarlamaları 1968-2015 [TRT local literature adaptations 1968-2015], *TRT Akademi, Geçmişten Geleceğe Televizyon Yayıncılığı* [*TRT Academy, Television Broadcasting from the Past to the Future*], *4*(7): 126–147.

Ko, Y. J. (2020). Intercultural intermediality: The unspoken text in intercultural film adaptations of Shakespeare. *Journal of Medieval and Early Modern English Studies*, *30*(2): 81–110.

Lan, Y. L. (2007). Returning to Naples: Seeing the end in Shakespeare film adaptation. In J. M. Welsh & P. Lev (Eds.), *The literature/film reader: Issues of adaptation*. MD: Scarecrow Press.

Leitch, M. T. (2007). *Film adaptation and its discontents: from Gone with the Wind to The Passion of the Christ*. MD: The Johns Hopkins University Press.

Lind, P. B. (2016). The film industry woos Shakespeare: Theatrical versus cinematographic space in the adaptations of Hamlet and Henry V by Kenneth Branagh. In P. B. Lind (Ed.), *Telling and re-telling stories: Studies on literary adaptation to film*. London: Cambridge Scholars Publishing.

North, D. (2019). Lev Troçki'nin Büyükada'daki can alıcı yılları: 1929-1933 [Leon Trotsky's crucial years on Princes' Islands: 1929-1933]. Retrieved from https://www.wsws.org/tr/articles/2019/09/25/intr-s25.html [Accessed on July, 25. 2022].

Tetik, T., & Özgüven, D. (2021). Reality crime programs in Turkish television: The notorious case of Palu Family on Müge Anlı. *Athens Journal of Mass Media and Communications*, *7*(2): 137–150.

Wagner, G. (1975). *The novel and the cinema*. London: The Tantivy Press.

Zatlin, P. (2005). *Theatrical translation and film adaptation a practitioner's view*. UK: Bristol: Multilingual Matters.

Dilay Özgüven Tetik

Reality (*Justice with Nagehan Tan*) in Quality (An Original Series on GAIN): From Hamlet to Hazar

Abstract: Scar kills Mufasa; then, takes the throne and eliminates Simba. *The Tragedy of Hamlet: Prince of Denmark* by William Shakespeare has been adapted to many works, many times, in various media, such as a worldwide-known feature-length animation, *The Lion King* (Roger Allers and Rob Minkoff, 1994) and a Turkish original series titled *Hamlet* (Kaan Müjdeci, 2021) on a Turkish SVODs called GAIN. This chapter focuses on the boundaries between appropriation and adaptation ways of Kaan Müjdeci in *Hamlet* (2021). In the original series, *Hamlet* is represented as a female character called Hazar. The series is based on the idea that what if Hamlet [Hazar] lives in 2020s' Turkey, where she attempts to take revenge from her uncle; then, along with her family, she participates in a "crime-based reality program" called *Justice with Nagehan Tan*. The fictional "crime-based reality program" in the series is portrayed as a kind of an appropriation of one of the most long-standing and popular "crime-based reality programs" in Turkey: *Müge Anlı ile Tatlı Sert* (2008-). The fictional program's host strives to solve the mystery behind the murder of Hazar's father, which is centered on an island. Significantly, this chapter proposes to illustrate a seminal work's transformation from the literature to a Turkish digital streaming service. Afterward, the narrative structure of the original series *Hamlet* (2021) is discussed. Crucially, the formats of the fictional "crime-based reality program," *Justice with Nagehan Tan*, and *Müge Anlı ile Tatlı Sert* (2008-) are compared.

Keywords: Reality Shows, Quality Series, *Hamlet*, Crime, Adaptation

What If? The Mysterious Homicide on the Island

The Turkish SVOD service GAIN was introduced to the audience in 2019. The SVODs, GAIN, describes itself as "a new generation content platform consisting of innovative, entertaining short and long content which values time. In addition to local and global TV series, and movies, documentaries, news, music, sports and entertainment programs, live broadcasts are also included in the content list for the audience to spend quality time." The list of original series between December 2020 to September 2022 on GAIN is presented in Tab. 1.

The first episode of the original series *Hamlet* commences with an opening crawl, explaining the situation of the horses on the Island. The opening crawl states that "the phaetons, which have been used as a means of transportation on the Islands, have turned into a means of income with the influx of tourists in the 2000s. In the absence of sufficient control, the carriage riders brought illegal horses to the Island and made more tours in order to earn more." The opening crawl continues that "the horses are getting ill due to insufficient care. Animal lovers react to the situation and create public opinion for the phaetons to be removed. On the other hand, rent fight begins. In 2019, 81 horses were culled in one night due to a plague." As a result, "this event marks the beginning of the end of the phaeton kingdom. Soon after, the municipality ends the phaeton kingdom on the island by paying compensation to the carriage owners." The original series *Hamlet* is an appropriation of the Shakespeare's *Hamlet*, while the series addresses to the contemporary situations in Turkey. Kaan Müjdeci defines the relation of the horses to *Hamlet* that "when retelling Shakespeare's story today, you cannot separate people's consciences from their relationship to good and evil, animals and nature. Therefore, I did not find it right to question this story and not to include animals and nature as a theme. I chose horses and many other animals to get the story on the right track." (Linville, 2021).

In *Hamlet*, the Hamlet character is portrayed by the actress Elit İşcan. Hence, the name Hamlet is transformed into Hazar. However, the director and writer of the series, Kaan Müjdeci states that "I actually do not see Hamlet as a man. And in the series, Hamlet is basically genderless. I believe the reason why he was a prince must have something to do with the climate of the era it was written in. To reflect on that in this structure, I divided Hamlet into three characters" (Linville, 2021). Müjdeci elaborates that "the main reason for this was, there were some things a 19-year old girl wouldn't be able to say. Maybe a prince would be able to say them 400 years ago, but in today's world, a daughter of a horse carriage man couldn't have said them" (ibid.). Müjdeci defines that he had separated Hamlet character into three personas. Müjdeci showcases that "in addition to Elit's character, I added a mysterious, eighty-five years old character as part of Hamlet, to be able to show that this character, in fact, had experience and was superior to the things happening around her. As the third Hamlet, I did need to reflect on the masculine aspects of Hamlet even for a little bit, so I added Nuh. And essentially, I wanted to present Hamlet as a combination of these three characters" (ibid.).

The story of the original series *Hamlet* on SVODs, GAIN, is "on a night in Büyükada, İstanbul, where 81 horses will be buried, the owner of the carriages is killed. The murderer is his brother. The victim's teenage daughter hatches a revenge plan to find her father's killer and uncover dark relationships: all the suspects will be brought together on stage in TV's most famous reality show" (Box Office Turkey, 2021). The original series *Hamlet* is defined as "a family drama with the elements of murder, revenge, grief, betrayal, and love" (Artful Living, 2021). The lead actors in the original series *Hamlet* are Elit İşcan as Hazar, Şebnem Bozoklu as Nagehan Tan, Hatice Aslan as Nazan, Ahmet Rıfat Şungar as Öner, Murat Kılıç as Serkan, Erdal Beşikçioğlu as Kadir, Mustafa Alabora as Ahmet, and Serdar Orçin as Kerem.

Tab. 1: The Original Series Between December 2020 and September 2022 on GAIN

Title	**Year**	**Release date**	**Season**	**Episode**
10 Bin Adım	2020–2022	December 30, 2020	2	20
Terapist	2021	January 1, 2021	1	7
Özelden Yürüyenler	2021	January 2, 2021	2	26
Metot	2021	April 7, 2021	1	4
Senkron	2021	April 7, 2021	1	6
Bizi Ayıran Çizgi	2021	April 24, 2021	1	5
Ayak İşleri	2021–2022	May 12, 2021	2	20
Orta Kafa Aşk	2021–2022	September 20, 2021	2	20
Hamlet	2021	October 19, 2021	1	7
#Etkileyici	2021	November 28, 2021	1	10
Duran	2022	January 11, 2022	1	9
Aslında Özgürsün	2022	May 9, 2022	1	8
Cezailer	2022	September 29, 2022	1	6

In the article "*Turkish Hamlets*," Savaş Arslan (2009, p. 165) points out that "an Islamic version of *Hamlet* might involve a risky engagement with an uncanny

Westernization and modernization whereby Islamism would have to respond to the cultural Westernization, which (of course) it absolutely rejects."

The concept by Arslan (2009) named "Turkification" could also be applied to Kaan Müjdeci's *Hamlet*. Arslan (2009) elaborates that "such a project may only be possible by reinterpreting Hamlet's oppositional characteristics through the framework of 'Turkification.'" The "Turkification" of *Hamlet* is highly demonstrated when Hazar's uncle and mother get married. The Turkish ritualistic essence is imported into the storyline where Hazar's uncle and her mother are married via imam. Turkish traditions often suggest for imam to marry two souls, where they are bound by marriage in the eyes of God. Hence, Islamism is not far behind in this series; even so it is highlighted in one of the major plots of the original series *Hamlet*.

The original series *Hamlet* is centered on an Island in Turkey where the suspicious activities caught the attention of a fictional crime-based reality program titled *Nagehan Tan ile Adalet* (*Justice with Nagehan Tan*).

The production crew agreed to discuss the events on the island, and the host of the show decided to present the case as; the mysterious homicide on the island. However, the first appearance of Nagehan Tan in the original series *Hamlet* is in Episode 3, at 39:59, the last 2 minutes of the series. The Close-Up camera angle focusing on Nagehan Tan pinning a headscarf. The Close-Up moves to the face of Nagehan Tan and the Turkish flag on the projection are visible behind her. The first line of Nagehan Tan in the show is that "my beloved audience, who are watching at home and my guests in the studio, you are welcome. First of all, I would like to ask a question to the guests in the studio. My beloved guests, 'Am I beautiful right now?'" The guests applauded Nagehan Tan and cheered, "beautiful, yes!" Nagehan Tan replies that "thank you so much, my beloved audience watching from home, I can feel that you are also find me beautiful. I can sense what you are thinking. Now, let's conduct a little experiment." Nagehan Tan removes her headscarf. She states that "I want to repeat the question. How do I look now? My beloved guests, am I beautiful?" The guests cheered, "Marvelous, very beautiful!" This sequence of the fictitious crime-based reality program within the series is conjunct with the "Turkification" and "Islamism" aspects cited earlier by Savaş Arslan. The emphasis on these two concepts is visible in the Hazar's storyline, whereas it is also underlined in the fictional crime-based reality program "*Justice with Nagehan Tan*."

In the fictional crime-based reality program, the host projects herself as a devotee of both religion and republicans. This notion could be showcased in this sequence of the original series. When Nagehan Tan is pinning the headscarf and conducting a dialogue with the audience, the Turkish flag is visible behind her on the projectors. Thus, the fictional crime-based reality program targets to impact the audience. This sequence could be derived from the attitude of Müge Anlı in *Müge Anlı ile Tatlı Sert*. It has been known that Müge Anlı is respectful for the religious beliefs and she is also admirer to Atatürk, the founder of Republic of Turkey. Anlı celebrates each national holiday, wearing Turkish flag or Atatürk pins on her show. Nonetheless, she often states that she visits mosques for prayer. In the original series *Hamlet*, this notion of Müge Anlı is attempted to be captured, even with a hint of mockery. The plot of the fictional crime-based reality program positions itself on the allegorical aspect of *Müge Anlı ile Tatlı Sert*, where the events and instances are exaggerated.

The following subchapter will compare the differences and similarities of *Justice with Nagehan Tan* to *Müge Anlı ile Tatlı Sert*. In this aspect, the modeled by Dilay Özgüven Tetik (2022, p. 80) table titled "Crime-Based Reality Programs in Turkish Television Between 1993 and 2022" will be utilized to define *Justice with Nagehan Tan*.

Müge Anlı ile Tatlı Sert Versus *Nagehan Tan ile Adalet*

The highlight of this chapter is to define and describe *Justice with Nagehan Tan* as a crime-based reality program. *Hamlet* is an original series on the Turkish SVOD, GAIN, which could be defined as a quality series. As it is mentioned in the previous subchapter, the series has been introduced and analyzed within the context of the adaptation of literature to digital streaming services. In this subchapter, the fictional crime-based reality program titled *Justice with Nagehan Tan* will be compared with factual crime-based reality program titled *Müge Anlı ile Tatlı Sert*. The crime-based reality programs under the genre of reality television will be observed and the comparison of both fictional and factual reality programs will be elaborated. In "*How Real Can You Get?: Recent Developments in 'Reality' Television*," Richard Kilborn (1994, p. 421) mentions that "ever since the earliest days of film, one of the abiding aspirations of moving image producers has been persuade their viewing publics that they are watching something which has a direct connection with the 'real world.'" Hence, Kilborn (1994, p. 422) defines that "there is now a general recognition that all notions of 'realism' are historically determined and that the criteria for judging the realism quotient of a text have just as much to do with the audience expectations and with sets of established conventions as with any objective measure for judging how much reality can be transposed on to the screen." This subchapter will analyze the reality show in a quality series, *Hamlet*.

Müge Anlı has been the host of a crime-based reality program titled *Müge Anlı ile Tatlı Sert* for over a decade. The program has been mainly focusing on murder cases, missing person cases, domestic violence, fraud, and several other criminal activities in Turkey. The show has been broadcasted on the private channel ATV since 2008. The show has been broadcasted from 9:00 to 13:00 until June 2022. However, the current season's (August, 2022) the time frame has been shifted to 10:00 – 12:00. In her thesis called "*The Uniqueness of Müge Anlı ile Tatlı Sert in Turkish Crime-Based Reality Programs: The Analysis of the Format's Evolution*," Dilay Özgüven Tetik (2022) models a table titled "Crime-Based Reality Programs in Turkish Television Between 1993 and 2022." The criteria in this table have been formed from the global research on the genre of reality television and have been applied to Turkish crime-based reality programs to be able to define their formats. The criteria in this table will be applied to fictional crime-based reality program "*Justice with Nagehan Tan*" to identify the format hence to compare the fictional crime-based reality program to the factual crime-based reality program. The table modeled by Özgüven Tetik (2022, p. 80) consists of 12 criteria as, "actual footage," "live broadcast," "consultants," "interview," "fiction," "reenactment," "scripted," "audience participation," "dramatic music," "narration," and "police involvement." In the Turkish crime-based reality program, "*Müge Anlı ile Tatlı Sert*," the following six criterion exists, "actual footage," "live broadcast," "consultants," "interview," "audience participation," and "police involvement."

The existence of the criteria from the table "Crime-Based Reality Programs in Turkish Television Between 1993 and 2022" (Özgüven Tetik, 2022) will be examined in this chapter by analyzing the fictional crime-based reality program titled *Justice with Nagehan Tan* within the original series *Hamlet*. The sequences of the show *Justice with Nagehan Tan* will be the groundwork. Hence, the fictional reality show will be defined based on sequences from the series solely. Because the analysis will be projected on the fictional show, only access to the format characteristics of this show lies within the series. Thus, the non-mentioned criteria will be ruled out, and the visual representation of the fictional reality show in *Hamlet* will define the format within the reality television genre. Thus, the fictional crime-based reality program, *Justice with Nagehan Tan* within the original series *Hamlet* includes the criteria of actual footage, live broadcast, consultants, reenactment, scripted, and audience participation.

The actual footage criterion is shown in Episode 7 of *Hamlet*, in the fictional crime-based reality program *Justice with Nagehan Tan*. Episode 7 is the final episode of the original series. The actual footage of the crime scene has been broadcasted in the fictional program when there is a murder case on the Island. The host of the program Nagehan Tan had aired footage in the actual location of the murder. The reporter states that "the crime scene investigators, our Turkish police enforcements, our district governor are present here. They are doing their best to solve the crime. You know that everyone knows each other on this Island. However, no one knows if this is a murder or fate." The actual footage criterion has been present in the Turkish crime-based reality programs since 1993, with the introduction of the first crime-based reality program titled *Sıcağı Sıcağına*. The actual footage criterion is the video from the actual crime scenes or actual locations of the events. There are only three crime-based reality programs which did not involve actual footage; *Gerçek Kesit*, *İtirazım Var*, and *İpucu Kriminal* in crime-based reality programs in the Turkish television history. *Gerçek Kesit* and *İpucu Kriminal* resembled the true-crime series, including none of actual footage, these programs only involved reenactments of the actual events. On the other hand, *İtirazım Var* is an appropriation of courtroom shows where actual footage is not needed.

The second criterion, which was showcased to the audience in the fictional crime-based reality program *Justice with Nagehan Tan* in the original series *Hamlet*, which is broadcasted live. The live broadcast criteria have been a part of crime-based reality programs since 1999. In the Turkish television history, the first live broadcasted crime-based reality program was *Film Gibi* which was hosted by Sinan Çetin. Although the show did not focus on the murder cases, it has been constructed on the missing person cases. Hence, it can be included in the format of crime-based reality programs. Since the debut of *Müge Anlı ile Tatlı Sert* in 2008, every crime-based reality program has met the criterion of the live broadcast. In the original series *Hamlet*, the fictional crime-based reality program *Justice with Nagehan Tan* is an appropriation of the Turkish crime-based programs. Thus, the fictional show includes the live broadcast criterion in its format. In the Episode 4, the family and relatives of Hazar are invited to the studio of *Justice with Nagehan Tan* to discuss the mysterious events on the Island. In the original series *Hamlet*, the live broadcast criterion had shown to the audience by the preparation of the guests in the studio. The microphones are attached to the guests and they are waiting for to show to go on live. On the other hand, the live broadcast criterion was implied by one of the crew members of the fictional crime-based reality program as "yes, we are going on air. Five, four, three, two, one…" While a crew member is counting down for the show to go on air, the backstage of the show is shown to the audience. The reason for this instance is that it is difficult to give the impression of the live broadcast in series. However, in the original series *Hamlet*, the live broadcast criterion is accomplished with this scene.

The consultant criterion is presented in the fictional crime-based reality program, *Justice with Nagehan Tan*. In the Turkish television history, the consultant criterion has been present since 2005 with the crime-based reality program *Kadının Sesi*. The existence of consultants in the studio has been one of the major criteria since the host address to consultants' professional opinion for ongoing cases. In *Müge Anlı ile Tatlı Sert*, there is a forensic scientist, and a lawyer present in the studio for the live broadcast. In *Justice with Nagehan Tan*, the consultant comments on the Öner's attitude. Nagehan Tan confronts Öner, and she claims that "when your girlfriend goes missing you should not stay quiet." Thus, the psychologist consultant in the studio comments that "we can clearly understand that Öner has psychological problems. It is certain. When we observe his behaviors, Öner has a serious psychosomatic disorder." In Episode 5 of *Hamlet*, in the fictional crime-based reality program, only Öner had been invited to the studio. The psychologist comments on the case of Öner, in which Öner is accused for the murder of his dog that "Miss Nagehan, the violence against animals could be defined as the worst side of human psychology. The suppressed emotions reveal these dark sides of human beings. Similar to the example of Öner's case. These suppressed emotions should be resurfaced and solved. I believe that we can solve this problem here." Nagehan Tan states that "I want to consult to our professor about the judicial aspect." The lawyer consultant in the studio defines that "once, there was no punishment for such crimes. However, now our laws have been expanded so that animals should also be protected, and if someone is violent against animals, there is a punishment for this act. The person who does violence on animals is obliged to serve for their crimes." After the accusations that have been created against Öner, he commits suicide. In Episode 6 of *Hamlet*, after the suicide of Öner, Nagehan Tan lets the psychologist to define the situation of Öner in the fictional crime-based reality program, *Justice with Nagehan Tan*. The psychologist examines that "Miss Nagehan, one thing is for certain. The science of psychology uses the method of observation to come through with an analysis. The whole observation we have demonstrated had led us to the same conclusion." The lawyer comments that "this is a long process. It is not easy to give a verdict. However, all of the evidence points to Öner. He is the murderer."

The criteria from the table, reenactment, and scripted are observed in the Episode 4, where Hazar and her family are invited to the studio regarding the suspicious events happening on the island. In the Episode 4, the fictional reality show commences with a reenactment segment. The team writes the reenactment sequences on reality programs of the show itself. Thus, the actors recreate the events in the studio, often with dramatic lighting effects and music. In "*The Rise of True Crime: 20th-Century Murder and American Popular Culture*," Jean

Murley (2008, p. 35) defines that "although the stories occur in recognizably real places, the textual reenactment of crime dramatizes and transforms them into fantasized locations, imaginary sites of real horror." The purpose of reenactment is to gasp the audience's attention. The reenactment in reality television could be defined as the "performing real events" on screen. For instance, the first example of reenactment was accomplished by Turkish actress Fatma Girik in her crime-based reality program, *Söz Fato'da*. Fatma Girik, as the host of the show, also participated in the reenactment segments as the victim. The effect of performing the actual events by the beloved Turkish actress gasped the audience's attention as well as to understand the situation of the victim. However, the reenactment segments are scripted; thus, which can lead the writers to exaggerate the actual events to create a dramatic outcome.

In the Turkish television history, the reenactment criterion was ruled out after it was observed that reenactment affected the emotions of the audience, most importantly, anger. The dramatization of actual events could cause heightened emotional reactions; therefore, within the period of the evolution of crime-based reality programs, the reenactment segment transformed into "storytelling" of actual people on television around the beginning of the 2000s. Thus, in *Müge Anlı ile Tatlı Sert* (2008-), the reenactment and scripted criteria could not be observed. Another reenactment in *Justice with Nagehan Tan* is in the case about Öner killing his dog. It has been revealed by the team of Nagehan Tan that Öner has murdered his dog. Thus, in the Episode 5 of *Hamlet*, the fictional crime-based reality program *Justice with Nagehan Tan* portrays a reenactment in the case of Öner. Hence Nagehan Tan creates a hashtag titled #katilöner[27].

The audience participation criterion is present in the fictional crime-based reality program *Justice with Nagehan Tan*. In "*Television Talk Shows*," Andrew Tolson (2000, p. 13) mentions that "new televisual spaces of performance, with their changing forms of audience participation, are involved in the construction of new types of the public sphere." Audience participation in crime-based reality programs mainly relies on the studio's phone connection. Anyone with valid information about the ongoing case can participate in the show by the given number on the header. The informants have the privilege to hide their names for security precautions. An example could be demonstrated from the show *Müge Anlı ile Tatlı Sert* is that Müge Anlı has been highly relied on the audience participation. However, the information that has been given by the participant could be false, exaggerated, or even misleading. Thus, the reliability of the information should be examined before the participant connected to the studio by phone. Müge Anlı has been analyzing and interfering this process and even in some occasions, she has excluded various information from the public. The unreliable information is not shared with the audience until it is verified. However, the depiction of the host within the original series *Hamlet*, Nagehan Tan, reacts to every piece of information given by the participant by phone, even heightening the tension in the studio. This depiction could be denoted as a criticism or allegory of *Müge Anlı ile Tatlı Sert*. In the Episode 4, in the reality show segment of the series, an audience participates in *Justice with Nagehan Tan*, and claims that he has witnessed that Öner has been shouting at Hazar. The participant claims that "the girl (Hazar) was running away, and he (Öner) was chasing her. He was making hand gestures to her. The gestures were like he was threatening her. The girl was terrified." Öner defends himself that "I have never threatened her. The whole Island knows who I am." Hence, Nagehan Tan states that "Öner, there is something wrong with you." Cornelia Ilie, in her article "*Semi-Institutional Discourse: The Case of Talk Shows*," elaborates the dynamic between host and audience/guests. Ilie (2001) examines the case of the talk shows; however, reality television being a hybrid genre formed around various reality formats. Thus, the statement by Ilie (2001, p. 211) refers that "although the show host is generally supposed to have control over the question- asking the show guests are also entitled to ask questions and make non- elicited comments; in this way, they can challenge the pre-established asymmetrical power relations." Hence, Ilie points out that "as a result, the relations between the hosts (presenters) and the guests (participants), on the one hand, and between the hosts and the audience, on the other, are constructed and re-constructed so as to involve new and unpredictable, sometimes even provoking, forms of interaction" (ibid.).

The police involvement criterion is vaguely mentioned in *Justice with Nagehan Tan*. The crew of Nagehan Tan is working with the police, where we can see in Episode 5. When Öner is accused of the kidnapping Hazar and murdering the dog, the producer of the show is involved in the police interrogations. Hence, in Episode 6, Nagehan Tan mentions that "I want to thank the police enforcements. We were able to punish criminals with the police's help and support." However, while the police factor is mentioned in several times, the actual police involvement in the studio is not visualized in the original series *Hamlet*, in the fictional crime-based reality program *Justice with Nagehan Tan*.

Concluding Remarks

The original series *Hamlet* on the SVOD service GAIN aired on October 19, 2021. The original series includes seven episodes, and each episode is around a 40–45 minutes timeframe. While the original series tells the story of Hamlet, it is appropriated to Turkey and Turkish traditions. On the other hand, the sequence of fictional crime-based reality program is embedded in the plot. Thus, the story is evolved into what if Hamlet is a woman who lives in Turkey and tries to solve the murder of her father in a crime-based reality program. The previous sub-chapter compared the existing factual crime-based reality programs with the fictional crime-based reality program titled *Justice with Nagehan Tan*. The original series adapted the persona of Müge Anlı to the fictitious Nagehan Tan.

The comparison of Müge Anlı and Nagehan Tan could be demonstrated within the attitudes of both factual and fictional identities. Müge Anlı have been broadcasting *Müge Anlı ile Tatlı Sert* on the private channel ATV since 2008. The show has been one of the most popular crime-based reality programs in the Turkish television history. The popularity of *Müge Anlı ile Tatlı Sert* is mostly relied on the persona of Müge Anlı. Anlı has been defined as a powerful, honest, merciful character. These character properties of her led the audience to trust her judgments. Anlı has been stating that she has been broadcasting the show with the support of her audience. Hence, Anlı is the only host of crime-based reality television whose show has never changed channel, canceled, or suspended. In this manner, the fictional character Nagehan Tan is clearly based on the persona of Müge Anlı. Nagehan Tan accommodates similar character properties with Müge Anlı. While the persona of Nagehan Tan is an appropriation of Müge Anlı, the fictional crime-based reality program *Justice with Nagehan Tan*'s format is not identical to *Müge Anlı ile Tatlı Sert*.

The criteria of *Justice with Nagehan Tan* include the actual footage, live broadcast, consultants, reenactment, scripted, and audience participation. These criteria in factual crime-based reality programs in the Turkish television correlate with the format of earlier crime-based reality programs, before *Müge Anlı ile Tatlı Sert*. In 2005, a new format was introduced to the Turkish audiences, which was different from earlier productions of crime-based reality programs. This new format includes the criteria such as, actual footage, live broadcast, consultants, reenactment, scripted, and audience participation. These criteria have only been seen in one crime-based reality program titled *Kadının Sesi* hosted by Yasemin Bozkurt. *Kadının Sesi* is the last program that included reenactment and scripted criteria in crime-based reality programs. The reason is that the program had been canceled in the same year when it was broadcasted. The reenactment and scripted criteria had a negative effect on the audience and caused several serious criminal activities. Thus, *Kadının Sesi* had been canceled, and reenactment and scripted criteria were moved from the format characteristic of crime-based reality programs. The resemblance of the program *Kadının Sesi* and *Justice with Nagehan Tan* is not only jointed by the format characteristics, but also by similar events that took place in these programs.

In the final episode of *Hamlet*, the whole family members and relatives are invited to the studio of *Justice with Nagehan Tan*. However, the broadcast is mired down when Hazar stabs the knife into her uncle's neck. While stabbing the knife, she shouts out, "murderer." Hazar decides to take revenge of her father's death. At this instant, the brother of Öner, Serkan takes out his gun, and starts to shoot everyone in the studio. Thus, the original series *Hamlet* ends with the death of the characters in the studio. Thus, the tragedy of Hamlet/Hazar is demonstrated in the studio of *Justice with Nagehan Tan*, while the original plot of the Hamlet story is merged with the fictional crime-based reality program plot.

Note

27 #murdereröner.

References

Arslan, S. (2009). Turkish Hamlets, *Shakespeare*, *4*(2): 157–168. DOI: 10.1080/17450910802083468.

Artful Living. (2021). Kaan Müjdeci'nin İlk Dizisi "Hamlet" 19 Ekim'de GAIN'de [Kaan Müjdeci's First Series "Hamlet" will be on GAIN on October 19th]. Retrieved from https://www.artfulliving.com.tr/gundem/kaan-mujdecinin-ilk-dizisi-hamlet-19-ekimde-gainde-i-24080 [Accessed on Sept., 17. 2022].

Box Office Turkey. (2021). Kaan Müjdeci, Gain'de Yayınlanacak Hamlet Dizisi Hakkında Konuştu [Kaan Müjdeci talked about the Hamlet series to be aired on Gain]. Retrieved from https://boxofficeturkiye.com/haber/kaan-mujdeci-gain-de-yayinlanacak-hamlet-dizisi-hakkinda-konustu--3608 [Accessed on Sept., 17. 2022].

Ilie, C. (2001). Semi-institutional discourses: The case of talk shows. *Journal of Pragmatic, 33*(2): 209–254. DOI: 10.1016/S0378-2166(99)00133-2.

Kilborn, R. (1994). 'How real can you get?': Recent developments in 'Reality' television. *European Journal of Communication*, *9*(4): 421–439. DOI: 10.1177/0267323194009004003.

Linville, J. D. (2021). Turkish series 'Hamlet' recasts tragedy for the Modern Equine Empire. *Variety*. Retreived from https://variety.com/2021/tv/festivals/turkish-series-hamlet-series- mania-1235055326/ [Accessed on Sept., 07. 2022].

Murley, J. (2008). *The rise of true crime: 20th-century murder and American popular culture*. London: Praeger Publications.

Özgüven Tetik, D. (2022). *The Uniqueness of Müge Anlı ile Tatlı Sert in Turkish crime-based reality programs: The analysis of the format's evolution* (Doctoral dissertation). İstanbul: Bahçeşehir University.

Tolson, A. (2000). Talking about talk: The academic debates. In A. Tolson (Ed.), *Television talk shows: Discourse, performance, spectacle* (pp. 7–31). London: Lawrence Erlbaum Associates, Publishers.

Ece Arıhan

The Transformation of Gender Representation in *She-Ra and the Princesses of Power*

Abstract: The concept of gender, its definition and implications have been at the center of many debates brought forward by feminist and queer scholars. Especially during the feminist waves, the socio-cultural construction of gender has been used as a basis for demanding equality and emancipation from oppressing patriarchal institutions. The impacts of these debates and ideas can be observed in mainstream media in the portrayal of women and men, particularly after the 1970s with the influence of second-wave feminism. Even though the change was taking place at a glacial pace in the 20th century, with the digitalization of the media and the broad use of the Internet, the fourth-wave feminism has been strongly affecting the media as the ideas of feminist and queer theorists are being widely circulated through social media in the 21th century. In addition, the increasing diversity of people working behind the camera and the production processes of media have immensely helped in transforming the media landscape, the portrayal of characters, the types of stories being told, and how they are depicted. This chapter concentrates on the representation of gender and its transformation in popular culture through the comparison of the cult popular American animated television series *She-Ra: Princess of Power* (1985-1987) and its reboot *She-Ra and the Princesses of Power* (2018-2020). *She-Ra: Princess of Power* was produced by Filmation and aired as a television series in the interval between the second and third-wave feminism, whereas its reboot was produced by DreamWorks and released digitally on Netflix during the fourth-wave feminism. In this chapter, an intersectional feminist lens is utilized to investigate how the portrayal of gender has changed and evolved from the original *She-Ra* to its reboot with the impact of feminist waves while highlighting the increased diversity of the characters and the narrative.

Keywords: Gender, Representation, Feminist Theory, Queer Theory, She-Ra, Animated Series

Introduction

Gender remains to be one of the pivotal elements pertaining to the way in which the world functions, embroidered into the fabric of social, cultural, political, and economic structures. In order to understand the concept of gender and the debates surrounding this term, it is necessary to define the concept of sex. Towards the end of the 19th century, scientists, scholars, physicians, and psychologists adopted an essentialist approach to describe sex and separated humans into binary categories, including woman and man, feminine and masculine, based on their biological differences (Robinson and Richardson, 2015, p. 4). They argued that sexual difference impacted the psychology and behavior of women and men and pointed out that while the binary sexes opposed one another, they also naturally complemented each other. Yet, in the 1960s, with the influence of second-wave feminism as well as the gay rights movement, scholars separated sex from gender and described gender as a social and cultural construct instead of a biological constant.

Third-wave feminists in the 1990s focused on the fluidity and multidimensionality of gender and sexuality propelled by postmodernism and queer theory. They denoted that the rigid binary categories of woman and man, femininity and masculinity, female and male were constructed by the patriarchy for the oppression of women by creating a social division (Robinson and Richardson, 2015, p. 10). This social division not only included discrimination based on gender but also on other types of social inequalities. So, feminist theorists and scholars utilized an intersectional approach by investigating the interchange and relationship between gender and various social inequalities such as class, race, ethnicity, and sexuality. Centralizing intersectionality paved the way for broadening the reach of feminism and shedding light on the experiences and issues of women with diverse backgrounds and identities. Today, intersectionality continues to be an essential element of fourth-wave feminism as the importance of reflecting the diversity and multiplicity of identities and perspectives is highlighted by feminist and queer theorists and activists fueled by social media (Munro, 2013, pp. 22–25). The impact of intersectionality and multivocality has begun to be mirrored in the media in the backdrop of the rapid flux of change brought on by the Digital Age. This is the reason why in this chapter, an intersectional feminist lens is utilized to examine gender representation and its transformation by comparing the popular animated series *She-Ra: Princess of Power* (1985-1987) and its reboot *She-Ra and The Princesses of Power* (2018-2020).

Construction of the Beauty Myth

Even though in the present, the gender representation in mass media somewhat reflects the diversity propelled by the feminist and queer movements, this shift has been occurring slowly, and the images in the mainstream media still often adhere to the traditional Western beauty standards. Naomi Wolf (2002, p. 9), one of the leading figures in third-wave feminism, denotes that even though feminist and queer movements have been mostly successful in providing the Western women with social and economic power, their physical appearance continues to be a source of oppression by the patriarchy which stands in the way of women's liberation. She points out that in the 1980s, a beauty myth was constructed by the media industry promoting the ideal woman that all women should aspire to be, who is "tall, thin, white, and blond" and has "a face without pores, asymmetry, or flaws" (Wolf, 2002, p. 1). According to Wolf (2002, p. 2), this era can be referred to as "*The Evil Eighties*" in which conservatism and the debates about reserving the traditional family values were on the rise.

During this time, the image of the perfect woman circulated by mass media was treated as absolute and transcendent, and arguing against the fixed feminine ideals was regarded as heresy. The intent behind the circulation of these images and ideals was not only to satisfy the financial needs of the corporations which produced and promoted products to attain the ideal feminine beauty but also was to achieve a political agenda. The more political and economic rights the women gained, the stricter the beauty myth and the image of the perfect woman became, which resulted in setbacks in the liberation of women. Nevertheless, with the impact of feminist and queer movements, girls and women today are more aware of the beauty myth and the propaganda of mass media, which has resulted in improvements to the representation of the female figure. The rigidity of the beauty myth has dissolved and opened up the space for the representation of diverse women with different races, ethnicities, sexualities, body shapes, age groups, and disabilities in the mass media. The increase in the diversity of representation is especially vital in media and products directed toward children, which is mirrored in popular toys, animated films, and animated series.

In order to present the ascension of plurality in the representation of toys, it is crucial to mention Barbie dolls, which are considered the most commercially successful and iconic dolls in modern times (Norton, Olds, Olive, and Dank, 1996, p. 287). Barbie dolls were produced in 1959 by Mattel, Inc., one of the most prominent toy companies, and quickly became a global phenomenon (Pinon, 2019). Similar to the ideal woman described in Wolf's beauty myth, Barbie was also tall, white, thin, and blonde, with the figure, posture, and clothes of a fashion model. Hence with the changing times, Barbie became exponentially controversial and was "criticized for promoting an unrealistic body image" (Gilblom, 2021). There was increasing concern among parents and scholars as Barbie served as a role model for children, and little girls identified with her during their play times. So, over the years, Mattel has redesigned Barbie frequently and created new dolls to keep up with the changing times while also addressing the critiques, which is particularly clear in their Barbie Fashionistas line (Pinon, 2019). The newest Fashionista line that has been released in 2022 is focused on inclusivity and diversity and is promoted on Mattel's (2022) website with the tagline "Barbie believes in the power of representation" which features more than 35 skin tones, 94 hairstyles, and nine body types. Furthermore, there are Barbie dolls that have prosthetic legs, hearing aids, and wheelchairs. So, as the awareness and consciousness around the importance of diverse representation rise significantly with the wide use of social media, it becomes clear that even one of the most iconic dolls in the toy industry must adapt to ensure its survival in the Digital Age.

The increase in the diversity of representation and inclusivity can also be observed in recent popular animated films, including *Moana* (2016), *Raya and the Last Dragon* (2021), *Encanto* (2021), produced by Walt Disney Animation Studios, *Turning Red* (2022) produced by Pixar Animation Studios, and *The Mitchells vs. the Machines* (2021) produced by Sony Pictures Animation. *Moana, Raya and the Last Dragon, Encanto,* and *Turning Red* all feature female protagonists of various ethnicities and races, and their culture is interwoven into the narrative of the films. Moreover, particularly *Encanto* and *Turning Red* portray female characters that have various body shapes and sizes. In addition, the female protagonist of *The Mitchells vs. the Machines* is openly queer and has a girlfriend in the film, which is a first in an animated family film (Feil, 2022).

In the case of the animated series, the multiplicity of representation can be recognized in *Adventure Time* (2010-2018) produced by Frederator Studios and Cartoon Network Studios, *Legend of Korra* (2012-2014) produced by Nickelodeon Animation Studio, *Steven Universe* (2013-2019) produced by Cartoon Network Studios, *She-Ra and the Princesses of Power* (2018-2020) produced by DreamWorks Animation Television and Mattel Creations, and *The Owl House* (2020-) produced by Disney Television Animation. All of these series feature characters of different races, ethnicities, body shapes and sizes, and also sexualities. In order to present the transformation of representation and the impact of the fourth-wave of feminism in the recent mainstream animated series, the prominent female characters and villains in the original animated series *She-Ra: Princess of Power* and its reboot *She-Ra and The Princesses of Power* are compared in this study. However, before this comparison, it is vital to investigate the origins of the series and the protagonist She-Ra.

The Origins of She-Ra

She-Ra: Princess of Power is a spinoff of the extremely popular American animated television series *He-Man and the Masters of the Universe* (1983-1985) and a part of the Masters of the Universe franchise, which includes toys, books, comics, magazines, animated films, animated series, and video games owned by Mattel. In the 1980s, Mattel was already a leader in the doll and toy car market with Barbie dolls and Hot Wheels, yet the company wanted to become prominent in the male action figure market (Frost and Stern, 2017). Thus, they created a toy line called Masters of the Universe featuring He-Man, a hypermasculine, muscle-bound male action figure, which was inspired by Conan the Barbarian, played by the renowned bodybuilder Arnold Schwarzenegger in the 1980s, in the cult sword and sorcery films *Conan the Barbarian* (1982) and *Conan the Destroyer* (1984). Furthermore, Mattel decided to have an animated series made to give the toys a context and backstory, which they believed would serve to promote their toy line and boost their popularity as the children would already be familiar with the characters and would want to purchase the toys. The company made an agreement with Filmation to produce the animated series *He-Man and the Masters of the Universe* and gave them creative control over the world-building, narrative, and history of the characters (Perlmutter, 2018, p. xxiii). After the series began to air in 1983, both the series and the toy line became a phenomenon.

An interesting development that was unexpected at the time for Mattel was that even though the Masters of the Universe toy line was marketed towards boys, the girls also began to purchase the action figures, He-Man in particular (Frost and Stern, 2017). So, Mattel produced a new female action figure called She-Ra, which combined their iconic doll Barbie's figure and looks that reflected the ideal feminine beauty and He-Man's power. Moreover, the first part of She-Ra's name "She" mirrored He-Man's "He" as his female counterpart, while the second part of her name Ra was given after the "god of the sun and creator god" (Encyclopaedia Britannica, 2021) in ancient Egypt. Afterward, similar to the marketing strategy they employed for the He-Man figures, Mattel partnered with Filmation to create an animated television series based on She-Ra and complementary action figures called *She-Ra: Princess of Power*. However, to build on He-Man's success, She-Ra was first introduced as He-Man's long-lost twin sister in an animated feature film released on March 22, 1985, called *He-Man and She-Ra: The Secret of the Sword*.

In the film, Prince Adam of Eternia, who becomes He-Man to fight evil and defend people in need, is given a mission by the Sorceress of Castle Grayskull to seek the worthy person that is preordained to wield the Sword of Protection. Prince Adam travels to Etheria, a beautiful planet occupied by the Horde, through a portal and discovers that the sword is fated for his twin sister Adora who was kidnapped as a baby by Hordak, the evil dictator and leader of the Horde. Furthermore, Adora was raised by the Horde, taught that the Horde was good, and The Rebellion led by Princess Glimmer was evil. Throughout the film, Adam helps Adora to learn the truth about the Horde and use the Sword of Protection to become She-Ra. The film concludes with Adora joining The Rebellion against the Horde to protect the people of Etheria from their evil forces. This film also serves as the first five episodes of *She-Ra: Princess of Power* animated series, which began to be aired on September 9, 1985, in the United States. *She-Ra* became a hit and was beloved by fans globally, which is the reason why it was revived as a reboot in 2018 as a digital animated series called *She-Ra and the Princesses of Power* on Netflix. The reboot modernized and diversified the designs of the characters while staying true to the original series' themes of friendship, good overcoming evil, and loyalty. In addition, the reboot reflected the humor of *She-Ra: Princess of Power* and was immensely successful both critically and commercially.

The Progression of Gender Representation from *She-Ra: Princess of Power to She-Ra and the Princesses of Power*

The animated series *She-Ra: Princess of Power* and its digital reboot *She-Ra and the Princesses of Power* are not only both globally popular but also mirror the eras in which they were produced. This is apparent in the transformation of their character design, character development, and narrative, as well as the representation of sexuality. Because an intersectional feminist lens is used in this chapter to investigate the evolution of *She-Ra* from the original to the reboot, and to better focus on the gender representation of the female characters and the impact of the fourth-wave feminism, the prominent female characters are examined and compared which include the protagonist Adora/She-Ra, the princesses of the Rebellion Glimmer, Perfuma, Mermista, Frosta, Netossa, Spinerella, Queen Angella, and the villains Catra, Scorpia, Entrapta, and Shadow Weaver.

To begin with, when the original and reboot are compared, the most striking evolution can be observed in the design of the characters. In the original *She-Ra*, because the characters were based on the figures of the Mattel toy line, all the female characters look alike and have an ultra-feminized body shape and size of the ideal woman, which is tall, thin, and busty with long hair. The only thing that lets the viewers differentiate the female characters from one another is their clothes, accessories, and hair color. Moreover, the characters are almost all white with the exception of Princess Netossa. All the prominent female characters are designed as adults that look like they are in their mid to late 20s and wear makeup. In addition, all their clothes are formfitting to showcase and sexualize the characters' bodies, including miniskirts, tights, and tops that resemble bustiers.

However, in *She-Ra and the Princesses of Power*, the first noticeable difference is the youthfulness of the characters, who mostly seem to be teenagers except for the adults Queen Angella (Princess Glimmer's mother), Shadow Weaver (Adora/She-Ra and Catra's mother figure), and the child princess Frosta aged 11. Additionally, all the female characters have different body shapes and sizes, such as tall, short, curvy, overweight, and thin, which makes each character unique and helps showcase their personalities. The diversity of design can also be observed in the representation of the race and ethnicity of the characters. Unlike the original, the reboot portrays female characters with various skin tones and facial features. Moreover, the female characters have a large variety of hair colors and styles, mirroring their diversity, and they wear no makeup or very little makeup with understated colors and highlights on their cheeks which emphasizes their youthful looks.

The clothing style of the female characters in the reboot also mirrors their youthfulness and personalities. The changes to the wardrobe of Adora/She-Ra, in particular, are crucial to mention. Adora's clothes in the original consist of a skintight bodysuit with her legs exposed, and the look is complete with high-heeled boots. Her blonde hair is down and settles in waves around her shoulders. Yet in the reboot, Adora's clothes and hair are more appropriate for her position in the Horde as the Force captain, who is ready for combat with pants, regular boots, a simple white blouse, a short-sleeved jacket, and her hair is in a high ponytail. This difference in clothes between the original and reboot is also paralleled in She-Ra when Adora transforms into her. In the original, She-Ra's costume is designed as a mini skirt and a bustier which are complemented by a cape and high-heeled boots, while her hair is long and cascades down her back in waves. In the reboot, She-Ra still wears a cape and has long, flowy hair, but her sleeveless top covers her upper body up to her neck, and instead of a skirt, she wears mini shorts. She also wears flat boots, and her arms and shoulders are much more muscular than the original She-Ra. In addition, it is crucial to note that in the reboot, as She-Ra matures towards the end of the series, her costume also changes to reflect the character's growth. The final version of She-Ra in the series has long white pants with flat boots, and her cape is turned into a bottom piece of her top which reaches to her knees and flows around her legs. Furthermore, her long hair is in a high ponytail which underlines her maturity and readiness for combat to fight and defeat evil.

The second transformation that stands out the most in the comparison of the original She-Ra and the reboot is the character development and narrative. In the original, Prince Adam/He-Man introduces Adora/She-Ra, and he is the protagonist in the first five episodes of *She-Ra: Princess of Power*. In addition, Prince Adam/He-Man makes appearances in various other episodes throughout the original series. Yet, in the reboot, although a part of the backstory of Adora/She-Ra still remains in which she was kidnapped by Hordak and brought to Etheria through a portal, He-Man does not exist and Adora/She-Ra is the sole hero of the series. Also, in the original *She-Ra*, because the characters are older, there is not much room for their development and their personalities stay mostly the same throughout the series. However, the creator of the reboot ND Stevenson (Nate Stevenson), who is a renowned cartoonist, author, and illustrator, approaches the new series as a coming-of-age story. Hence, all of the prominent female characters are given story arcs that prioritize their character development and journey towards maturity. This journey is best showcased through the protagonist Adora/She-Ra, and the antagonist Catra.

In the original *She-Ra*, the character development for Adora mainly occurs throughout the first five episodes in which she learns about her origins, wields the Sword of Protection to transform into She-Ra, and becomes the hero and protector of Etheria. Afterward, the series continues with the adventures of Adora/She-Ra and The Rebellion, but there is not much more focus on character growth in the rest of the episodes. In the same vein, Catra, who is one of the main villains and adversaries of Adora/She-Ra in the original series, is portrayed as evil and remains that way in the series with no change to her character. In contrast to the original, in the reboot, Adora and Catra are presented as close childhood friends, taken by the Horde, who grew up together and protected each other. Yet a drift occurs between them when Adora learns that the Horde is actually evil, becomes She-Ra, and joins The Rebellion. Although Adora/She-Ra asks Catra to join her in The Rebellion, Catra refuses and takes Adora/She-Ra's place as the Force Captain to lead the Horde. Throughout the seasons of the reboot, the adversary between Adora/She-Ra and Catra remains as one of the primary and most intriguing conflicts of the series as the viewers are presented with these characters' journeys and development. Towards the end of the fifth and last season, after all the confrontations between them, Catra finally faces her inner demons and insecurities, becomes reformed, and joins Adora/She-Ra and The Rebellion in the fight against the Horde Prime, the emperor and dictator of the Horde Empire. Throughout the reboot, the struggles and insecurities of Adora/She-Ra are also shown as her character matures while discovering her powers, abilities, and who she is. So, upon the comparison of the original and reboot, the former approaches the structure of the characters as more rigid, strictly divided into categories such as absolute good and evil, right and wrong, while the latter presents characters as more fluid, open to change, growth, and improvement which makes the characters more nuanced and complex.

Furthermore, the character development and narrative surrounding Adora/She-Ra and Catra are closely interwoven into the exploration of their sexuality in *She-Ra and the Princesses of Power*, unlike the original, which only portrays heterosexual relationships. In the reboot, while Adora/She-Ra and Catra go through the coming-of-age journey, they also discover that despite their rivalry against one another, they love each other, which is always presented as bubbling just under the surface. In the final season, when Adora and Catra acknowledge their feelings and confess their love, this becomes a catalyst for Adora to transform into She-Ra and save Etheria from destruction by the Horde Prime. Hence, the reboot positions the love between Adora/She-Ra and Catra as the central relationship of the series with the message of true love overcoming all obstacles, which is extremely rare in an animated series targeted toward children. In addition, the reboot portrays other queer couples, such as Bow's fathers, George and Lance, as well as Princesses Netossa and Spinnerella, who are openly together and married. There is also a new character in the reboot called Double Trouble with the ability to shapeshift who is nonbinary.

In closing, both *She-Ra: Princess of Power* and *She-Ra and The Princesses of Power* are revolutionary for the eras in which they are produced. Although there is some room for improvement and a need for better representation in the areas of gender, race, ethnicity, body image, and sexuality in the original series, Adora/She-Ra and all the prominent female characters are portrayed as leaders that are powerful and independent which pave the way for the empowered titular female heroes in the popular series created in the 1990s such as Xena in *Xena: Warrior Princess* (1995-2001) and Buffy Summers in *Buffy the Vampire Slayer* (1997-2003) during the third-wave feminism. When compared with the original, the reboot fixes many of the representation issues and addresses the need for the portrayal of diverse characters and their multifaceted experiences through attention to detail in character study and nuanced storytelling. This transformation is also signaled in the change to the name of the series from the more singular focused *She-Ra: Princess of Power* to the ever more inclusive and diverse *She-Ra and the Princesses of Power* centered on the plurality of experiences of the characters. Hence, the transformation of gender, race, ethnicity, and sexuality in *She-Ra and the Princesses of Power* reflects the impact of fourth-wave feminism through the deconstruction of the beauty myth and the rapid shifts occurring in representation in the mass media in the Digital Age.

References

Encyclopaedia Britannica. (November 18, 2021). Re. In *Encyclopaedia Britannica.* Retrieved from https://www.britannica.com/topic/Re?utm_campaign=b-extension&utm_medium=chrome&utm_source=ebinsights&utm_content=Re [Accessed on Sept., 2, 2022].

Feil, C. (March 16, 2022). The year that queer animated characters made history. *Vanity Fair.* Retrieved from https://www.vanityfair.com/hollywood/2022/03/awards-insider-the-year-that-queer-animated-characters-made-history [Accessed on Sept., 2, 2022].

Frost, B. J. (Writer), & Stern, T. (Director). (2017). *He-Man* [Television series episode]. In B. Volk-Weiss (Creator), *The toys that made us.* Los Angeles, CA: The Nacelle Company.

Gilblom, K. (February 24, 2021). How a barbie makeover led to a pandemic sales boom. *Bloomberg.* Retrieved from https://www.bloomberg.com/news/articles/2021-02-24/barbie-s-pandemic-sales-boom-followed-yearslong-revamp-at-mattel#xj4y7vzkg

Nadel, A. H. (Producer), Friedman, E., Kachivas, L., Lamore, M., Reed, B., & Wetzler, G. (Directors). (1985). *He-Man and She-Ra: The secret of the sword* [Motion picture]. United States: Filmation Associates; Mattel.

Norton, K. I., Olds, T. S., Olive, S., & Dank, S. (1996). Ken and Barbie at life size. *Sex Roles, 34*(3): 287–294.

Mattel, Inc. (August 24, 2022). Barbie believes in the power of representation. *Mattel.* Retrieved from https://shop.mattel.com/pages/barbie-diversity [Accessed on Sept., 2, 2022].

Munro, E. B. (2013). Feminism: A fourth wave?. *Political Insight, 4*(2): 22–25.

Perlmutter, D. (2018). *The encyclopedia of American animated television shows.* Maryland: Rowman & Littlefield.

Pinon, N. (December 23, 2019). She's a Barbie girl in a new world. *Mashable.* Retrieved from https://mashable.com/feature/barbie-diverse-inclusive

Robinson, V., & Richardson, D. (Eds.). (2015). *Introducing gender and women's studies.* Macmillan International Higher Education.

Scheimer, L. (Executive Producer). (1983-1985). *He-Man and the Masters of the Universe* [TV series]. Filmation Associates; Mattel.

Scheimer, L. (Executive Producer). (1985-1987). *She-Ra: Princess of power* [TV series]. Filmation Associates; Mattel.

Stevenson, N. (Executive Producer). (2018-2020). *She-Ra and the princesses of power* [Digital streaming series]. DreamWorks Animation Television; DreamWorks Animation; Mattel Creations.

Wolf, N. (2002). *The beauty myth: How images of beauty are used against women.* New York: HarperCollins Publishers.

Hakan Erkılıç and Servet Can Dönmez

On VR Filmmaking

Abstract: Emerging in almost every field of daily life, such as architecture, medicine, tourism, advertising, education, etc., VR applications have become one of the most rapidly advancing areas of digital transformation in the audiovisual field. VR applications evolve at the junction point of entertainment, business and science. Structured on the basis of filmmaking practice and game infrastructure, VR applications have begun to create a unique narrative and style of their own, and have introduced such attributes as experience instead of view, and user instead of viewer. The key determinants of VR applications, which are often mistaken for 360-degree filmmaking, include interactivity, immersion and the sense of "being there" (telepresence) created thereby. The user is thus prompted to interact through the simulation or imaginary design of the real world. From screenwriting to shooting/filmmaking as well as to the viewing experience, VR applications represent a departure from traditional filmmaking practice. This chapter[28], after outlining the basic terminology of VR, seeks to describe the practice of screenwriting, shooting (camera positioning), audio design and editing based on VR applications, although a standard has not yet been established.

Keywords: VR, VR Applications, Screenwriting, Camera Positioning, Audio/Sound, Editing

Introduction

The most fundamental difference between humans and other living beings on Earth is the ability of humans to transfer their memory and experiences between generations. The curiosity and the desire to know what the reality is lie at the heart of humanity's various inventions. Sherman et al. (2003, p. 6) define the history of mankind as the history of the various media tools invented to enable this intergenerational transmission. From this point of view, the cave paintings are the first tools that serve this purpose, which, as Hamit (1993, p. 57) points out, are also considered to be the first examples of virtual reality in the sense that they recreate a lived reality.

The term "virtual" refers to "what does not exist in reality but is conceived in the mind," whilst the term "real" implies a more complex and philosophically debatable concept: "the real" is defined as "what actually exists," or "all things that are recognized as existing." Basically, the human desire to know what is real is a topic that falls within the sphere of ontology. The question as to what reality is has been answered differently throughout the ages. Berkeley, a philosopher who lived about a century after Descartes justified existence and reality based on the mind, was the first to bring these two opposing concepts closer together in the context of virtual reality technology known to us today. Berkeley argues that all reality is mind and matter, that beings depend merely on perception, and that existing in the mind depends on being perceived by the mind (Luce, 1941). The two concepts, "virtual" and "real," which appear to be antonyms given their definitions in the dictionary, take on a different meaning when brought together. Castells (2010) argues that a new culture, a culture of virtuality, has emerged as virtuality has become a fundamental dimension of our reality since digitized communication networks have become inclusive of all cultural manifestations and personal experiences. Castells (2010, p. 403) defines the terms "virtual" and "real" with reference to the Oxford Dictionary: "virtual: being so in practice though not strictly or in name," and "real: actually existing." Drawing on this definition, Castells points out that the reality, as how we experience it, is always virtual.

Technological and medical advances have confirmed that human perception of the outside world occurs entirely in the brain. When the data from the five sense organs find a response in the brain, there occurs perception. The rapid advances in the computer and electronics industry lead to the rapid development of technologies that can replace these five senses. However, it was long before today's virtual reality technology that cinema began to manipulate sight and hearing, the most basic senses through which humans receive their first data about the outside world. This manipulation by cinema takes place in the movie theater, just like in Plato's cave, through the film images reflected on a screen in the dark within its own spatial reality. Through this reflection, viewers find themselves in a different reality. Therein lies a crucial detail: in the movie theater, the viewers are always at a safe distance. This represents the most fundamental point where virtual reality and cinema diverge. For Steuer (1992, pp. 79–87), the most prominent aspect of virtual reality technology is its ability to create "telepresence," i.e. "the sense of being there." This powerful aspect of virtual reality makes the "viewer" who watches the movie at a safe distance a "user," a "participant," or a "player" in the story. Technologically speaking, virtual reality is an interactive technology that gives users feedback by tracking their positions and actions (Jerald, 2016, p. 9; Sherman and Craig, 2003, p. 13). Virtual reality technology is an interactive computer technology that manipulates perceived external reality to create the sense of being in a place where one is not physically present. A virtual reality experience requires four basic components: virtual representation, virtual environment, sensory feedback and interaction (Sherman et al., 2009). The sense of being physically present in some environment, "presence," emerges as a perceptual, cognitive and psychological outcome in virtual environments. The sense of presence falls into three different dimensions (Mestre and Vercher, 2011; Heeter, 1992, pp. 262–265), including subjective personal presence, which is achieved through movements, feedback and avatars; social presence, which is confirmed by other users and entities; and environmental presence, which arises from interaction with the environment and space.

VR productions are increasingly evolving, from medicine to tourism and documentaries to education. The intense interest attracted by VR productions in both fictions and documentaries in cinema has prompted film festivals to launch new sections/competitions dedicated to VR. Besides major festivals such as Cannes, Venice, Sundance, Toronto, Busan, IDFA, etc., there are also film festivals that are dedicated exclusively to VR productions such as VRFest/Las Vegas, VRSci Fest, Vancourve VR Film Fest, Australian Virtual Reality. This paper focuses on the practice of VR content production. The paper will first outline the basic concepts of VR filmmaking and then discuss the relationship between cinema and virtual reality. After drawing a distinction between user-centric True Virtual Reality content, where the flow depends on the user's preferences, and 360-degree content, an overall evaluation of filmmaking will be presented, drawing on the practical applications of VR content production.

From Cinema to Virtual Reality

Cinema's relationship with virtual reality technology dates back to Morton Heilig's invention of the "*Sensorama*" in 1956 (Sherman and Craig, 2003, p. 25). Apart from three-dimensional visualization, the device aimed to provide the viewer with a new experience by giving feedback to other senses such as sound, movement and smell. By the 21st century, however, virtual reality, after having faded in the meantime, has started to attract people's attention once again with the emergence of headsets that can be used more comfortably physically with the evolving technology and shrinking microchips. Another factor that brings virtual reality and cinema closer together is the approach "*The Myth of Total Cinema*" of Andre Bazin (2005, pp. 17–22), one of the most important figures of realist cinema theory. Bazin proposes that the reality is spatial and that imaginary objects in an image do not destroy the illusion of reality. Hence, in much the same way that the transformations in digital technology have marked not the death but the rebirth of cinema (Erkılıç, 2017), it is possible to say that the same is true for virtual reality technology. It is through digital cinema and virtual reality applications that Bazin's theory of reality moves into a new phase.

One of the leading theories on how cinema creates reality at the cognitive level is the apparatus theory. Jean-Louis Baudry (1986) argues that the viewer feels a sense of mastery in the movie theater, which is analogous to Plato's cave, just like Lacan's child looking in the mirror for the first time. Making the subject the master of the gaze, a movie creates a perception of reality through image continuity (Elsaesser and Hagener, 2010). In virtual reality, however, the master of the scopophilic view in the movie theater is replaced by users who experience and witness the story spatially. The viewer is now, in the 21st century, a user in virtual reality technology. Jerald (2016) believes that the virtual reality stands as a candidate to replace direct communication. As such, content producers are required to have a human-centric perspective. This has a direct impact on the structure and codes of the narrative. Another aspect that distinguishes virtual reality content from traditional movie narratives is that the content and flow can be changed depending on the user's decisions.

Virtual reality contents differ from traditional motion pictures not only in experiential but also in stylistic terms. At this point, it is once again essential to distinguish between the user-centric True Virtual Reality content, where the flow is customized depending on the user's preferences, and the 360-degree content. Essentially, the fully interactive virtual reality contents represent a simulation of a story. 360-degree contents, on the other hand, are basically a limited experience with the freedom of view of a viewer who is freed from the director's frame. A comparison of movie narratives and virtual reality experiences reveals some codes that are common to both 360-degree video contents and fully interactive virtual reality experiences: we see that there are important elements of the narrative such as establishing shots, dialogue and ambient sounds, visual effects as well as sound and movement in the mise-en-scene to guide the viewer (Erkılıç and Dönmez, 2020, pp: 337–338). Yet, we find that almost none of the most basic elements of narration in traditional cinema, such as the director's framing, scales of shots and plans, dramatic lighting, cuts and transitions, are explicitly present in virtual reality.

Jenkins (2006, p. 21) argues that storytelling has become a means of "world-making," creating environments which cannot be explored with traditional tools or with a single tool. The real world is much bigger in the world of the movies, and the world of the movies grows and expands with the contribution of the viewers. In the face of such advances, virtual reality technology opens new doors as it offers new possibilities. Pointing out that traditional codes fail and are inadequate when producing content with this new tool, Bailenson (2016) also argues that in virtual reality, it is not possible to fully experience the content without a guide. For Bielskyte (2016), the focus should not be on storytelling, but on creating experiences. Creating an experience, however, requires both spatial design and plot design. It is therefore possible to argue that virtual reality content differs from traditional cinema not only in terms of viewing or experiencing, but also in terms of production. In a world where traditional cinema still serves as the dominant narrative tool, this differentiation evokes the question "how is it made?" for both the producer and the user.

The underlying reason why virtual reality content is often referred to as "virtual reality movies" is that 360-degree videos create a telepresence effect when viewed with virtual reality headsets. However, 360-degree videos constitute a video format in which images are recorded globally by multiple cameras (Fonseca, 2016). In this regard, Sarah Thomas (2019, p. 454) provides two different conceptualizations, regarding "*True Virtual Reality*" and "*Cinematic Virtual Reality*." The distinction proposed by Thomas is important to clarify this point. True Virtual Reality describes fully interactive virtual reality experiences, whilst Cinematic Virtual Reality stands for 360-degree stereoscopic videos that offer a limited experience and are viewed with virtual reality headsets. The primary underlying reason for comparing virtual reality contents with motion pictures is the fact that those who create such works have a background in cinematic works. Additionally, the fact that the history of the motion picture continues to evolve with virtual reality results in the application of previous practices and theory (predominantly, of cinema) in virtual reality (Dönmez and Erkılıç, 2018). The theory and practice of cinema can support the cinematic editing of VR contents. In much the same way that cinema continues to renew storytelling with its own linguistic and aesthetic style based on the previous experience, VR applications also keep on evolving by transforming cinematic storytelling. However, recent studies show that virtual reality should be considered as an independent field.

How Is It Made? On VR Practice

Advancing by differentiating from cinematic practice, VR content production represents an emerging field. As with any new creative production, VR content production also poses its own set of challenges. Gödde et al. (2018) identified six main challenges for cinematic narrative in Virtual Reality:

Guiding the viewers' attention to the relevant story elements,
Choosing the role of the viewer between an active participant and a passive observer,
Choosing the right place for the camera, the action and story elements and what consequences this has for seated viewers,

Balancing spatial and temporal story density,
Rethinking framing,
Rethinking editing (Gödde et al., 2018).

Recognizing these challenges as well as designing and planning VR content in consideration of them allows us to minimize potential barriers. These challenges also lead to opportunities for creativity. Drawing on the study of Gödde et al. and other literature reviews, the paper will describe these challenges and suggest possible solutions.

Taking into account the current technological form of virtual reality technology, it is important to note that the first step is to create content around the topic of virtual reality. However, this varies in direct proportion to the limits of the human body. To create an experience through the human body and its senses, it is first necessary to be aware of the limits of the human senses. Speaking of virtual reality, the first limits to be recognized are the senses of sight and hearing. To ensure that a sense of presence is created, the experience must be stereoscopic. Hence, this corresponds to a field of 114–120 degrees. A 175-degree field of regard does not allow people to see in three dimensions, whereas the total field of regard of humans is 220 degrees (see Fig. 1).

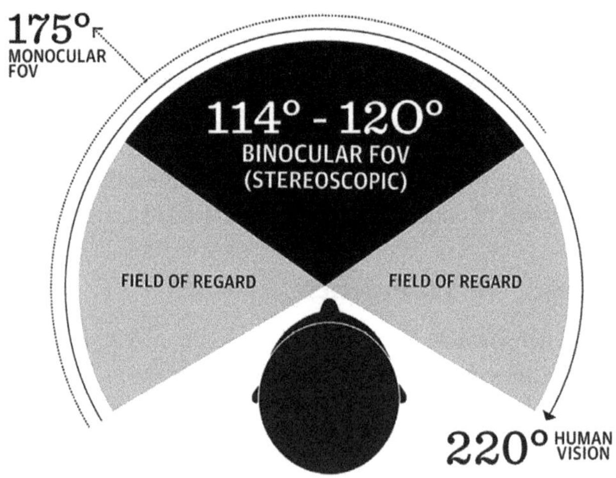

Fig. 1: Human Vision and Field of Regard (Williams, Love, and Love, 2021, p. 154).

The vertical field of regard, on the other hand, is approximately 55-degree, of which 35 degrees is the area where text and symbols can be read most easily (see Fig. 2).

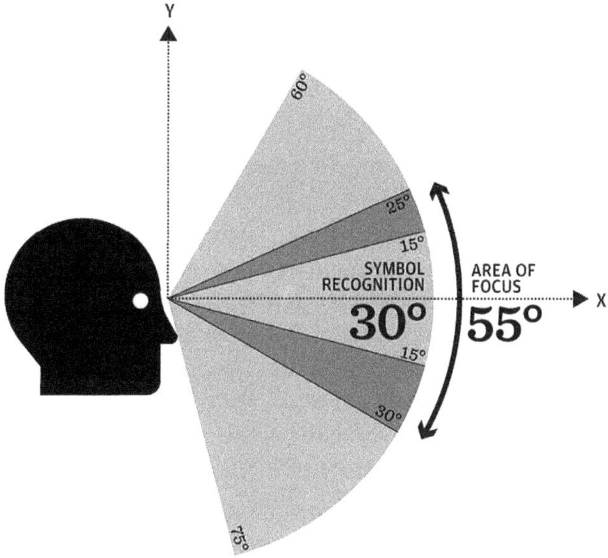

Fig. 2: Vertical Field of Regard (Williams, Love, and Love, 2021, p. 155).

The fundamental building blocks of all stories are the characters, the conflict and the resolution. For storytelling, however, each tool has its own advantages and disadvantages. At this point, what distinguishes virtual reality from other tools is that it enables us to experience things that we cannot experience in the real world. Having conducted one-on-one interviews with teams that produce professional contents in the field of virtual reality and compiled these interviews in a book, John Bucher (2018) provides important anecdotes on the foundations of virtual reality narrative. Pete Billington, screenwriter at *Dreamwork Animation* and *Oculus Story Studio*, believes that virtual reality technology is bringing storytelling back to its primitive roots. Virtual reality is similar to how stories were historically told around the campfire. Being drawn into stories and using our imagination to fill in the gaps, in this case, is akin to virtual reality experiences in terms of establishing a connection with an individual (Bucher, 2018, p. 72). Jessica Shamash, filmmaker at *Pixar* and *Oculus Story Studio*, who agrees with

Billington's views, asserts that this primal connection is established through empathy. Samash, who believes that the more layers are added to the virtual reality experience, the more effective the experience will be, suggests that the traditional three-act structure should not be ignored while adding layers (Bucher, 2018, p. 78). In her book "*Cinematic Virtual Reality: A Critical Study of 21st Century Approaches and Practices*," Kath Dooley (2021), a filmmaker and academician, summarizes the main conclusions she has drawn from her own experiences and interviews with professionals working in this field as follows:

- At this point, the challenge is to write a detailed description of the story agents (items, characters and action) presented in the 360-degree environment. The screenplay may be formatted according to the traditional movie screenplay, but it is considerably longer than the traditional one (see Fig. 3).
- For Martin Taylor, co-screenwriter and director of *Awake* (2016), the notion of "guiding" the viewer through a spatialized screenplay seems to mean emphasizing directional cues in the story to ensure that "key moments" are not missed. Therefore, *Awake*'s screenplay features detailed descriptions of the spatialized action, as well as the basic actions that the filmmakers want the viewer to follow at specific times (see Fig. 4).

There is an oddness to the room. Far too many lamps. Papers pinned to the walls with patterns and geometric designs. Items in the room are tagged with small WHITE LABELS. A curious mind has been at work here, mapping the place. Questioning everything.

THE VOICE (V.O.) (CONT'D)
...because what consciousness is, is a rather specialized form of awareness...

A large mirror above the fireplace is smashed. Shards and cracks spidering out from a single impact.

An unkempt man sits alone, sleeping in a WHEELCHAIR. This is **HARRY** (60) and he wakes with a start, almost dropping a framed PHOTOGRAPH he was nursing in his lap. It is a picture of himself in better days. Beside him stands **ROSE,** the love of his life, with an OAK TREE in the background.

You recognise the same scene from the DIORAMA. HARRY was a man clearly fit in his earlier days, but now bound to a WHEELCHAIR. He looks exhausted, like he hasn't had a good night's sleep in a year.

The RADIO is revealed to be the source of THE VOICE. A broadcast of Philosopher, Alan Watts - the details on the radio's glowing digital readout.

THE VOICE (V.O.) (CONT'D)
(on the radio)
...When you look around the room, you are conscious of as much as you can notice, and you see an enormous number of things which you do not notice...

CLICK - HARRY abruptly turns the RADIO off with the remote. The room is now quiet save for the sound of TICKING and a FLUTTER -- The Ticking is a small METRONOME steadily clocking away on a side table next to HARRY's Wheelchair. The Flutter is from a tiny BLUEBIRD in a cage in the corner of the room hopping from perch to perch.

HARRY gathers himself, groggy and still half asleep. Whether he is mumbling to himself or the Bluebird is hard to tell.

HARRY
(under his breath)
This is never going to work you know. Just like all the others.

The Bluebird twitters. HARRY looks over.

HARRY (CONT'D)
Don't you start. We can rest when we're done.

Fig. 3: Page 2 of the 6th Draft Screenplay for Awake (Dooley, 2021, p. 64).

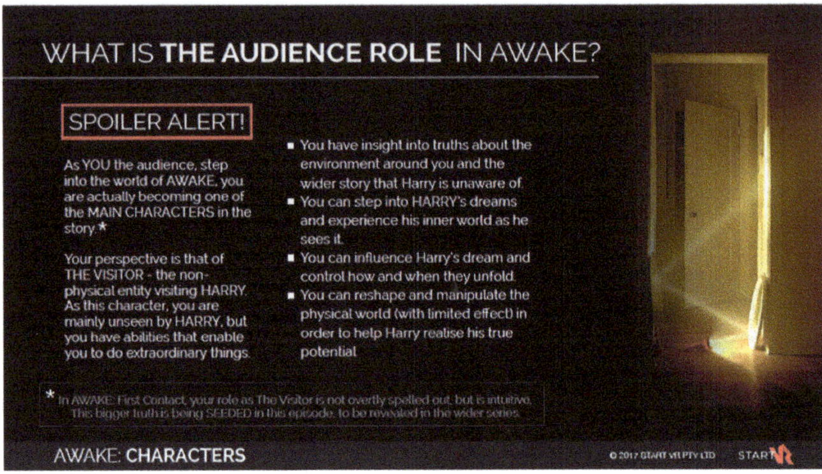

Fig. 4: *Awake* Story Bible (Dooley, 2021, p. 71).

In VR screenwriting, coding 360 degrees by dividing it into a set of parts, i.e. front, rear, left, right, and expressing it with color is a different and functional method to write 360 degrees by defining it (see Fig. 5). This makes it easier to identify 360-degree movements simultaneously within the continuum of events. In the flow, writing each scene in its respective color makes it possible to see the 360-degree flow of events at a glance. This method allows the screenwriters to master their story and build the plot in 360 degrees.

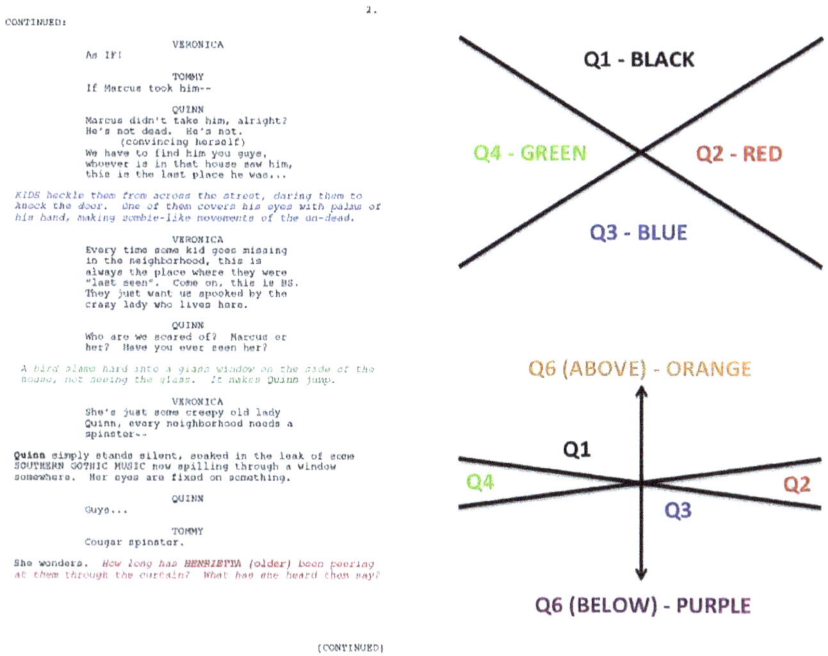

Fig. 5: Screenwriting for Virtual Reality (Damiani, 2017).

Damiani (2017) notes that there are two paradigms evident in VR storytelling: the traditional Teller-Listener Storytelling Paradigm, which has been prevalent since we started telling stories around a fire, where the narrator relays the story and the user understands the story, and the Builder-Participator Storytelling Paradigm, a storytelling style where the user participates in story settings and creates the story. It can be argued that 360-degree videos are dominated by the Teller-Listener Storytelling Paradigm, whereas VR cinematic narratives are dominated by the Builder-Participator Storytelling Paradigm. In virtual reality contents, the flow needs to be thoroughly planned and designed at the screenwriting stage to ensure that the user understands the story and the director does not miss the plot. Gödde et al. (2018) found that it was the initial viewing direction (IVD) that determined the placement of action and story elements. In VR, the first-person perspective implies that the user sees through the eyes of a character. In the third-person perspective, on the other hand, the user has no direct involvement in the story and perceives the story in a disembodied way (Damiani, 2017).

The multifaceted nature and interactivity of 360 video, which plays a decisive role in this framework, also opens up new possibilities for storytelling. A prime example of this interaction and the multifaceted screenplay and mise-en-scene structure is the virtual reality experience *Afterlife* (2019). This experience allows users to have a multiple flow with 29 different options and combinations. The screenplay of the content is also designed in a structure that shifts in line with the user's choices (Erkılıç and Dönmez, 2021, pp. 505–525).

The key point that should be considered while creating virtual reality content is the positioning of the camera and mise-en-scene in accordance with the distance that the human eye can focus and follow. Laurent Lescop and Bruno Suner (2020) describe in detail the design of a 360-degree set, which differs from a traditional movie set, through the set they designed for *Dans le Luna with Marc Caro*. Lescop and Suner (2020, pp. 545–554) suggest that the key points to consider when designing a 360-degree set in order to solve the problem completely during the shoot without dealing with post-production are as follows:

- The acting area should not be more than 3 m away. This is because, beyond 3 m, the resolution of cameras loses detail due to human vision and attention span. This corresponds to a diameter of roughly 5–6 m around the camera.
- The details in the background which are so far away that they lose resolution should be unrelated to the flow of the story. This can lead to loss of attention for the user.
- As conventional scales of shots cannot be used, close-ups etc. are not possible. This conventional cinematic framing that is sought to be achieved through the movements of the actor is therefore directly related to the focal length and quality of the camera. In cases where the actor moves too close to the camera or too far away from the camera to the point of losing details, this leads to distorted images and a loss of impact.
- Characters should be positioned in the right places at the right time.
- The lighting should be diegetic and evenly distributed.
- As far as possible, the editing process as used in traditional cinema should be avoided, as this goes against the nature of the apparatus. An uninterrupted flow should be preferred. This bears similarities with theater in terms of acting. The actors' gestures, facial expressions and movements should be explicit and understandable.
- The user's position in the story has a direct impact on the design of the set. The positions of the invisible viewer, the passive viewer and the participating viewer-actor constitute a fundamental element that needs to be considered

in the design of the camera and other actors, objects and the set (Lescop and Suner, 2020, pp. 545–554).

A viewer who is merely an observer with no connection to the stage is a passive viewer, whilst a viewer who is part of the stage is a participating viewer. Gödde et al. (2018) show the results of active and passive positions on the experience in the table below (see Tab. 1).

Tab. 1: Features of Active and Passive VR Experiences (Gödde et al., 2018).

Viewer is part of the scene	**Viewer is observer**
Active experience/ "Lean Forward"	Passive experience/ "Lean Back"
Interaction possible and expected	No interaction
High involvement	Lower involvement
High potential for a feeling of presence	Lower potential for a feeling of presence
Story might fade into background	Emphasis on narrative
More control for the viewer	More control for the storyteller

Given Gödde et al.'s findings on active and passive positions and Lescop and Suner's notes on set design and acting, it is clear that they are in line with the INFO wheel layout suggested by Williams et al. for set design (see Fig. 6).

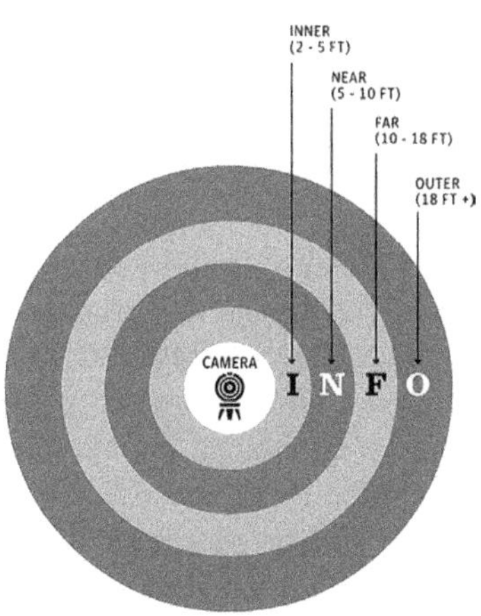

Fig. 6: INFO Wheel (Williams, Love and Love, 2021, p. 23).

In the wheel (on Fig. 6), I [Inner] stands for the main character and events, N [Near] for secondary characters and events, F [Far] for figuration and other indirect elements, and O [Outer] for everything that is irrelevant and out of focus. Moreover, Williams et al. suggest that the mise-en-scene and plot should be designed according to two different camera positionings: one where the camera is in the middle of the action or one where the camera follows the action from the sidelines (see Fig. 7).

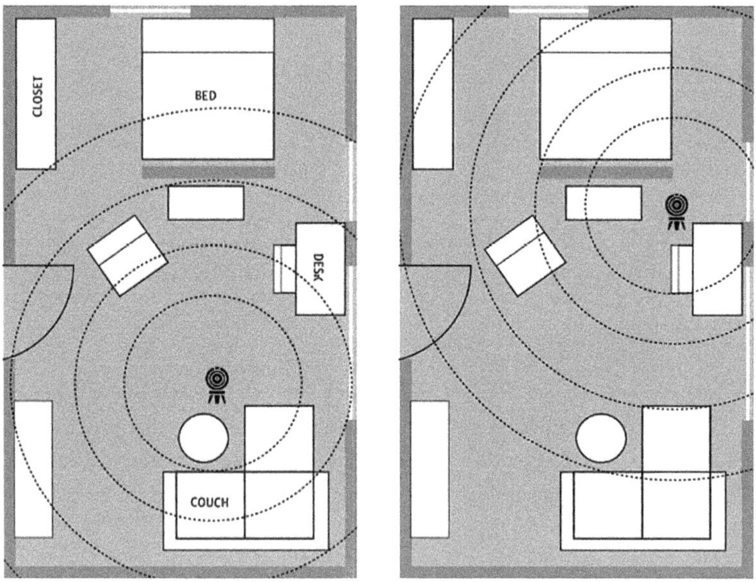

Fig. 7: Dual-Option Camera Positioning (Williams, Love, and Love, 2021, p. 24).

However, it is also necessary to consider how users perceive the environment and narratives so that we can understand the structures of virtual reality narratives. Quin, Rau, and Salvendy (2009) suggest 4 items in response to this question: flow, cognitive assimilation, immersion and presence. Flow indicates the state of total involvement in an experience, i.e. the more seamless and engaged the user is in the experience, the more effective the flow is. Cognitive assimilation represents the cognitive connection that the user establishes with the space, which may vary for each individual in proportion to the socio-cultural background and the persona of the user. The sense of presence, just as Heeter (1992) points out, is the user's sense of being present in that environment and the elements incorporated into the content to create this sense. Immersion is one of the key concepts in virtual reality terminology and technology. This concept reflects the extent to which and how users are able to be involved in virtual reality experiences. Although it varies depending on the context, immersion usually involves activities that serve a sense of presence. Immersion is divided into four categories: physical or sensory, challenge-based or involvement-based, cognitive or imaginative, and emotional immersion.

- In physical or sensory immersion, activities performed in virtual reality are perceived as real by the brain, just like the sense felt when an activity is performed in the physical world (e.g. swimming) (Qin, Rau, and Salvendy 2009; Fagan, 2018).
- Challenge-based and involvement-based immersion requires the active involvement of the user; such involvement creates a sense of being part of the story (ibid.).
- Sensory immersion is a condition inherent in the virtual reality tool, whilst cognitive and imaginative immersion is a passive experience, like reading a book (Douglas and Hargadon, 2000).
- Emotional immersion is the type of immersion that can affect one's emotions and thoughts, and is so effective that it can lead to physical and therefore mental changes in emotional state, e.g. empathy, compassion, morality (Brown and Cairns, 2004, p. 1299).

Neal Tyler Heaton (2020) argues that, in order to solve the problems of creating "environmental storytelling," which constitutes one of the key elements of creating a sense of being there in the virtual reality experience created by him, a number of elements need to work together and function properly. These elements include the quality of the spatial sound (in terms of amplitude, frequency and reflection), interactivity and mobility. Emphasizing that these basic elements need to be used efficiently to enhance the user's spatial experience and draw them further into the narrative, Heaton underlines the importance of the effective use of spatial sound as the user interacts with the space and objects in a setting of free movement. For example, it is preferable to use a spatial audio that makes the user feel like heading towards its source, rather than an off-voice of unknown source. An ambosonically-recorded 360-degree audio is quite effective for directing the user's attention. The quality of the 360-degree audio is related to the correct use of many factors such as tone, timbre, geometry of the space, various dynamics and their attributes (see Fig. 8).

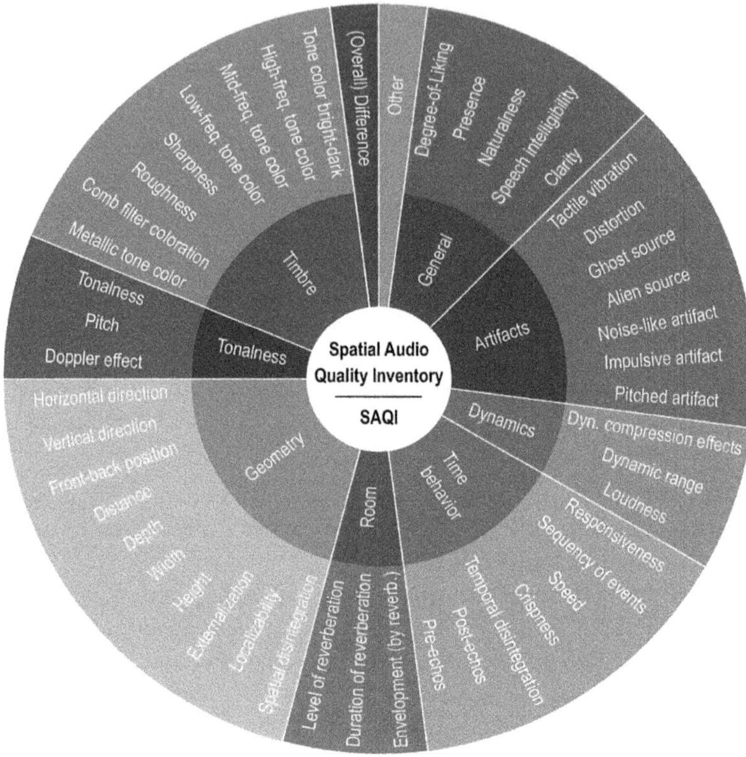

Fig. 8: SAQI Wheel for the Evaluation of Virtual Acoustic Environments, Structured into Informal Categories [Inner Ring] and Attributes [Outer Ring] (Serafin, 2022, p. 163).

Deniz Tortum (2019), the director of the 360-degree film *Floodplain VR* (*Sel Yatağı VR*), states that the first challenge they faced during the filmmaking process was to direct the viewer's gaze since there was no frame. Other challenges faced during the shooting include remote casting, extra post-production for audio and concealment of the set crew. Celine Tricart (2018) argues that, in virtual reality, there exists no camera in the traditional sense, so a rectangular framing cannot be used as a composition within this framing. This makes it difficult to make edits within and between scenes. In virtual reality, just like in the theater, it is possible for the viewer to lose track of the flow if the next scene is not edited and connected effectively. The editing of virtual reality content and

360-degree films does not have a cut-and-paste logic in the conventional sense; for scene transitions, such edits as camera movement, character gaze direction, mise-en-scene, audio, graphical orientation and lighting are utilized (see Fig. 9).

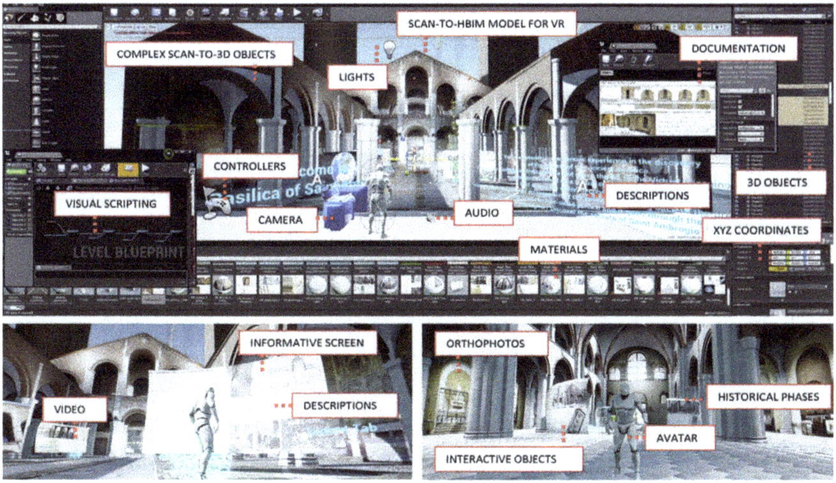

Fig. 9: The Unreal Engine 4 Editor Allows the Development of a VR Project Using Different Types of Contents (Banfi et al., 2019, p. 22).

These also serve as tools for the user to follow the story. Although it is too early to talk about a new editing language for VR, there are huge opportunities ahead for its development.

Conclusion

As a tool that is still in the process of technological evolution, the basic filmmaking practices of virtual reality also continue to evolve. There is a growing body of data and studies on these filmmaking practices and codes. Yet, when it comes to creating a human-centered design, it is of course possible to lay down certain rules and limits, at least in terms of practices of experience. To articulate these rules more clearly, it is first necessary to keep in mind the distinction that the only aspect shared by cinematic virtual reality content, i.e. 360-degree videos, and fully interactive virtual reality content is the act of viewing with virtual reality headsets. After shooting, a number of interactive objects and options can be added to 360-degree videos through game engines. For a complete virtual reality experience, however, the user should have full freedom of movement. This is because it is still not possible to move within the video recording. Full freedom of movement is a quality that is unique to fully computer-generated virtual reality contents. Hence, 360-degree videos tend to be more widely used in documentaries, news and travel videos. Computer-generated graphics have become almost photorealistic as a result of advances in digital technology and artificial intelligence software. Once this technology is combined with virtual reality technology, there will be an opportunity to have an experience that we will find it difficult to distinguish it from the real thing. Referring to such content as a movie or a game would be misleading. It would be fairer to call them "experiences." This is because such content now combines, as a new form, the image quality of cinema with the unlimited possibilities of the digital game world.

The perception of the human being as an individual and the replacement of the divine gaze by the individual during the Renaissance gave rise to the perspective gaze. The cinematic aesthetics was primarily shaped by the window (frame and screen) built on the perspective gaze that develops at the center of the individual. However, VR marks the beginning of a new phase. Now, we are faced with a new form and narrative that again puts the individual at the center, but synthesizes the "window," "frame," and "mirror" (Elsaesser and Hagener, 2010), immersing him/her 360 degrees and interacting with him/her, where the viewer has become the user, the lens-front reality has become a computer-generated CGI reality, and the view has become an experience. Unlike the director's gaze and framing in traditional cinema, the user has the freedom of 360-degree vision in virtual reality technology. A new production is being developed, which moves from the cinematic practice and narrative, but transcends it. It is, however, still not possible today to claim that there are standards established for the practice of VR filmmaking. Not only is VR an experience, it is also a pursuit. In this regard, there is a need for further research based on VR filmmaking experiences. With enormous potential for creative innovation, exciting advances are expected in VR applications.

Note

28 This chapter includes findings from the study was supported by Mersin University Scientific Research Project no. 2019-1-AP4-3395.

References

Bailenson, J. (December 5, 2016). The trials and tribulations of narrative in VR: The Stanford Ocean Acidification Experience. *Standford*. Retrieved from https://www.youtube.com/watch?v=G6mmXcNE7co [Accessed on Aug., 21. 2022].

Banfi, F., Brumana, R., & Stanga, C. (2019). Extended reality and informative models for the architectural heritage: From scan-to-bim process to virtual and augmented reality. *Virtual Archaeology Review*, *10*(21): 14–30.

Baudry, J. L. (1986). Ideological effects of the basic cinematografic apparatus. In P. Rosen (Ed.), *Narrative, apparatus, ideology: A film theory reader* (pp. 286–298). New York: Columbia University Press.

Bazin, A. (2005). *What is cinema?* Vol. I. (H. Gray, Trans.). Berkeley: University of California Press.

Bielskyte, M. (2016). The new storytellers II: World-building: Best practices for creating story worlds. *Phi*. Retrieved from https://www.youtube.com/watch?v=jtr0AZK64Do [Accessed on Aug., 21. 2022].

Brown, E., & Cairns, P. (2004). A grounded investigation of game immersion. *Extended abstracts of the 2004 conference on human factors and computing systems*, CHI '04: 1297–1300.

Bucher, J. (2018). *Storytelling for virtual reality: Methods and principles for crafting immersive narratives*. New York: Routledge.

Castells, M. (2010). *The information age economy, society, and culture: The rise of the network society*. Vol. 1. Oxford: Blackwell Publishing

Damiani, J. (March 23, 2017). The beginner's guide to VR scriptwriting & storytelling. *VRSCOUT*. https://vrscout.com/news/vr-scriptwriting-beginners-guide-writing-unframed/. [Accessed on Apr., 21, 2018].

Dooley, K. (2021). *Cinematic virtual reality: A critical study of 21st Century approaches and practices*. Palgrave Macmillan, Springer International Publishing.

Douglas, Y., & Hargadon, A. (2000). The pleasure principle: Immersion, engagement, flow. In *Proceedings of the eleventh ACM on hypertext and hypermedia*. Association for Computing Machinery (pp. 153–160).

Dönmez, S. C., & Erkılıç, H. (2018). 360 Derece sanal gerçeklik uygulamalarını sinema kuramı üzerinden okumak mümkün mü? [Is it possible to read virtual reality applications through cinema theory?]. *Mersin Üniversitesi Sosyal Bilimler Enstitüsü Dergisi*, *2*(1): 40–56.

Elsaesser, T., & Hagener, M. (2010). *Film theory: An introduction through the senses*. New York: Routledge.

Erkılıç, H., & Dönmez, S. C. (2020). Sanal gerçeklik anlatısının izini sürmek: Trinity VR ve Selyatağı VR örnekleri. [Tracing virtual reality narrative: Trinity VR and Selyatağı VR examples.] *SineFilozofi*, Özel Sayı [Special issue]. (2): 318–344.

Erkılıç, H., & Dönmez, S. C. (2021). Sanal gerçeklik anlatısının temelleri üzerine: After Life sanal gerçeklik deneyimi analizi. [On the fundamentals of VR narrative: After Life VR experience analysis.]. In E. A. Ahmet (Ed.), *Neo-Sinema* [Neo-Cinema] (pp. 505–524). İstanbul: Doruk Publishing.

Erkılıç, H. (2017). Dijital sinema teorisi üzerine: Akışkan sinema ve akışkan sinema teorisi. [On digital film theory: Liquid cinema and liquid film theory.] *SineFilozofi*, *2*(4): 56–72.

Fagan, K. (March 4, 2018). Here's what happens to your body when you've been in virtual reality for too long. *Business Insider*. Retrieved from https://www.businessinsider.com/virtual-reality-vr-side-effects-2018-3 [Accessed on Aug., 21. 2022].

Fonseca, D. (2016). *Effect of immersive (360) video on attitude and behavior change*. Master Thesis. Aalborg University, Denmark.

Gödde, M., et al. (2018). Cinematic narration in VR – Rethinking film conventions for 360 degrees. *International Conference on Virtual, Augmented and Mixed Reality*. Las Vegas. DOI: 10.1007/978-3-319-91584-5_15

Hamit, F. (1993). *Virtual reality and the exploration of cyberspace*. Sams Publishing.

Heaton, N. T. (2020). *Narrative presence in virtual reality experiences.* University of Lethbridge Research Repository OPUS.

Heeter, C. (1992). Being there: The subjective experience of presence. *Presence Teleoperators & Virtual Environments*, *1*(2): 262–271.

Jenkins, H. (2006). *Convergence culture: Where old and new media collide.* New York: New York University Press.

Jerald, J. (2016). *The VR book human-centered design for virtual reality.* ACM Books.

Lescop, L., & Suner, B. (2020). Designing intradiegetic and extradiegetic spaces for virtual reality. *eCAADe 2020*. Institute of Architecture: 545–554.

Luce, A. A. (1941). Berkeley's existence in the mind. *Mind, 50*(199): 258–267. Retrieved from https://www.jstor.org/stable/2250980 [Accessed on Sept., 1. 2022].

Mestre, D. R., & Vercher, J. (2011). Immersion and presence. In P. Fuchs, M. Guillaume, & G. Pascal (Eds.), *Virtual reality: Concepts and technologies* (pp. 93–100). New York: CRC Press.

Qin, H., Rau, P. P., & Salvendy, G. (2009). Measuring player immersion in the computer game narrative. *International Journal of Human-Computer Interaction*, *25*(2): 107–133.

Serafin, S. (2018). Sonic interactions in virtual environments. In N. Lee (Ed.), *Encyclopedia of computer graphics and games*. Cham: Springer.

Sherman, R. W., & Craig, A. B. (2003). *Understanding virtual reality*. California: Elsevier Science.

Steuer, J. (1992). Defining virtual reality: Dimensions determining telepresence. *Journal of Communication*, 42: 73–93.

Thomas, S. (2019). The star in VR. *Celebrity Studies, 10*(6): 453–468.

Tortum, D. (2019). Sanal gerçeklik atölyesi. *8. Atıf Yılmaz Kısa Film Festivali. Atölye ve Söyleşiler. [Virtual reality workshop. 8th Atıf Yılmaz Short Film Festival. Workshops and talks.]* Mersin.

Tricart, C. (2018). *Virtual reality filmmaking: Techniques & best Practices for VR filmmakers*. New York: Routledge.

Williams, E., Love, C., & Love, M. (2021). *Virtual reality cinema: Narrative tips and techniques* (First edition). New York: Routledge.

Sırrı Serhat Serter

Online, Physical (In-Person) or Hybrid: New Digital Era and Film Festivals

Abstract: Cinema was one of the sectors most negatively affected by the changing daily life practices with because of the coronavirus. In 2020 and 2021, almost all film festivals in the world have had been canceled or forced to move online forcibly. However, no matter how successful it was, film festivals that moved online could not replace physical screenings. Because online festivals could only allow people to come together and share an experience in a very limited way. With the easing of the epidemic scene as of the end of 2021, movie theaters started to fill up again and festivals started to return. However, at a time when everyone was at home during the pandemic, a new era began in which the movie watching practices of the audience changed, and many audiences preferred to watch movies in the comfort of their home by digital platforms. Film festivals had to adapt themselves to digital era and these new conditions considering these of changing viewing habits. Thus, two types of approaches emerged in terms of festivals as of 2022; big and well-established film festivals completely switched to physical screenings from online with the help of their financial opportunities, brand values and already existing audience potential. Smaller-scale festivals, which do not have these facilities, have accepted that some events such as online screenings or talks are now part of the festivals, not ignoring the changing viewing practices during the pandemic. The subject of this article is the recent digitalization of film festivals and to what extent and how they use these digital opportunities.

Keywords: Film Festival, Cinema, Online Screening, Digital Cinema, Hybrid Screening

Introduction

Film festivals had already started to face a transition even before the pandemic in 2020. The rapid growth of streaming has increased the demand for new distribution channels with rich content. Following new investors and buyers entering the film festival market, festival organizations have launched online film programs and activities. The lockdowns and public measures responding to individual health concerns during the pandemic have limited the possibility of experiencing crowded theater halls. As a result, film festivals were either delayed or organized online instead of face-to-face activities. This transition has encouraged questioning the benefits and challenges of the digital as life turned into normal: Where do the film festivals lead?

Online festivals may initially seem inefficient and even harm the magic of the traditional festival culture. However, the transition to remote and hybrid models has proven a significant development compared to pre-pandemic conditions: Accessibility. Pre-pandemic film festivals were already inaccessible to many people. Considering the economic challenges, attending a film festival in-person used to be costly and a privilege for limited communities. Because of the high travel and accommodation prices, attending a festival presented major economic difficulties, not alone for the youth but for the people with higher socio-economic status as well. In fact, festivals with digital programming introduced a democratic option through remote access. As a result, people -especially cinephiles- could enjoy festivals for a cost-effective price, an experience that they could not have earlier.

It should be noted that such a radical change in the mechanisms of the festivals brought both benefits and challenges, especially for film producers and directors. Firstly, film festivals function as hubs of networking and distribution. The usual competition among the distributors getting the top-rated films was hammered due to the pandemic. This is because face-to-face meetings and negotiations (through private screenings, parties, or spontaneous meetings) in festivals between producers and distributors could not be accomplished. While a distributor had a chance to show his/her interest in the work presented by the producer or director through face-to-face gatherings right after the film screening, it became much harder to create such opportunities online.

In addition to the disruption of the communication between the distributors and movie creators, independent filmmakers started to feel threatened since their work does not target mass audience. Despite such difficulties online, it is highly possible that online agents consolidate their market position more and more. In a survey by Film Festival Alliance (2021), %94 of film producers whose films were exhibited in 2020, admitted that they attended a virtual festival. According to Whistler Film Festival survey, %74 of attendants remarked that they joined (or hosted) a virtual festival since March, 2020 (Heck, Rickaby, and Quade, 2021, p. 7). Such data shows that the film industry reached a point of no return thanks to its advantage of access.

Following the COVID-19 pandemic, film festivals faced the threat of cancellations and even find an end. Here, online platforms have offered a chance to continue through the bypass of face-to-face screenings and attracting the participants online, thus, saving the day. Many major festivals decided to present online screening such as Sundance, New York and Toronto, yet some, including Cannes, preferred to cancel the event. These tactical divergences highlight the differences of opinion among the festivals. Then, the question is, what will happen to online festivals as face-to-face events turn back? Will festivals remain online? And if so, what is to lose and to win?

The Characteristics of Online Film Festivals

Wide accessibility and facility of interaction can be seen as the most significant advantages of online festivals. Moreover, they welcome a wider and diversified population. Face-to-face festivals' limitations may cause industry inequality, meaning that those on the margins will remain there (Sealy, 2022). Additionally, online festivals may offer better access for visually disabled or the hearing-impaired people because online platforms generally provide voice commentaries and subtitles, which is not a priority in face-to-face festivals constantly.

Physically attending a festival has other added values than the screening itself. Since they attract people and encourage them to discuss on various topics, the effects the viewers/participators experience are much different such as getting excited to see the directors or actors after the screening, waiting in the box office for the last-minute tickets and to interact with newly met people, etc.

Online festivals, on the other hand, challenge the aim of the audience, directors/producers and industrial professionals coming together. Physical (in-person) screenings offer a beneficial environment for filmmakers to observe how the audience interacts with a film in a way an online screening cannot imitate. Eliza Sealy (2022), after the screening of Khadar Ahmed's *The Gravedigger's Wife* (2021) in London Film Festival's Q&A section, remarked that the participants expressed how important and meaningful the film is to them and how excited were they for Somalian culture presented in the silver screen. Nevertheless, when a film is exhibited online, filmmakers generally have a limited opinion on how the audience interacted with their work. As a result, the conversations with the audience at the film festivals serve to the producers and filmmakers in order to obtain instant and observable feedback of their work.

Video-on-demand (VOD) platforms and online viewing have been developing rapidly since the 2010's. Despite different film watching habits of a global audience with different cultural backgrounds, watching TV and film during the curfew became a valuable option to cope with the isolation (Taylor et al., 2020, p. 712). In fact, the history of online film festivals is much older, a VOD webpage in Bulgaria carried out an online film festival in 2013 (Nedyalkova, 2016, pp. 140–141). So, online streaming infrastructure had already well developed before 2020 and was ready for online film festivals when the pandemic came up. As a result, the year of 2020 witnessed the increase of the consumption of online streaming.

Powers (2020) claims there are three main reasons that film festivals all over the world started online streaming. Firstly, it is the desire to reach potential audience living in different cities and countries and those who suffer difficulties to access the festivals due to disability or parenting. The second reason is to provide the attendance of film producers who cannot travel to certain festivals. Thirdly, watching films online has become the main way of viewing and it became the new normal whose rejection would put the actors behind the new reality.

Additionally, the role of streaming changes from festival to festival. While some use it to spice up the conventional format, others take it as an essential part of the whole event. It mainly depends on the distributors' and filmmakers' desire to join such an exhibition. Noticeably, there is a correlation between the changing status of the exhibition type and the increasing prestige of the films made by streaming platforms. Looking in this direction, Alfonso Cuaron's *Roma* (2018), produced by Netflix and awarded with the Oscar of the best film category, played a major role in this change. The director himself also presented Netflix as a respectable producer (Hanzlik and Mazierska, 2022, p. 44). Therefore, it is not surprising that some festivals, like in the example of Roma, merge their powers with VOD services.

In a year with international travel restrictions, delayed exhibitions and closed theatres due to the COVID-19, every festival had to adopt the new situation or cancel their programs. The lack of long waiting lines or fanfares of the premieres have been filled with quick online organizations which developed the streaming platforms as a medium of fierce competition and limited know-how of its technology. That situation increases the importance of question of how the film festivals could remain up-to-date while the entire industry in turmoil attracted the participants including industry representatives, audience.

Film Festivals during COVID-19

Despite its capacity to reduce stress and provide escapism, movie theaters could not function in this way during the pandemic. After social distance measures taken by the governments, they were shut down as well as suspended exhibitions of studios and distribution companies. However, film lovers and festival creators have chosen not to give up. The reason is not only being keen on sharing this experience with the crowds in a traditional sense but also it is a vital way of co-experiencing film art. Thus, organizers redefined the festivals by creating new categories focused on online streaming, video games and virtual reality experiences.

Marijke de Valck and Antoine Damiens (2020) claim that festival organizers have proven their skill, adaptation and creativity by finding very fast and effective local solutions against a global catastrophe. Many festival organizers overcame this difficulty using their creativity. Organized in April, 2020 for example, *CPH: DOX* and *Visions du Réel* festivals were the first ones presenting streaming alone. Fantasia Film Festival of Montreal followed the same path in the following summer. Some of the majors in the industry accustomed to welcoming tens of thousands of guests and high profile famous film producers preferred to present a limited face-to-face screening for locals along with the online streaming. Additionally, in 2019, Toronto Film Festival (TIFF) reduced the number of films to 60 from 245, New York Film Festival's (NYFF) program was reduced to 60 from 75. Organizers tried to create a community atmosphere as much as possible to generally isolated streaming world, while producer promotions and Q&A sections on Zoom after the screening became usual (Strong, 2021).

It is important to take into account the prices as attending a film festival might generally be difficult due to its prices. This is also valid for the Sundance Film Festival especially which is organized in a luxurious mountain resort. According to festival organizers, 2021 Sundance Film Festival welcomed the greatest number of audience within its 40 years of history. Compared to its face-to-face version in 2020, this record exceeded the number of 600.000 total audience with an increase rate of 2,7. 2021 Sundance Film Festival was generally organized as an online, shortened festival. In a seven day-schedule, movies have been streamed on 40 satellite screens which were operated by 20 movie theaters and various corporations nationwide along with 73 feature films, 50 shorts, 4 Indie Series, 23 interviews and events and 14 projects of the New Frontier episode. Attendants watched the organization from more than 120 countries and all the 50 states. During these 11 days in Sundance, an approximately 120 films were shown in the Park City, near Utah and its surroundings (Lindahl, 2021).

In addition to the above examples, some online festivals cooperated to reach the mass audience during the pandemic. Boston Underground Film Festival in October, 2021, Brooklyn Horror Film Festival, North Bend Film Festival and Overlook Film Festival for example, were united to create an online Horror Movie Festival the *Nightstream*. Each festival targeted their own audience's sensitivity and together they created a national event appealing to a greater number of audience that they could not be able to manage separately (Kohn, 2021).

Cinema is one of Turkey's worst negatively affected industries due to the COVID-19 restrictions nationwide. Movie theatres were open at intervals from the mid 2020 to summer 2021, and the festivals were sometimes canceled, sometimes converted to online or organized in the open air with a limited audience under tight restrictions. Following the decline of the pandemic since the end of 2021, movie theaters started to regain its audience as well as the film festivals. Finally, the 41st İstanbul Film Festival met its audience between the 8–19 April, 2022.

Major film festivals organized in Turkey are perceived as very strong since they managed to survive inspire of the impacts of the pandemic. Ahmet Boyacıoğlu, for example, director of the Antalya Golden Orange Film Festival (Antalya Altın Portakal Film Festivali), claims that he stands against the idea of "online festivals" because a film festival is an event that should create an atmosphere where the audience meet the artists in-person and ask questions to each other. While he finds it weird that the festivals are converted to online during the pandemic, he highlights that they organized the Antalya Golden Orange Film Festival physically without delay. Boyacıoğlu also adds that they turned the festival to an open-air format serving to a limited number of audience thanks to warm weather conditions of Antalya and they also requested PCR tests and vaccination cards from all the attendants (Tatar, 2022).

Kerem Ayan, the director of the İstanbul Film Festival (IFF), states that İKSV (İstanbul Culture and Art Foundation), the organizing entity, responded early when the pandemic had just emerged in March 2020 and they, founded their own online film platform in order to stream movies online throughout May and June on this platform. As these screenings have drawn great interest, IFF continued open-air screenings in June and then in October, they kept *Film October* (Film Ekimi) screenings both physically and online. According to Ayan, these online screenings during the pandemic targeted people from all the strata and received appreciation because they provided time and location flexibility for different audience demand (Taşçı, 2021). IFF continued both physical (in-person) and online exhibitions in 2021 and they organized April 2022 film festival entirely physically in the movie theaters.

İrfan Demirkol, the chairman of The World Mass Communication Research Foundation (Dünya Kitle İletişimi Araştırma Vakfı) which has been organizing Ankara International Film Festival (Ankara Uluslararası Film Festivali) for 32 years, states that what makes a film festival a "festival" is "bringing together the masters and pupils," and the "existence of the audience." Primary duty of the festivals, according to Demirkol, is to collect the quality films and bring the audience and directors of those films together in order to create a special space for them so that they can discuss and share their opinions about films, thus transferring to younger generations a deeper knowledge on cinema. Demirkol also states that they placed a great emphasis on the health of the audience by effectively applying regulations such as mask usage, social distance, HES Code (government application showing the infection risk level of people) or PCR tests, as they respected watching films physically on location (Tatar, 2022).

Virtual Elements in Film Festivals

Virtual platforms provide remote consumption of the festival without going out of the house at a reasonable cost. Virtual screening works efficiently if the idea of festivals is to bring divergent audience with various films. However, it is not possible to revive the collective experience of a physical festival despite its limited accessibility. Therefore, virtual exhibitions saved the day during the COVID-19 for the festival organizers.

Of course, it is crucial to consider a particular festival's goals and targets, because these goals and targets may vary for each festival. Against the pandemic, festivals reproduced their identities and values. Venice VR Expanded event during Venice Film Festival in 2020 for example, proved that it was possible to attend a festival regardless of the location thanks to the virtual reality. VR Headsets the users put on allowed people to attend Venice Film Festival, taking photos with famous directors and celebrities on the red carpet, seeing them closely and to chat while enjoying the comfort of their couches in their homes. For many who lack financial means to be there in Venice, this technology offered a very big step forward for the accessibility of film festivals and democratizing them (Hackl, 2020).

Likewise, Sundance Film Festival in 2022 designed a virtual and different space called the *Spaceship* during the festival. It is a virtual space where both online and face-to-face participants could come together through their avatars and get in touch with each other. At the same time, *Spaceship* is a part of Sundance's the *New Frontiers* program which is focused on developing technologies. Users are able to join to parties or to experience the live performances with the help of a scanner or a VR headset in this virtual space and they can interact in virtual spaces (Wilhelm, 2022).

Film festivals at the same time are the discovery of art through the method of narrating. Traditionally, this medium refers to a film or films though video games also entered the scene and started to impress the film festival society. Rockstar Games' *LA Noire* was the first video game ever acknowledged in a film festival, in 2011. Since that day, organizers have appreciated the impact of the video games on the movies and there is a special division in Tribeca Film Festival, for example. Casey Baltes, Vice President of Tribeca Games, states that the video games are one of the most sophisticated tools of storytelling, not alone with the narration but with incredible artistic mastery creating fascinating worlds and setting up business connections with societies worldwide (Beresford, 2020).

A lot of elements such as episodic programs, video games and VR content are taking a place in many festival programs. These programs do not attract the attention as much as the feature films which still dominate the applications. However, beyond the movie, any festival that doesn't take into account the importance of an effective storytelling faces the risk of losing its interest. Virtual elements offer opportunities to those who do not wish to attend an event in-person or cannot attend for any reason. As Kohn (2020) stated at the joint press brief during the major film festivals: "We believe that cinema has an unmatched power to illuminate both the world surrounding us and the perception within us. Movies may hold on to us in crisis. They can grow, inform, provoke and heal."

This can be applied to virtual reality and video games as well. What the pandemic has taught us is that storytelling and artistic expression have intertwined with the new dimensions offered by the new media. All these contributions mentioned above promise more audience, access and convenience; thus, the ideal future cannot exclude the co-existence of virtual and physical events in harmony. A future where different festivals accomplish their goals and provide more options and accessibility to their clients.

Film Festival of the Future

The future of the film festivals is changing and it has gained speed following the effects of the pandemic undoubtedly. Festival directors and creators see the future of the film festivals as a space where art and storytelling are expressed like in the Venice VR Expanded and they see the benefits of technology as a way of expressing the creative experience of a film festival. Meanwhile, festival directors see this future as a hybrid model. Even after the relaunch of the silver screen in the post-pandemic era, online and virtual events would most likely become parts of the film festival experience. On the other hand, nothing could be compared to the face-to-face experience and expectations of sitting in a movie theatre for a newly released film.

Even before the pandemic, events like festivals, concerts, shows, and premieres had already been experiencing a transformation. In previous years, dozens of independent movies were shown in a film festival, and they used to get requests for a global distribution by the studios, yet such marketing habits started to change around 2016. Suddenly, the financially strong companies such as Netflix and Amazon emerged and they started to buy the favored movies of the festivals for an astonishing amount of money adding them to content of their streaming services (Watercutter, 2022).

Parallel to such developments, audience and film relations are changing as well. People got used to switch between few story theaters and home cinema. Directors such as Dennis Villeneuve and Christopher Nolan rightfully demand their works to be shown in the theaters but these filmmakers are much different than the independent directors who desire their films to be watched by everyone. Festivals give them a chance to act as they like, yet, when festival turns to online what they lose is to observe real-time reactions of the audience, the opportunity of feeling the hall.

Conclusion

It is evident that most of the film festivals coped well with the COVID-19 pandemic, the demand to screen online in 2020 and 2021 affected them strongly. Additionally, some parts of the festivals, especially film industry events successfully accomplished online organizations with advantages and disadvantages like in the old days (pre-2020 period) whatever the type of the festival was. However, as it seems that these types of events could not be as successful and smashing as pre-pandemic physical (in-person) festivals, and most likely same success will probably be gained only when the festivals could be accomplished entirely physically again. In every condition it seems, festival organizers are planning to return to physical theatres as soon as they are allowed to.

Festivals could learn from each other and share their experiences. In this context, film festivals were not put aside, on the contrary, they developed methods to reach the audience in the most challenging times testing all the options. These options were supported by various methods such as open-air film screenings, online screenings, virtual reality applications and VR headsets. A hybrid format bringing together face-to-face and online screenings may become a conspicuous model for the future of festivals in these days where the pandemic not entirely ended (and again be in increase trend at the moment).

Producers and directors miss the opportunity of excitement of their films' premieres in a fully crowded movie theater partly for the last two years, yet, festival organizers seem like they rediscovered the festival experience both for the artists and the audience. Even though film producers are grateful for these novelties, they are facing contradictions about their benefits and drawbacks. Following years will probably offer more options for both physical (in-person) and virtual events. Most likely, online festivals will be organized for people who cannot afford traveling but have a desire to watch films and contact film producers online.

However, attending a film festival in-person with its added value of "being there" feeling, would hardly be replaced by virtual and distant festivals.

Against all those obstacles and difficulties, film industry still suffers the effects of the pandemic. Additionally, the future for per element of the industry seems ambiguous. Despite the fact that nothing can imitate the collective cinema experience, it is impressive to observe the methods festivals have taken overcoming the difficulties the pandemic has introduced. Thus, festivals may democratize the events, which for a very long time symbolized the privileged section of the film industry, and may offer a new method to audience establishing a connection with films rather than the press news.

COVID-19 has not lost its effect entirely and some various viruses are mentioned as well. It seems not only pandemics but other issues like economic difficulties, war, migration and etc. prevent people coming altogether and watch films in a movie theater occasionally. However, nothing or no one can detain them from the pleasures they have as long as humans exist on Earth and live. There will always be cinephiles who admire and love watching films. Because no matter what happens as they will run and fill the movie theatres, festivals will develop and move forward thanks to them. Every festival will place online or virtual elements in their programs considering their special conditions or they will choose a hybrid method. Then again movie theatres always and definitely maintain their existence, because this has been the story of cinema since the first screening in 1895 in *La Grand Café*. Neither a disease or technology nor the economics will be able to break this story.

References

Beresford, T. (September 24, 2020). Tribeca Film Festival to Add Video Games to Official Selections. *The Hollywood Reporter*. Retrieved from https://www.hollywoodreporter.com/movies/movie-news/tribeca-film-festival-add-video-games-official-selections-4065885/ [Accessed on July, 19. 2022].

De Valck, M., & Damiens, A. (December 06, 2020). Film Festivals and the First Wave of COVID-19: Challenges, Opportunities, and Reflections on Festivals' Relations to Crises. *Necsus*. Retrieved from https://necsus-ejms.org/film-festivals-and-the-first-wave-of-covid-19-challenges-opportunities-and-reflections-on-festivals-relations-to-crises/ [Accessed on July, 11. 2022].

Film Festival Alliance. (2021). Filmmaker and Audience Survey Results. *Film Festival Alliance*. Retrieved from https://filmfestivalalliance.org/2020-film-festival-organizer-audience-and-filmmaker-survey-results/ [Accessed on August, 03. 2022].

Hackl, C. (November 17, 2020). The Future of the Film Festival. *Forbes*. Retrieved from https://www.forbes.com/sites/cathyhackl/2020/11/17/the-future-of-the-film-festival/?sh=297920f64d8a [Accessed on June, 25. 2022].

Hanzlik, J., & Mazierska, E. (2022). Eastern European film festivals: Streaming through the Covid-19 pandemic. *Studies in Eastern European Cinema*, *13*(1): 38–55.

Heck, A., Rickaby, C., & Quade, S. (2021). The Future of Film Festivals: Emerging models and relevant practices for media arts organizations. *Whistler Film Festival*. Retrieved from https://whistlerfilmfestival.com/research/ [Accessed on August, 02. 2022].

Kohn, E. (July 08, 2020). How Venice, Telluride, NYFF and TIFF's 2020 Collaboration Will Affect the Festivals Circuit. *IndieWire*. Retrieved from https://www.indiewire.com/2020/07/fall-film-festivals-working-together-1234572013/ [Accessed on July, 20. 2022].

Kohn, E. (July 23, 2021). American Film Festivals Have a Future If They're Willing to Change (Almost) Everything. *IndieWire*. Retrieved from https://www.indiewire.com/2021/07/future-of-film-festivals-collaboration-1234652935/ [Accessed on July, 17. 2022].

Lindahl, C. (February 08, 2021). Sundance Announces Record Audience in 2021: Over Half Million Views. *IndieWire*. Retrieved from https://www.indiewire.com/2021/02/sundance-2021-viewing-numbers-largest-festival-audience-1234615605/ [Accessed on July, 18. 2022].

Nedyalkova, M. (2016). Festivals gone digital: A case-study of Netcinema.bg and the online European Film Festival in Bulgaria. In J. Dudkova & K. Misikova (Eds.), *Transformation processes in Post-Socialist screen media* (pp. 138–152). Bratislava: Academy of Performing Arts in Bratislava and Slovak Academy of Sciences.

Powers, T. (May 16, 2020). Film Festivals Aren't Just Surviving Online, They're Creating a Better Future. *IndieWire*. Retrieved from https://www.indiewire.com/2020/05/film-festivals-online-future-1202231417/ [Accessed on July, 11. 2022].

Sealy, E. (April 07, 2022). Virtual Film Festivals: A Temporary Solution or Here to Stay? *Independent Cinema Office*. Retrieved from https://www.independentcinemaoffice.org.uk/blog-virtual-festivals-a-temporary-solution-or-here-to-stay/ [Accessed on June, 28. 2022].

Strong, H. (March 09, 2021). How Film Festivals Have Managed the Shift to Virtual. *Hyperallergic*. Retrieved from https://hyperallergic.com/626125/virtual-festivals-covid-19/ [Accessed on July, 11. 2022].

Taşçı, B. (January 25, 2021). Sinema, Tiyatro, İKSV ve Ötesine: Kerem Ayan ile Röportaj [Cinema, Theatre, İKSV, and Beyond: An Interview with Kerem Ayan]. *Film Hafızası.* Retrieved from https://filmhafizasi.com/sinema-tiyatro-iksv-ve-otesine-kerem-ayan-ile-roportaj/ [Accessed on August, 05. 2022].

Tatar, D. A. (April 24, 2022). Film Festivalleri: Sinemada Dijitalleşme, Nereye Kadar? [Film Festivals: Digitalization in Cinema, To What extent?] *Journo.* Retrieved from https://journo.com.tr/film-festivalleri [Accessed on July, 17. 2022].

Taylor, S., Landry, C. A., Paluszek, M. M., Fergus, T. A., Mckay, D., & Asmundson, G. J. G. (2020). COVID stress syndrome: Concept, structure, and correlates. *Depression and Anxiety*, *37*(8): 706–714.

Watercutter, A. (January 21, 2022). Film Festivals Are Evolving for the Better. *Wired.* Retrieved from https://www.wired.com/story/film-festivals-hybrid/ [Accessed on July, 06. 2022].

Wilhelm, K. A. (January 26, 2022). Creating A New Familiar: Film Festivals in the Covid Era. *Documentary.* Retrieved from https://www.documentary.org/online-feature/creating-new-familiar-film-festivals-covid-era [Accessed on July, 30. 2022].

Volkan Hacıtahiroğulları, Hüseyin Kutay Tinç, and Tolga Ovatman

How User Reviews and Achievements Can Be Correlated with Player Engagement

Abstract: User reviews are one of the leading factors of judging player engagement and popularity of digital video games. They not only provide sentimental feedback but also give insight on what the player likes or dislikes about a product. Game achievements provide objective data related to the successes of a player in terms of engagement. A comparison between the subjective sentimental nature of user reviews and the objective data gathered from user achievements should be a credible comparison which gives us a fresh alternative in the analysis of player engagement. Looking through previous research on player experience, player engagement and player enjoyment aspects presents us with research, questionnaires, and sentiments. From this investigation we can summarize three categorization topics for analyzing player engagement in Western action role-playing games. We identify these topics with the game flow elements in this genre of video games as "gameplay," "story," and "exploration." Regarding these three topics a categorization of user reviews based on subject focus and a categorization of player achievements based on the engagement aspects of these achievements should give us clear correlations between these data and player engagement for Western action role-playing games. This chapter will summarize the correlation of these player engagement and player experience aspects and the data collected from user reviews and achievements, while also detailing the three topics of player engagement created for Western action role-playing games.

Keywords: Player Experience, Player Engagement, User Reviews, Achievements, Action Role Playing Games

Introduction

Games are meant to be played and completed. Stories told and presented in this interactive narrative of digital video games asks the player, the user controlling the events and characters which progress the story, to invite themselves into their vast worlds. Players are encouraged to explore, interact and care about these stories told and characters who tell them during their game experience.

A structured player experience leads to a credible player engagement which is important for people both making and playing these games. Players want to be immersed and engaged in these game experiences they've bought, and developers want to give these experiences to players based on sales and artistic merit.

When a game designer can analyze player engagement correctly, they will design better and more successful games. Because of all these upsides, player engagement has been a topic of research for quite some time with factors discussing its description and analysis. It is a motivating factor for player experience, and thus impacts various types of games ranging from commercial to educational to serious games. Analysis of player engagement is also a possibility for producing of game design breakthroughs with analysis of current success and failure stories. Assessing player engagement has been done with multiple approaches and questionnaires in the past and is a popular topic of game design and impact of video games in academia.

Product reviews, specifically user made ones, give future consumers and product developers useful information regarding the experience the product provides in all fields they are used. They also provide valid, codable datasets for language processing, text and sentiment analysis. Their complex and multi-aspect nature leads to the creation of a variety of tools for better understanding of its different aspects. When looking at user reviews generated through *Metacritic* and *Steam*, we see the expression of experiences with storylines and characters of a game just as much as their gameplay experience such as combat, choice and exploration mechanics. And one way to validate these opinions are achievements.

User oriented experiences see a lot of examples of gamification in their implementation. It is useful in improving user experience and increases engagement in different applications, activities, and services. This practical usage of game design elements is unsurprisingly also used in video games themselves under the name of achievements. For academic studies they are a good measurement tool of effective applications of game elements as they are the objective results of players in game actions. These results can be used for game or player analysis both on an individual or group level.

Using both these datasets we propose the creation a new measurement method for player engagement by taking the objective data of player achievements and comparing them to the subjective opinions presented in user reviews. Because of the multi-aspect nature of user sentiments, we require a categorization of relevant player engagement aspects which we've reduced to three main categories of "story," "gameplay," and "exploration" which our research suggests as the unmistakable result. This measurement should present a unique alternative to already existing questionnaire-based tools and allow for a more dynamic testing method.

A game's story, gameplay, and exploration are aspects which we will focus this new measure for understanding player engagement. Throughout this research we will see correlations with these three aspects, further solidifying our categorization.

Player Experience

The goal of any game developer is to create successful, engaging and, enjoyable games. These are the key baselines of player experience. Combination of the aspects a player experiences personally is defined as player experience. These player experience aspects are separated on physiological, behavioral and psychological levels. Some of these aspects include presence, immersion, flow, being open to procedures and outcomes occurring in a game, symbolic or fictional actions which are constrained by context to list a few (Wiemeyer, Nacke, Moser, and Floyd'Mueller, 2016).

The actual player experience starts way before the actual start of gameplay (Mäyrä, Stenros, Paavilainen, and Kultima, 2017). Video games can draw people in (Jennett et al., 2008), glue them in the gaming experience (Brown and Cairns, 2004), and have the player continue playing (Rigby and Ryan, 2011).

Quantifying player experience is necessary for academics to better understand these aspects, compare games in relation to player experience and improving our understanding of what makes a game successful. For quantifying player experience two questionnaires, PENS and GEQ have been constructed and widely used because of their broad nature and accuracy (Johnson, Gardner, and Perry, 2018).

Developed from the Self-Determination Theory (STD); PENS, also known as the Player Experience of Need Satisfaction Questionnaire (Ryan, Rigby, and Przybylski, 2006), assesses competence, autonomy, relatedness, intuitive controls, and presence/immersion aspects of player experience. A game's sales, series loyalty, duration of player interest, positive affect, and enjoyment have been recorded to be in relation to the usage of PENS. PENS questionnaire has been used for measuring the aspects of presence in terms of physical, emotional, and narrative. These three aspects create the baseline for our three categories of our study. While the physical presence can be correlated with gameplay, the emotional presence of the game world can be correlated with exploration, and the narrative presence of a game is correlated with its story.

PENS is not the only measure developed and gained a wide use in the academic world. GEQ, also known as the Game Experience Questionnaire, was developed to measure the player engagement of video games (IJsselsteijn, Kort, and Poels, 2013). Focusing on seven factors; flow, immersion, challenge, competence, frustration, positive affect and negative affect, GEQ explores focus-groups of players for these factors. GEQ was used in psychophysiological and social experience studies as well as designing video games for specific groups of people (IJsselsteijn et al., 2008). Modified versions of GEQ have been used in showing the platform a game is played to affecting the game experience as studied by Aker, Inal, and Rızvanoğlu (2020) This revealed a positive response from players playing a game's PC version in comparison to its mobile version. However, as found in a case study by Bostan and Berkman (2017), who conducted a study on the *PlayStation* game *Horizon Zero Dawn*, latent variables of GEQ and gameplay elements showed a low correlation. This low correlation was a result of a sub-optimal association between a single variable from GEQ and a single gameplay factor. For a better correlation between single gameplay factors and player experience, we believe we can find a new alternative to questionnaires such as PENS and GEQ.

One of the important things a developer can do in creating a better player experience in their games is personalizing this experience for the player. For such personalization Vanhatupa (2011) created guidelines specifically for computer based role-playing games (CRPGs). These guidelines suggest that the static storyline structure of a CRPG, which limits player engagement which in turn diminishes player experience, can be accomplished using adaptation, presence, and sense of control, all aspects covered in player engagement. These can again be correlated with our categories as adaptation to player actions can be correlated with story, presence of the player represented in NPC reactions can be correlated with exploration and their sense of control through game balancing with the player character in mind is correlated with the gameplay elements of a game.

Player Engagement

Schoenau-Fog's (2011) exploration into digital games and their player engagement process reinforces to us that correct application of game design elements creates engaging player experiences. It is one of the core aspects of what a player experiences (Adams, 2014). The basis of this concept coined player engagement is created from the involvement of a player in the game, flow, presence and immersion (Wirth et al., 2007). As expressed by Brown and Cairns, "an engaged gamer is interested in the game and wants to keep playing." (2004, p. 1). One of the aspects of player engagement, flow, is expressed as wanting to stay in the experience of an action of play simply for its own sake (Csikszentmihalyi and Csikzentmihaly, 1990). There have already been methods created in measuring flow, one of which was a questionnaire developed by Choi and Kim (2004) which assessed a player's sense of control and immersion, their sense of curiosity, and a game's intrinsic interest. The intrinsic interest of a game is created by its story, while the player's sense of curiosity is the catalyst for exploration and their sense of control and immersion is created from the gameplay elements of the game they are playing, reinforcing our study.

Immersion as another aspect of player engagement, like player experience, doesn't require the action of play which was discovered by Denisova and Cairns (2019). Learning of a feature for example can also immerse a player through creating expectation. Throughout their research Denisova and Cairns (2019) found that learned aspects of a game increased immersion and this increase was tied to a perceived feeling of these features instead of whether they were implemented or not.

While player experience can be quantified using PENS and GEQ, player engagement has also been investigated throughout academia. Player gameplay is highly context-sensitive and the models which try to quantify player engagement vary because of this. One investigation by Sawyer et al. (2018) found from comparable contextual data, a hierarchical Bayesian method can be effective in modeling player engagement. Brockmyer et al. (2009) developed a tool for analyzing the measures of player engagement which was coined the Game Engagement Questionnaire (GEnQ). Sullivan et al. (2010) created a game manager (GrailGM) and the aspects we have questioned previously have been a factor in structuring of this game manager. This game manager was then used to highlight the structural aspects of computer role-playing games (CRPGs) further reinforcing our categorization especially for the CRPG genre. Continuing with role-playing games, in their research Iten, Steinemann, and Opwis (2017) mention choice having a correlation with player engagement. These choices however need to be meaningful to have a positive effect. Similar to our method they used player responses as well, citing previous studies where specific experiences of players are used to understand player experience and engagement.

The Engagement Questionnaire (EQ) was created by Mayes and Cotton (2001) to specifically measure engagement in video games. Mayes and Cotton found five factors related to engagement in video games which include interest, authenticity, curiosity, involvement, and fidelity. Interest takes into factor a game's content and how interesting, appealing, and exciting it is. Authenticity is how controllable and responsive the game is when the player initiates an action, as well as how natural the response of the game is to these actions. Curiosity focuses on the themes of exploration and characters. Involvement is factored in using the focus and playtime of the user. Fidelity is the graphical and mechanical consistency of the game, and it is the closest tie-in to the development challenges and the technology of a video game. Factors found in EQ also provide us with similarities to our research categories as interest is created through the story, authenticity with the successful implementation of gameplay and curiosity by the creation of the game environment and encounters. Involvement can also be compared to choice, which is one of our possible sub-categories.

What all this research done in player engagement suggests is a positive correlation between playtime, completion of game objectives and increased engagement. This result leads us into looking at achievements as achievement completion rates should give us insight in measuring player engagement.

Achievements

Ludivestigum is the term used for the collected statistics of games and scores on different sports. These ludivestigums date back to a time before video games ever existed and these records would include more than just a player's final score. However, since *Space Invaders* could allow players to earn a high score in 1978, achievements have been a part of video games. They are rewards and extrinsic motivators for a player's in-game accomplishments and have been a standing stone of video games, their design and consumption for generations. Today, games are required to have a list of achievements just to be able to put on the digital libraries of *Sony* and *Microsoft*'s console home entertainment systems (Medler and Eludamos, 2009). For these systems as well as *Steam* (one of the biggest digital distribution platforms for computer games (Graft, 2009) players can both check their own achievement rates as well as their friends and the entire player base around the world of the selected game. The importance of game achievements for player experience is explored in Salen and Zimmermann in their book *Rules of Play* and is expressed by Medler as "a player's gameplay history is the recording of a player's experiences." (Medler, 2009, pp. 177–194).

For some players, completion of a list of achievements becomes an entire goal by itself. For some players these achievements entice them to play in a certain style and take actions they might not have planned without the motivation of these achievements. This mentality and effort shown correlates with research done in cognitive and behavioral goal setting (Locke and Bryan, 1969; Rothkopf and Billington, 1979). Achievements also show up in game development to increase motivation for continuous playing. One advanced example of this is seen in *BioWare*'s *Mass Effect* game series (BioWare, 2006) as achievements and choices from one game in the series are saved in the save file of the player and can be transferred to the sequel which then might have impacts on the sequel's narrative and gameplay.

Achievement types will vary (Blair, 2011; de Salas and Lewis, 2013; Montola et al., 2009) regarding on their accomplishment type, their focus and playstyle.

Some achievements simply require the player to play the game and will be unlocked as they progress throughout the story. Others will be focused on challenges and difficulty forcing the player to play in increased difficulty settings or just in a more challenging way to complete the objectives. Some achievements encourage the player to explore, requiring them to search the entire game area for sighs, collectable items, side story continuation and unique sets of inventory items. Most games with story or gameplay-based choices that change the way the game is played or changes the narrative also have achievements that reward and differentiate these players for the choices they make. Sometimes this encourages players to play the same game in multiple playthroughs. Some other ways to vary achievements are based on whether the player is expecting the achievement to appear, whether it is incremental with progression, or dependent on how players are notified of these achievements. The combination of these three variations is called the combined achievement (Blair, 2011). A combined achievement seems to have the most impact on player engagement as results show.

Video game achievements also effect many aspects of player experience and engagement which is our entry for usage of achievements in this measurement. Groening and Binnewies (2019) investigated the motivation and performance of players when achievements are used as gamification elements to reinforce player engagement. It is important to note how gamification is already the use of game design elements of video games in non-game contexts (Hamari, Koivisto, and Sarsa, 2014) and they are being used in games already because of course they should be. We see from Groening and Binnewies' investigation (2019) that the needs of autonomy, closure and ability can be achieved by achievements better than goal setting with longevity. Johnson et al. (2018) also measured these effects of achievements using the post-experimental Intrinsic Motivation Inventory (IMI). They questioned the subjective and physiological experiences and the perceived tension and effort of players which resulted in their findings where the diversity of rewards seems to have the most improvement in motivation and experience for a player. To increase player engagement in terms of longevity and playtime, Park et al. found achievements to be initially important but not as important as social features in games as they seem to be more useful for engagement predictions, especially in multiplayer games.

Our focus on this measure is to analyze player engagement instead of improving it, which proves achievements as a good dataset for understanding the objective data of players' experience. Achievement completion rates don't give us players' feelings or opinions about the game they are playing instead they give us information about what they are accomplishing during the act of play. If we can understand the objective acts of players from achievements, we also need to find their subjective opinions to compare with the data we gather from achievements. This is where user reviews come into the equation.

User Reviews

A game review is one of the first interactions a player has with a video game. Outside of game trailers and disc covers, game reviews create a lens for players to view the game through. The total result of a video game (whether from 0 to 10 or 0 to 100) coming from a combination of user reviews or a renowned publication is the first criticism the player will have of the game. Expectations and understandings created from these words and numbers they gather will become a basis for their entire player experience just as we mentioned when defining player experience. We can see this on practice as expressed by game publishers as they mention how reviews impact sales and future funding of games (Sherrick and Schmierbach, 2016; Zhu and Zhang, 2010). User reviews also impact games post release. One example being the 2016 indie game *No Man's Sky* starting its post-release lifecycle with overwhelmingly negative reviews, taking feedback from these reviews and publishing free game updates until in 2020 where *No Man's Sky* won The Game Award for "Best Ongoing Game" while having a *Steam* review rating of "Mostly Positive" from one hundred and seventy thousand plus owing to their support for the betterment of the game post launch (Borman, 2018).

There is a comparison between professional and user (peer) reviews necessary when it comes to game reviews' impacts. This difference of importance shows itself on impacting game sales (Sherrick and Schmierbach, 2016) and developer usage to maximize player experiences (Staffor, 2016). This distinction is a result of a difference of focus between user and professional reviews. Johnson et al discussed these differences (2014) and the aspects critics focus on were defined by Zagal et al. (2009). The same research suggests users reviewing games are more passionate about the games they are reviewing, and this passion might come from positive or negative reasonings. These users will be judging a game based on its operational state (bugginess) and design choices instead of what professional reviewers focus such as accessibility. These emotionally charged reviews are also more polarized than professional reviews as stated by Santos et al. in their research (2019). For this research we can focus on aspects focused by the players and what they feel important in user reviews much better than in professional reviews.

The two major epicenters for user reviews include *Metacritic* and *Steam*. *Metacritic* is an online website for user and professional critic reviews which are then used in calculation of different *Metacritic* Review Scores respectively while *Steam* is one of the biggest digital game distribution platforms for computer games (Graft, 2009). The *Steam* client allows users to write public or private game reviews for any game they own while *Metacritic* allows any user to create reviews for any game regardless of their ownership of said game. *Steam* also gives users the ability to express their like or dislike of a game with their detailed review while *Metacritic* uses a scoring system. *Steam* allows other users to see the reviewers' playtime and the number of other reviews they've made as well as whether other users found said review helpful or not. Both *Metacritic* scores and reviews (Johnson, Watling, Gardner, and Nacke, 2014; Livingston, Nacke, and Mandryk, 2011) and *Steam* user reviews (Bais, Odek, and Ou, 2017; Lin, Bezemer, Zou, and Hassan, 2019) have been used in academic research including research done on player experience and engagement. Research on user attitudes using user reviews from *Metacritic* was already done by Strååt et al. in 2017 for *BioWare*'s *Dragon Age* and *Mass Effect* game franchises (Strååt and Verhagen, 2017; Strååt, Verhagen, and Warpefelt, 2017) where they manually analyzed the sentiment of reviews to create a method for developers to compare with the success rate of their previous titles to gauge the possible success of their future titles and make necessary changes in their design stages. Looking at all this previous research, we believe the binary nature of *Steam* achievements allows for better sentiment analysis of these user opinions.

With the better understanding of achievements and user reviews, we need to look at what type of games are needed for the base measurement in this method.

Action Role-Playing Games

From 1970s onwards, video games have been divided into categories called genres based on whether a game provides an experience focused on either hand-eye-coordination, management skills, or narrative (Donovan, 2010; Liu, 2011).

Role-playing games (RPGs) are the foundations of the video games coined with the same name, but on pen and paper originally. These games, specifically their pioneer *Dungeons & Dragons* (Barton and Stacks, 2019) also include a set of rules which both player and enemies adhere by and have statistics while players pursue quests during play. Action RPGs are then a combination of these pen and paper examples and the hand-eye-coordination based genre of action games (Donovan, 2010). These games task the player with combat with non-player character opponents to gain experience and improve their playable characters. For this, these games usually include an open to traverse world for the player to traverse between missions and locations. This world also includes an overarching story that ties the player character into this game world (Van Der

Heijden, Bakkes, and Spronck, 2008). This genre also "provides interactive virtual environments capable of offering experiences analogous to real life" (Bostan, 2009, pp. 1–26), being relevant in studies of player motivation. The main reason of using western ARPGs in this method of analyzing player engagement is an overall ease of comparison as many games with "ARPG" or "Action Role-Playing" tags in their *Steam* pages, professional and peer reviews shows us these games to include an interactive story, an open world for players to traverse and skill trees consisting of options for different playstyles and upgrade paths. All these elements are also available in our measurement categorization of player engagement.

Sentiment Analysis

According to Liu, B. (2011) opinions are "simply a positive or negative sentiment, view, attitude, emotion, or appraisal about an entity or an aspect of the entity." (2011, p. 1). Also known as opinion mining, the research of these opinions is called sentiment analysis, used in the field of information processing. Sentiment analysis helps researchers with subjectivity and emotion (Serrano-Guerrero, Olivas, Romero, and Herrera-Viedma, 2015). Sentiment analysis is not the first research done on opinions (Morinaga, Yamanishi, Tateishi, and Fukushima, 2002; Pang, Lee, and Vaithyanathan, 2002; Tong, 2001; Turney, 2002; Pang and Lee, 2009) but when the term was first coined (Nasukawa and Yi, 2003) five steps were created in the procedure of this analysis as follows: data collection, text preparation, sentiment detection, sentiment classification, presentation of output.

In academia, sentiment analysis has been used to probe user opinions in game reviews (Strååt and Verhagen, 2017; Islam, 2014), and improvement of game elements (Stafford, 2016). It has also been used in evaluation of the usefulness of game-based education (Barr, 2018; Miles and Huberman, 1994; Coknaz et al., 2019). Sentiment analysis of user reviews should also allow better understanding of in category sentiment to correlate with achievement categories.

Definition of Methodology

When combined with Klimmt's model of three dimensions of game enjoyment (Klimmt, 2003), our research provides us with three core categories we've previously coined story, gameplay, and exploration. Achievements and user reviews will be divided based on these categories separately. Achievements categorized as story (main story mission achievements which are unmissable and focus on game completion), exploration (exploring the open world, collecting hidden items, and playing non-main story related missions and encounters), and gameplay (rewarding player skill or hand-eye-coordination, gained from earning experience points or performing certain unique tasks) achievements while user reviews can be categorized by scanning the reviews manually or by using already existing sentiment analysis tools to define references to used words as nodes (codes) and split into categories based on context (a horse is an exploration tool but can also be a story character) and then sentiment of these references reflecting the overall sentiment of players on each category specifically. When compared with the user review analysis, average percentage of achievements completed by category will give us a preview of the level of engagement the game has achieved on said category. These categorizations can then be compared separately and in cohesion with a game's total game recommendation rates from *Steam* to understand the correlation between these categories and player engagement the game provides.

References

Adams, E. (2014). *Fundamentals of game design*. Pearson Education.

Aker, Ç., Inal, Y., & Rızvanoğlu, K. (2020). A multi-modal approach for evaluating player experience on different gaming platforms. *International Journal of Mobile Communications, 18*(2): 175–195.

Bais, R., Odek, P., & Ou, S. (2017). *Sentiment classification on steam reviews.* Stanford University.

Barr, M. (2018). Student attitudes to games-based skills development: Learning from video games in higher education. *Computers in Human Behavior, 80*, 283–294.

Barton, M., & Stacks, S. (2019). *Dungeons and desktops: The history of computer role-playing games 2e*. CRC Press.

BioWare. (2006). *Mass effect.* [Video game]. Edmonton, Alberta, Canada: Electronic Arts.

Blair, L. (2011). The Use of Video Game Achievements to Enhance Player Performance, Self-Efficacy, and Motivation. Retrieved from https://stars.library.ucf.edu/cgi/viewcontent.cgi?article=2826&context=etd [Accessed on Sept., 5. 2022].

Borman, M. (2018). Maxwell Borman, 'No Man's Sky': The Greatest Redemption in Gaming History. Retrieved from http://ndsuspectrum.com/no-mans-sky-the-greatest-redemption-in-gaming-history/ [Accessed on Sept., 5. 2022].

Bostan, B., & Berkman, M. I. (2017). Explorations in Game Experience: A case study of 'Horizon Zero Down'. In *Proceedings of the Eurasia Graphics* (pp. 4–5).

Bostan, B. (2009). Player motivations: A psychological perspective. *Computers in Entertainment (CIE)*, *7*(2): 1–26.

Brown, E., & Cairns, P. (2004, April). A grounded investigation of game immersion. In *CHI'04 Extended Abstracts on Human Factors in Computing Systems* (pp. 1297–1300).

Brockmyer, J. H., Fox, C. M., Curtiss, K. A., McBroom, E., Burkhart, K. M., & Pidruzny, J. N. (2009). The development of the Game Engagement Questionnaire: A measure of engagement in video game-playing. *Journal of Experimental Social Psychology*, *45*(4): 624–634.

Choi, D., & Kim, J. (2004). Why people continue to play online games: In search of critical design factors to increase customer loyalty to online contents. *CyberPsychology & Behavior*, *7*(1): 11–24.

Coknaz, D., Mirzeoglu, A. D., Atasoy, H. I., Alkoy, S., Coknaz, H., & Goral, K. (2019). A digital movement in the world of inactive children: favourable outcomes of playing active video games in a pilot randomized trial. *European Journal of Pediatrics*, *178*(10): 1567–1576.

Csikszentmihalyi, M., & Csikzentmihaly, M. (1990). *Flow: The psychology of optimal experience* (Vol. 1990). New York: Harper & Row.

de Salas, K., & Lewis, I. (2013, July). Identifying types of Achievements. In *Proceedings of CGAMES'2013 USA* (pp. 23–30). IEEE.

Denisova, A., & Cairns, P. (2019). Player experience and deceptive expectations of difficulty adaptation in digital games. *Entertainment Computing*, *29*, 56–68.

Donovan, T. (2010). *Replay: The history of video games*. Yellow Ant.

Eberhard, L., Kasper, P., Koncar, P., & Gütl, C. (2018, October). Investigating helpfulness of video game reviews on the steam platform. In *2018 Fifth International Conference on Social Networks Analysis, Management and Security (SNAMS)* (pp. 43–50). IEEE.

Graft, K. (2009). Stardock reveals impulse, steam market share estimates. *World Wide Web Electronic Publication*, *11*.

Groening, C., & Binnewies, C. (2019). "Achievement unlocked!"-The impact of digital achievements as a gamification element on motivation and performance. *Computers in Human Behavior*, *97*, 151–166.

Hamari, J., Koivisto, J., & Sarsa, H. (2014, January). Does gamification work? -A literature review of empirical studies on gamification. In *2014 47th Hawaii international conference on system sciences* (pp. 3025–3034). IEEE.

IJsselsteijn, W. A., De Kort, Y. A., & Poels, K. (2013). The game experience questionnaire. 46.

IJsselsteijn, W., Van Den Hoogen, W., Klimmt, C., De Kort, Y., Lindley, C., Mathiak, K.,... & Vorderer, P. (2008, August). Measuring the experience of digital game enjoyment. In *Proceedings of measuring behavior* (Vol. 2008, No. 2008, pp. 88–89). Maastricht, The Netherlands: Noldus.

Islam, M. R. (2014, April). Numeric rating of Apps on Google Play Store by sentiment analysis on user reviews. In *2014 International Conference on Electrical Engineering and Information & Communication Technology* (pp. 1–4). IEEE.

Iten, G. H., Steinemann, S. T., & Opwis, K. (2017, October). To save or to sacrifice? Understanding meaningful choices in games. In *Extended Abstracts Publication of the Annual Symposium on Computer-Human Interaction in Play* (pp. 495–502).

Jennett, C., Cox, A. L., Cairns, P., Dhoparee, S., Epps, A., Tijs, T., & Walton, A. (2008). Measuring and defining the experience of immersion in games. *International Journal of Human-Computer Studies*, *66*(9): 641–661.

Johnson, D., Gardner, M. J., & Perry, R. (2018). Validation of two game experience scales: the player experience of need satisfaction (PENS) and game experience questionnaire (GEQ). *International Journal of Human-Computer Studies*, *118*, 38–46.

Johnson, D., Klarkowski, M., Vella, K., Phillips, C., McEwan, M., & Watling, C. N. (2018). Greater rewards in videogames lead to more presence, enjoyment and effort. *Computers in Human Behavior*, *87*, 66–74.

Johnson, D., Watling, C., Gardner, J., & Nacke, L. E. (2014, October). The edge of glory: the relationship between metacritic scores and player experience. In *Proceedings of the First ACM SIGCHI Annual Symposium on Computer-Human Interaction in Play* (pp. 141–150).

Klimmt, C. (2003, November). Dimensions and determinants of the enjoyment of playing digital games: A three-level model. In *Level Up: Digital Games Research Conference* (pp. 246–257).

Lin, D., Bezemer, C. P., Zou, Y., & Hassan, A. E. (2019). An empirical study of game reviews on the Steam platform. *Empirical Software Engineering*, *24*(1): 170–207.

Livingston, I. J., Nacke, L. E., & Mandryk, R. L. (2011, August). The impact of negative game reviews and user comments on player experience. In *Proceedings of the 2011 ACM SIGGRAPH Symposium on Video Games* (pp. 25–29).

Liu, B. (2011). *Web data mining: exploring hyperlinks, contents, and usage data* (Vol. 1). Berlin: Springer.

Locke, E. A., & Bryan, J. F. (1969). Knowledge of score and goal level as determinants of work rate. *Journal of Applied Psychology*, *53*(1): 59.

Mayes, D. K., & Cotton, J. E. (2001, October). Measuring engagement in video games: A questionnaire. In *Proceedings of the Human Factors and Ergonomics Society Annual Meeting* (Vol. 45, No. 7, pp. 692–696). Sage CA: Los Angeles, CA: SAGE Publications.

Mäyrä, F., Stenros, J., Paavilainen, J., & Kultima, A. (2017). From social play to social games and back: The emergence and development of social network games. In *New perspectives on the social aspects of digital gaming* (pp. 11–32). New York: Routledge.

Medler, B. (2009). Generations of game analytics, achievements and high scores. *Eludamos: Journal for Computer Game Culture, 3*(2): 177–194.

Montola, M., Nummenmaa, T., Lucero, A., Boberg, M., & Korhonen, H. (2009, September). Applying game achievement systems to enhance user experience in a photo sharing service. In *Proceedings of the 13th International MindTrek Conference: Everyday Life in the Ubiquitous Era* (pp. 94–97).

Morinaga, S., Yamanishi, K., Tateishi, K., & Fukushima, T. (2002, July). Mining product reputations on the web. In *Proceedings of the Eighth ACM SIGKDD International Conference on Knowledge Discovery and Data Mining* (pp. 341–349).

Miles, M. B., & Huberman, A. M. (1994). *Qualitative data analysis: An expanded sourcebook*. Los Angeles: Sage Publications.

Nasukawa, T., & Yi, J. (2003, October). Sentiment analysis: Capturing favorability using natural language processing. In *Proceedings of the 2nd International Conference on Knowledge Capture* (pp. 70–77).

Pang, B., & Lee, L. (2009). Opinion mining and sentiment analysis. *Foundations and Trends in Information Retrieval, 2*(1–2): 1–135.

Pang, B., Lee, L., & Vaithyanathan, S. (2002). Thumbs up? Sentiment classification using machine learning techniques. *arXiv preprint cs/0205070*.

Rigby, S., & Ryan, R. M. (2011). *Glued to games: How video games draw us in and hold us spellbound: How video games draw us in and hold us spellbound*. AbC-CLIo.

Rothkopf, E. Z., & Billington, M. J. (1979). Goal-guided learning from text: Inferring a descriptive processing model from inspection times and eye movements. *Journal of Educational Psychology, 71*(3): 310.

Ryan, R. M., Rigby, C. S., & Przybylski, A. (2006). The motivational pull of video games: A self-determination theory approach. *Motivation and Emotion, 30*(4): 344–360.

Sawyer, R., Rowe, J., Azevedo, R., & Lester, J. (2018, September). Modeling player engagement with Bayesian hierarchical models. In *Proceedings of the AAAI*

Conference on Artificial Intelligence and Interactive Digital Entertainment (Vol. 14, No. 1, pp. 257–263).

Santos, T., Lemmerich, F., Strohmaier, M., & Helic, D. (2019). What's in a review: Discrepancies between expert and amateur reviews of video games on metacritic. In *Proceedings of the ACM on human-computer interaction, 3*(CSCW), 1–22.

Schoenau-Fog, H. (2011, September). The Player Engagement Process-An Exploration of Continuation Desire in Digital Games. In *DiGRA Conference.*

Serrano-Guerrero, J., Olivas, J. A., Romero, F. P., & Herrera-Viedma, E. (2015). Sentiment analysis: A review and comparative analysis of web services. *Information Sciences, 311*: 18–38.

Sherrick, B., & Schmierbach, M. (2016). The effects of evaluative reviews on market success in the video game industry. *The Computer Games Journal, 5*(3): 185–194.

Stafford, P. (2016). *Brain wave: The PhDs changing games.* Retrieved from http://www.polygon.com/features/2016/1/18/9882430/brain-wave-the-phds-changing-games

Strååt, B., & Verhagen, H. (2017). Using User Created Game Reviews for Sentiment Analysis: A Method for Researching User Attitudes. In *GHITALY- CHItaly.*

Strååt, B., Verhagen, H., & Warpefelt, H. (2017, September). Probing user opinions in an indirect way: an aspect based sentiment analysis of game reviews. In *Proceedings of the 21st International Academic Mindtrek Conference* (pp. 1–7).

Sullivan, A., Mateas, M., & Wardrip-Fruin, N. (2010, June). Rules of engagement: moving beyond combat-based quests. In *Proceedings of the Intelligent Narrative Technologies III Workshop* (pp. 1–8).

Tong, R. M. (2001, September). An operational system for detecting and tracking opinions in on-line discussion. In *Working notes of the ACM SIGIR 2001 workshop on operational text classification* (Vol. 1, No. 6).

Turney, P. D. (2002). Thumbs up or thumbs down? Semantic orientation applied to unsupervised classification of reviews. *arXiv preprint cs/0212032.*

Van Der Heijden, M., Bakkes, S., & Spronck, P. (2008, December). Dynamic formations in real-time strategy games. In *2008 IEEE Symposium On Computational Intelligence and Games* (pp. 47–54). IEEE.

Vanhatupa, J. M. (2011, June). Guidelines for personalizing the player experience in computer role-playing games. In *Proceedings of the 6th International Conference on Foundations of Digital Games* (pp. 46–52).

Wiemeyer, J., Nacke, L., Moser, C., & Floyd'Mueller, F. (2016). Player experience. In *Serious games* (pp. 243–271). Cham: Springer.

Wirth, W., Hartmann, T., Böcking, S., Vorderer, P., Klimmt, C., Schramm, H.,... & Jäncke, P. (2007). A process model of the formation of spatial presence experiences. *Media Psychology*, *9*(3): 493–525.

Zagal, J. P., Ladd, A., & Johnson, T. (2009, April). Characterizing and understanding game reviews. In *Proceedings of the 4th International Conference on Foundations of Digital Games* (pp. 215–222).

Zhu, F., & Zhang, X. (2010). Impact of online consumer reviews on sales: The moderating role of product and consumer characteristics. *Journal of Marketing*, *74*(2): 133–148.

Murat Durusoy

NFTs and Art: A New Fertile Battleground

Abstract: With the emergence of blockchain technologies, decentralized applications (dApps), and the evolution and accessibility of cryptocurrencies, non-fungible tokens started to flourish in the digital art world. Non-Fungible-Tokens' marketplaces enable an easy path for digital artists to meet with their potential buyers while raising questions and problems about the nature of the digital arts and the speculative art world in general. For example, are NFTs just another scarcity created by economics, or are they a valuable product of technological advancements?

This chapter examines the earlier epoch of the NFT scene and analyses the subjects related to the authenticity of artworks, the democratization of the art scene, copyrights and authorship issues, preservation and storage of digital arts, environmental impacts of the technology, and digital security while sketching a general understanding also aims to formulate a robust founding argument for the relationship with NFTs and digital art and their possible future.

Keywords: NFT, Blockchain, Digital Art, Remediation, Preservation

Introduction

Non-Fungible Tokens and art are two unrelated and unconnected concepts. Non-Fungible Tokens (NFTs) and the idea of an "Art Market" are tied from their roots. In order to understand how this conception came to be, one must understand what NFTs are, how they function via "blockchain" technology, and Art-Market's delicate ways of creating new arenas of selling art. This study will briefly explain the phenomenon it mentions and then clarifies specific misconceptions and relations between NFTs and Art. Since blockchain technologies and NFTs are developing rapidly, some concepts might change or become obsolete when this work is released.

In order to understand what Non-Fungible Tokens are, one needs to identify what fungibility items are. Fungible items or fungibility is, to put it in simple terms, interchangeability. An example of fungible items is if one has $10 in their pocket, it is the same as $10 in any other person's pocket. Therefore, any $10 is the same as any additional $10. Not only that, but they tend to be divisible. Unlike a commodity like a house which cannot be divisible, money, on the other hand, can be divided and exchanged separately. Therefore, one can divide $10 into two and have two $5; one does not have to give the same $5 to exchange them. This applies to cryptocurrencies like bitcoin, ether, and alike since their exchange units are identical to any other currency.

Non-Fungible items, on the other hand, are unique items. According to Majer (2019, p. 5), "they each have characteristics and properties that uniquely distinguish them." These characteristics can be different one way or another, but the main idea of Non-Fungibility is that they cannot be a substitute for one another. If you have a "token," there is no other "token" in the world with the same qualities. Therefore, it is a unique pointer to a unique asset. Those assets can be digital, from game skins to digital art or other artifacts.

NFT and Blockchain

This system of NFTs needs to rely on a financial mechanism, which is cryptocurrencies like Bitcoin. Ethereum, Tezos, etc. There is no NFT without a cryptocurrency because one needs to verify that the transaction of goods (in this case, cryptocurrency) can be done on a blockchain.

This study's aim is not to describe blockchain technologies but to give an idea of their utility within the range of NFTs. The production of NFTs is called minting. In order to create an NFT, one has to prepare its artwork, digital image, etc., for a particular marketplace and turn its artwork into a smart contract.

The basic premise of any blockchain technology for NFTs is that the transaction between the buyer and the seller is authenticated and validated in a decentralized network. All the buyer has at the end is proof of the transaction. With that "receipt," the buyer can claim authorship of the work or collectible they purchased. This is where things get interesting because the artwork is not the NFT that has been purchased. It is a pointer to a place on the Internet where the image is stored. There are a couple of ways to store this artwork. It can be on a single server prone to be lost or disappear like MySpace lost 50 million works in 2019 (Royster, 2019). Another solution is to use networked storage like IPFS [interplanetary file system] (IPFS Powers the Distributed Web, n.d.), but it also comes with its discontents.

According to Ippolito (2022), "[p]eer-to-peer systems are more likely to suffer gradual degradation due to peers abandoning the system; how many Napster or Gnutella nodes are still in use today?" This fate has been shared between all the digital assets we put on the Internet. According to Ippolito (2022), this is a problem for future digital historians and anthropologists. With the emergence of new technologies, today's new technologies may become obsolete, and they might need to decode digital symbols. Ippolito (2022) gives a not-so-long example; Imagine the technology of NFTs and saving them on that networked storage that existed in the 2010s. The dominant way to create those kinds of animations would have been Adobe Flash (Ippolito, 2022). McNamara (2020) states that "unfortunately, due to increasing concerns about security and memory usage, Flash has since been superseded by languages such as HTML5. As a result, Flash files no longer run on any current browser or operating system."

Assuming that the creation medium did not go obsolete, there are still problems with another medium, the marketplace of the NFT that has been minted. Since different marketplaces are running different cryptocurrencies, there is no guarantee that the marketplace you choose to mint will last; even so, NFT that you create will stay in that marketplace. Since those marketplaces change rapidly because of environmental concerns or popularity concerns, assuming your artwork/NFT did not become obsolescent, your choice of marketplace or cryptocurrency might be.

Democratization of the Art World

Until that point in this work, one can quickly draw attention to the fact that instead of talking about art, one needs to lay the ground for the technological and financial aspects of NFTs. Without proper knowledge of the medium, one can get lost in its hypermediated structure. As Bolter and Grusin pointed out, every emergent medium oscillates between hypermediacy and immediacy (Bolter and Grusin, 2003). Clearing up this distinction is straightforward. Assuming you encounter a sculpture, you confront it directly without any need for mediacy. You directly experience the artwork. In the case of NFTs, there are several mediations in place. First is the mediation of the digital, or computer. Then, the abstract mediation of the cryptocurrencies, or decentralized finance [Defi], comes the mediation of several marketplaces. In the light of Bolter and Grusin's insights in 2003, there will come a time when NFTs and NFT art world will be immediate, but until then, what people pay is not the artwork or art, in general, itself but the mystification of the technology underneath and the possibility of re-selling this NFT. Unfortunately, once we talk about an art market, we need to talk about money.

NFT sales indeed created the disruption that the art world needs in a moment of COVID crisis. The allure of Beeple's $69 million sale (Kastrenakes, 2021) at a Christie's auction in 2021 is the pinnacle of the NFT hype. Through this transaction, NFTs come into the spotlight. The piece was named "*Everydays – First 5000 Days*" and is a collage of the artist's works that he created in 5000 days every day, consisting of small doodles, collages, etc. The ease of creating digitally and the generic style of the animations, gifs, and jpegs give rise to an increase in NFT creators worldwide. According to NFT Market Report 2021, Crypto Art Market reached a total volume of $2. 798. 220, 643 with a total number of sales of 774.304 (Yearly NFT Market Report 2021, 2022). One has to keep in mind that these numbers exclude other NFT purchases like collectibles, gaming goods, and metaverse purchases. Famous collectibles like "*Bored Ape Yacht Club*" and "*CryptoPunks*" are also excluded from the Crypto Art section. To put a perspective on general NFT sales; in 2021, $17. 694. 851, 721 (Yearly NFT Market Report 2021, 2022).

Compared with the worldwide art market, these numbers are still a small percentage. According to "The Art Market 2021," total sales in 2020 reached $50,1 Billion (McAndrew, 2021). It also should be noted that in 2019 the total sales were much higher, $64,3 Billion. The diminishing sales can be easily speculated to be a result of the global COVID-19 pandemic. It is important to note that the emergence of the NFT art market, the global pandemic, and the diminishing sales in the Global Art Market happening simultaneously cannot be just coincidence.

It is easily seen that NFTs create a new marketplace in which everyone can create and sell through those without any intermediaries. One of the premises of the NFTs is the democratization of the art market. Without any intermediaries like galleries, auction houses, or art connoisseurs, digital artists could reach out and connect with their buyers directly. Without the commissions paid to the intermediary agent, artists now instantly gain access to the funds people pay for their work. Or so it seems. According to the NFT Market Report 2021, The Crypto Art market is primarily dominated by several large emerging corporations like SuperRare, ArtBlocks, etc. and traditional auction houses like Sotheby's and Christie's. All of them apply specific fees on sales for artists. For example, SuperRare gets %15 of the original sale, %10 of the secondary sales, and on all sales gets %3 of the total money paid (What Is the Fee Structure on SuperRare?, 2022). Unfortunately, these fees do not stop here. The artist should "mint" their works on the blockchain. Which also has a fee called "gas fee." Minting an NFT means converting your digital artwork into crypto assets to be stored on the blockchain, and the "gas fee" is the fee you have to pay; surprisingly, it is not a constant fee due to the volatility of the crypto market, it might raise or fall during a particular time of the day, or time of the month. There is nothing new under the sun.

Parallelisms with the traditional art world do not stop there either. A naive art enthusiast can though contemporary art as a solitary practice. If that is not the case, we can see NFTs as created by an artist's creative genius. A simple search on site Fiverr, "a global online marketplace for freelance services" (Fiverr, 2022), returns 12,253 services as of September 2022 (Find the Best Global Talent., 2022). Services include titles like, "I will create quality pixel nft collection," "I will create 10k nft [NFT] art collection in any unique style," and so on. The price tags vary around €10 to €1000. On the other hand, in traditional contemporary art, hiring assistants or artists to create unique artworks is not something new. Worldly renowned artist Jeff Koons is a good example.

At its peak, in 2015, the Koons studio reportedly employed more than 100 painters to finish his Gazing Ball series: 35 well-known paintings, many of them Impressionist, each one exactingly reproduced, with the addition of a blue glass "gazing ball" image to provide a Koonsian touch (Shnayerson, 2019, p. 369).

In light of these examples, NFT space creates a sub-class of artists/workers that greater and richer investors/artists can exploit, just like the working class in the physical art world, which is not what democratization of the art world literally means.

Authorship and Ownership Issues

The idea of owning an NFT is somewhat counter-intuitive to owning an artwork. Even though forgeries of paintings are widespread worldwide, they are still hard to come by. As for installations and site-specific works, it is much more difficult because the artwork is realized at that place exclusively. But as for NFTs, there is no judicial constraint on somebody who right-clicks and saves a minted image and then mints it again. According to Ippolito (2022, p. 2), "when you buy an NFT, you do not buy the original assets so much as you buy the idea of owning that asset."

Unlike collecting physical art, NFTs are basically a "receipt" confirming that somebody made a transaction to show that they bought the artwork. It is a transaction recorded on a blockchain. On that record, metadata, there is a pointer to an asset somewhere on the web, as discussed before. Therefore, there can be thousands of the same image on the web, but since somebody bought its NFT, "the original" belongs to them and has bragging rights. One does not buy the artwork but the idea/receipt of the purchase of the artwork. According to "Conditions of Sale of Christie's," what somebody buys is explained as:

> [P]urchase of the lot means you have full ownership rights in the NFT itself, including the right to store, sell and transfer your NFT. Your purchase of the lot does not provide any rights, express or implied, in (including, without limitation, any copyrights or other intellectual property rights in and to) the digital asset underlying the NFT other than the right to use, copy, and display the digital asset for your own personal, non-commercial use or in connection with a proposed sale or transfer of the NFT and any other right

> expressly contained in these Conditions of Sale. For the avoidance of doubt, you do not have the right to distribute or otherwise commercialize the digital asset or to represent or imply any sort of sponsorship, endorsement, affiliation, or other relationship with the seller and/or the creator of the digital asset without the prior authorization of the seller or the party(ies) that holds such rights. (Conditions of Sale for Christie's Inc., n.d., p. 44)

To overcome this authorship issue at hand, artists and creators started to give out physical copies of the artwork with the purchase. With services like Meural (NETGEAR, n.d.) and Infinite Objects (Infinite Objects, n.d.), one can showcase their NFTs on a physical, digital display. But they do not solve ownership problems because one can still copy and display other people's digital assets by just copying and showcasing them on those glorified and overpriced digital displays. At first sight, it may seem to solve the authorship and showcasing issues besides the Internet, but NFTs are not artworks themselves but just pointers to a space on the Internet. Not only that, but creating a physical copy of an artwork is against the essence of NFTs because they tend to change hands rapidly. The average ownership duration during the second quarter of 2022 is 47.9 days (Quarterly NFT Market Report 2022 Q2, 2022).

Consequently, physical objects create more issues than they solve. As mentioned in the Skeptics' Introduction to Crypto art and NFTs, "when you link a physical object to your NFT, you're shackling a bowling ball to a cheetah" (The Skeptics' Introduction to Crypto art and NFTs for Digital Artists and Designers, 2021). Ownership of the NFTs happens in moments, so questions like how those physical objects change hands, who will keep track of the logistics of those operations, and how one knows where their NFTs are in a given time are hard to answer and have nothing to do with the technology. Hence, attaching physicality to an NFT is just a gimmick. And also, people have complicated reasons for buying things.

> Yet the presumption that NFT buyers are being ripped off misses an important paradox of certain digital goods: The less of a link they have to tangible, non-internet stores of value, the higher the price they might command. NFTs' abstraction, their seemingly arbitrary valuation, and even the paltriness of the privileges they convey to their owners are, for now, big selling points, especially to buyers purchasing directly from artists. People have complex reasons for buying things, and NFTs are no exception. (Marks and Zittrain, 2021)

Besides, the ownership problems in the purchasing section, there are also problems of forgery of digital artworks as well as physical artworks. For example, Anish Kapoor's and David Bailey's artworks were photographed, turned into NFTs, and marketed for millions of pounds without their consent (Art by Anish

Kapoor and David Bailey for Sale as NFTs without Their Consent, 2021). Similar issues have arisen in the NFT space, especially with the well-known trademarked characters of Marvel and DC comics. Both parties' legal teams warned freelance artists not to use copyrighted materials to sell as NFTs ($7.5 Million NFT Collection Accused of Using Art Without Permission Threatened by Legal Action – Bitcoin News, n.d.). There is no system of anti- infringement in place in any NFT marketplace as of this work's writing. Instead, websites like "Deviantart," which is a long-standing digital artwork database in which people can showcase their digital illustrations and works, rolled out their own anti-infringement systems (DeviantArt Protect, n.d.).

Environmental Hazards and NFTs

The decentralized computational power required for minting an NFTs is energy-consuming and can be regarded as environmentally destructive. It is essential to keep in mind that the figures shown in this work will be solely based on Ethereum networks transactions. Therefore, the cost of preserving, showcasing, and maintaining websites has been omitted. As of September 2022, according to the website 'digiconomist' the cost of a single Ethereum transaction costs 194.55 kWh, which is "equivalent to the power consumption of an average US household over 6.58 days," and its carbon footprint is 108.51 kgCO2, which is approximately "equivalent to the carbon footprint of 240,496 VISA transactions or 18,085 hours of watching YouTube" (Ethereum Energy Consumption Index, n.d.).

Additionally, a single NFT can involve many transactions, and these include minting, bidding, canceling, sales, and transfer of ownership. According to Memo Akten (2022a), through research and calculation, "a single NFT's footprint is equivalent to an EU resident's total electric power consumption for more than a month, with emissions equivalent to driving for 1000 Km, or flying for 2 hours." Not only that, but an average NFT artist's existence and production of NFTs is equivalent to an EU resident's electricity consumption for three years (Akten, 2022b). At the time of writing this work, there are new studies of proofing the transaction that will be implemented in the future on to the blockchain, which is more environmentally friendly. Hopefully, things will get better, but as Akten states that "if we are building new systems, we should build them aligned with the values that we hope to carry into the future" (Akten, 2022a).

Conclusion

The prominent stance of this study is not to take sides for or against the NFTs. On the contrary, the idea of expanding the field so artists from all over the world who have an internet connection can produce, sell, and earn money without intermediaries is remarkable. However, the pitfalls mentioned above and dangers like environmental hazards, authorship dilemmas, and the decentralization deception and democratized art world parable disguises the same capitalist financial elite and their systems taking over the NFT space at a peculiar pace. When the art world and the financial elite cross paths, talking about the art and the artwork itself becomes ineffectual and pointless. At the intersection of those paths, the solitary artists, without a doubt, will still be solitary struggling artists.

Before the NFTs and blockchain technologies, in 2014, Georgina Adam analyzed the explosion of the art market in the 21st century. At the end of the book, she makes an insightful remark about finance and the art world:

> From the deceptive transparency of the auction process to imprecise pricing in art galleries, from currency arbitraging to tax evasion to money laundering, the art market, at its upper end, has always had its secret deals, insider trading and speculation. But with internationalisation, the Internet and a closer alignment of the worlds of art and finance, the opportunity for wrongdoing is greater than ever before. (Adam, 2014, p. 162)

Unfortunately, with the volatile and cryptocurrencies emerging, the news about individual artists' blockbuster sales, and the FOMI [Fear of Missing Out] effect, artists flock to the NFT Market blind. It is no coincidence those two facts happened in the same period; during the effects COVID-19 pandemic, which spans most of 2020 and 2021, the art markets' volume of sales decreased by %23 (McAndrew, 2021) to $31.4 million, its lowest point after the effects of the global economic recession of 2008. As a result, the art market turned its face to NFTs and cryptocurrencies. Putting all the positive sides of NFTs aside, the main argument of this study is that the explosion of the NFT market is just another way of the capitalist art markets' expansionist agenda to the new playgrounds and unaware artists.

References

$7.5 Million NFT Collection Accused of Using Art Without Permission Threatened by Legal Action – Bitcoin News. (n.d.). Retrieved from https://news.bitcoin.com/7-5-million-nft-collection-accused-of-using-art-without-permission-threatened-by-legal-action/ [Accessed on Sept., 4. 2022].

Adam, G. (2014). *Big bucks: The explosion of the art market in the twenty-first century*. Lund Humphries.

Akten, M. (2022a, March 24). The Unreasonable Ecological Cost of #CryptoArt. *Medium*. Retrieved from https://memoakten.medium.com/the-unreasonable-ecological-cost-of-cryptoart-2221d3eb2053 [Accessed on Sept., 5. 2022].

Akten, M. (2022b, March 24). The Unreasonable Ecological Cost of #CryptoArt (Part 2: Extras). *Medium*. Retrieved from https://memoakten.medium.com/analytics-the-unreasonable-ecological-cost-of-cryptoart-72f9066b90d [Accessed on Sept., 5. 2022].

Art by Anish Kapoor and David Bailey for Sale as NFTs Without Their Consent. (2021, November 22). *Financial Times*.

Bolter, J. D., & Grusin, R. (2003). *Remediation: Understanding new media*. New York: MIT Press.

Collins-The Collins Word of the Year 2021 is... (n.d.). Retrieved from https://www.collinsdictionary.com/woty [Accessed on Aug., 31. 2022].

Conditions of Sale for Christie's Inc. (n.d.). Retrieved from https://www.christies.com/pdf/onlineonly/ECOMMERCE%20CONDITIONS%20OF%20SALE%20-%20NEW%20YORK%206-16-21%20(002).pdf [Accessed on Aug., 22. 2022].

DeviantArt Protect: Helping Safeguard Your Art by Team on DeviantArt. (n.d.). Retrieved from https://www.deviantart.com/team/journal/DeviantArt-Protect-Helping-Safeguard-Your-Art-884278903 [Accessed on Sept., 4. 2022].

Ethereum Energy Consumption Index. (n.d.). *Digiconomist*. Retrieved from https://digiconomist.net/ethereum-energy-consumption/ [Accessed on Sept., 4. 2022].

Find the Best Global Talent. (2022). Fiverr.Com. https://www.fiverr.com/search/gigs

Fiverr. (2022). *Wikipedia*. Retrieved from https://en.wikipedia.org/w/index.php?title=Fiverr&oldid=1104507180 [Accessed on Sept., 4. 2022].

Hasan, H. R., & Salah, K. (2018). Proof of delivery of digital assets using Blockchain and smart contracts. *IEEE Access*, *6*: 65439–65448.

Infinite Objects. (n.d.). *Infinite objects*. Retrieved from https://infiniteobjects.com/ [Accessed on Sept., 4. 2022].

IPFS Powers the Distributed Web. (n.d.). Retrieved from https://ipfs.tech/ [Accessed on Aug., 8. 2022].

Ippolito, J. (2022). Crypto-preservation and the ghost of Andy Warhol. *Arts*, *11*(2): 47. https://doi.org/10.3390/arts11020047

Kastrenakes, J. (2021, March 11). Beeple sold an NFT for $69 million. *The Verge*. Retrieved from https://www.theverge.com/2021/3/11/22325054/beeple-christies-nft-sale-cost-everydays-69-million [Accessed on Sept., 4. 2022].

Majer, A. (2019). *NON-FUNGIBLE TOKENS: Transforming the worlds of assets, gaming, and collectibles*. Blockchain Research Institute. https://www.blockchainresearchinstitute.org/project/non-fungible-tokens/

Marks, W., & Zittrain, J. (2021, April 7). What critics don't understand about NFTs. *The Atlantic*. Retrieved from https://www.theatlantic.com/ideas/archive/2021/04/nfts-show-value-owning-unownable/618525/ [Accessed on Sept., 4. 2022].

McAndrew, C. (2021). *The art market 2021, An Art Basel UBS report*. Art Basel and UBS.

McNamara, R. (2020, December 18). *RIP Adobe flash: Five takeaways about the plug-in's legacy in Net Art*. Hyperallergic. Retrieved from http://hyperallergic.com/609682/rip-adobe-flash-five-takeaways-about-the-plug-ins-legacy-in-net-art/ [Accessed on Sept., 4. 2022].

NETGEAR. (n.d.). *Meural digital canvas—Digital art frame. NETGEAR*. Retrieved from https://www.netgear.com/home/digital-art-canvas/ [Accessed on Sept., 4. 2022].

Noh, M. E., Odenkirk, S. C., & Shionoiri, Y. (2022). GM! Time to wake up and address copyright and other legal issues impacting visual art NFTs. *The Columbia Journal of Law & the Arts*, *45*(3).

Quarterly NFT Market Report 2022 Q2. (2022). NonFungible Corporation.

Royster, P. (2019). Your internet data is rotting. *The Conversation*. Retrieved from http://theconversation.com/your-internet-data-is-rotting-115891 [Accessed on Sept., 4. 2022].

Shnayerson, M. (2019). *Boom: Mad money, mega dealers, and the rise of contemporary art* (First edition). PublicAffairs.

The Skeptics' Introduction to Cryptoart and NFTs for Digital Artists and Designers. (2021, January 1). Justin Cone. Retrieved from https://justincone.com/posts/nft-skeptics-guide/ [Accessed on Sept., 4. 2022].

Trautman, L. J. (2021). *Virtual art and non-fungible tokens*.

What is the fee structure on SuperRare?. (2022). *SuperRare*. Retrieved from https://help.superrare.com/en/articles/5662523-what-is-the-fee-structure-on-superrare [Accessed on Sept., 4. 2022].

Yearly NFT Market Report 2021. (2022). NonFungible Corporation.

Çisil Sohodol, İdil Karademirlidağ Suher, and Nilüfer Geysi

Social Media as a Gift and Curse in Crisis Communication: A Study on Turkish PR Practitioners

Abstract: The purpose of this chapter was to examine how Turkish PR practitioners evaluate social media in terms of its threats and opportunities for crisis communication, and its effects on the crisis consulting process. Additionally, it attempted to elicit their advice on how to use social media more effectively during crisis communication. In-depth interviews were conducted with twenty senior PR practitioners from agencies that are members of the Turkish Public Relations Association (TUHID) and the Communication Consultancies Association of Turkey (IDA). The findings showed that Turkish PR practitioners mostly regard social media as a curse rather than a gift due to the number of threats they asserted about it. The findings pointed out that they recognize the importance of social media for issues and risk tracking. Our research demonstrated the high awareness level of PR practitioners about the role of social media to build relationships with key stakeholders; however, it was argued that social media is underutilized for this purpose.

Keywords: Turkish PR Sector, Crisis Management, Social-Mediated Crisis Communication, Digital Media

Introduction

Since the day social media have come into our lives, it has been causing a redefinition of communication, marketing, and management strategies. It has an advanced influence on marketing communication, media relations, community relations, customer relations, government relations, and business relations (Luttrel, 2015) since it forces companies to build two-way communication (Pavlik, 2007). The ongoing change and development of social media have made the crisis ecosystem much more complicated (Lee, 2020) and it continues to create a new era in crisis communication practice, and literature (Cheng, 2020). This situation has led to the evolution of crisis communication understanding, too.

The impact of social media on crisis communication has been seriously debated all around the world. However, the studies that include recommendations for use of social media in crisis communication are majorly unstructured (Lachlan et al., 2014) and research on how public relations (PR) practitioners in Turkey approach social media in terms of crisis communication is extremely limited. Therefore, this study aims to find out the views of Turkish PR professionals about changes that social media has created in the field of crisis communication and to take their recommendations about the use of social media in the crisis communication process.

Defining Crisis and Crisis Communication

A crisis can be defined as "a major occurrence with a potentially negative outcome affecting an organization, company or industry as well as its publics, products, services or good name" (Fearn-Banks, 2016, p. 1). Therefore, the viability of an organization is closely related to crises that require a fast decision-making mechanism (Pearson and Clair, 1998, p. 60). A crisis may be a breaking point for an organization since it may cause financial losses (Roux-Dufort, 2007), brand damage (Fan et al., 2013), injuries or deaths (Bundy et al., 2017), or environmental harm (Clayton et al., 2013). The damage has the potential to impact organizations' reputation to a certain extent (Barton, 2001).

The extensive crisis literature suggests that although crises cannot be stopped, their impacts can be minimized. The process "to prevent or lessen the negative outcomes of a crisis and thereby protect the organization, stakeholders, and/or industry from damage" is defined as crisis management (Coombs, 1999, p. 4). One of the most referred frameworks of crisis management is Mitroff's (1988) which includes five phases: signal detection, preparation/prevention, containment/damage limitation, recovery, and learning. This process is divided into three basic phases by Coombs (2010) as pre-crisis, crisis, and post-crisis.

The organization's dialog with its publics in these stages defines the crisis communication concept (Fearn-Banks, 2016, p. 2). Crisis communication is "a structured approach to the handling of such events, aiming to put in place a communications strategy designed to direct the right information to the right people with maximum speed, minimizing the risk of misinformation and helping overall damage limitation" (Murray, 2005, p. 8).

Public relations and corporate communication executives have duties like improving communication with key stakeholders, handling media relations, defining the role of the spokesperson, and training relevant employees (Coombs, 1999). Crisis management and crisis communication are not always run by organizations alone, companies generally consult PR agencies or PR consultancies (Crandall et al., 2014; Jugo, 2017). In the PR industry, there are divisions in most of the PR agencies that are devoted to crisis communication or there are entire agencies that only focus on crisis communication (Bussey, 2011).

Social Media and Crisis Communication: Changes, Contributions and Challenges

Social media is a common term for online tools and websites that create mutual interaction. Social media is "activities, practices, and behaviors among communities of people who gather together online to share information, knowledge, and opinions using conversational media which are web-based applications that make it possible to create and easily to transmit content in the form of words, pictures, video, and audio" (Safko, 2009). Social media platforms such as Facebook, Twitter, LinkedIn, Instagram, FourSquare, YouTube, Flickr enable people to share ideas and information on various topics and have become a part of the daily life of many people (Saroj and Pal, 2020).

In the crisis communication field, social media is generally considered both a gift and a curse (Prentice and Huffman, 2008; Cheng, 2016). Although "gift and curse" do not seem to be compatible concepts, they are both inseparable parts of social media. Social media can trigger or escalate crises (Pang et al., 2014) and can help organizations to prevent them, respond better or learn from crises (Lin et al., 2016). There are studies that have highlighted the coexistence of these two concepts -gift and curse- in crisis communication. For example, Apuke and Tunca (2018) examined the sources and data obtained from an electronic database and concluded that social media has negative and positive effects on crisis management. According to Argenti and Barnes (2009, p. 246), "the dichotomous nature of digital channels as both blessing and a curse is a common theme in their emerge into the world of business communication, and this holds true for crisis management and communication as well."

The research on the advantages of social media in crisis communication shows how it facilitates two-way symmetrical communication (Duhe and Wright, 2013; Honisch and Manchon, 2020) by enabling dialogue (Wright and Hinson, 2009; Ki and Nekmat, 2014), interactivity (Ott and Theunissen, 2015), engagement (Guidry et al., 2017; Jiang et al., 2016), relationship building (Xu, 2018), and mutual understanding (Tench and Yeomans, 2006). Another vital opportunity of social media is that organizations can monitor emerging issues, trends, and threats; therefore, social media can work as an early warning or sensor system (Avery, 2017). During a crisis, real-time monitoring may provide insights to define or redefine the crisis response strategy (Taylor and Kent, 2007).

Social media allows rapid dissemination of information which is advantageous for organizations to give, and update messages (Lovejoy et al., 2012) cost-effectively (McLean and Power, 2009). Organizations, via social media, can identify, and map stakeholders related to the crisis (Walker, 2014), and can educate internal or external stakeholders regarding risks (Veil et al., 2011). Social media can convey crisis narratives (Yang et al., 2010) so organizations can create meaning among the publics (Fog et al., 2010). Thanks to social media, organizations have their own media, and they can publish crisis information without the control of journalistic gatekeeping (Duhe and Wright, 2013). Lastly, social media is convenient to evaluate the effectiveness of crisis strategies (Jiang et al., 2016).

The functions and characteristics of social media that can be considered threats or challenges for crisis communication are substantial. According to (Holloman, 2014, p. 131), crisis become more frequent because of the nature of social media. Although it was previously discussed as an opportunity, the intensive and rapid flow of information makes it difficult for companies to control the crisis situation (Valentini et al., 2018). Due to the virality, a greater number of stakeholders are exposed to the negative content. Organizations control their own messages on social media; however, it is not possible to control comments, explanations, or interpretations of stakeholders. User-generated content (UGC) on social media contributes to the further spread of negative news (Veil et al., 2011). A company's misuse of social media can also set off the crisis (Griffin, 2014). Another challenging issue is that it has been becoming a public sphere where activists can challenge the dominant understanding and companies (Ciszek 2016). Cases such as fake sites, imitative websites, cyber terrorism, hacking of corporate websites, or social media accounts can be listed as other types of crises that social media puts in the lives of companies. Social media also causes the long-lasting effect problem (Swann, 2017). It is almost impossible to completely eliminate the footprints of the crisis experienced by the companies (González-Herrero and Smith, 2010).

The discussed issues show that social media has a huge impact on crisis communication both positively and negatively. Based on the reviewed literature, the following research questions were proposed for this study:

- **Research question 1 (RQ1):** How do Turkish PR practitioners who work in public relations and consultancy firms approach social media in terms of its threats and opportunities?
- **Research question 2 (RQ2):** How is social media affecting the practice of crisis consulting?
- **Research question 3 (RQ3):** What do they recommend to crisis managers to use social mediamore effectively in crisis communication?

Methodology

The present study followed an exploratory approach, and utilized a qualitative in-depth interviewing method (Denzin and Lincoln, 2011) to find out the views of Turkish PR practitioners about threats and opportunities that social media has brought to the field of crisis communication, identify how social media has been affecting the practice of crisis consulting and to take their recommendations about the use of social media as a crisis communication tool.

The interviews were semi-structured, and conducted with senior PR executives who work in PR agencies that are members of TUHID and IDA and include crisis consulting as one of their services. All the participants were chosen through purposive sampling, a non-probability sampling technique. Purposive sampling is "randomly selecting units without replacement from the particular section of the population believed to yield samples that will give the best estimate of the population parameter of interest" (Guerte and Barrios, 2006, p. 278). The interviews were ended when researchers explored "depth" and identified "various properties and dimensions" in main categories (Corbin and Strauss, 2014, p. 140).

In total 20 PR executives were included in the study, 11 of which were men and 9 were women. Participants had an average of 15 years of work experience in the PR consulting field, ranging from a minimum of 5 to a maximum of 40 years of experience. Job titles held by the participants included founder president, deputy general manager, senior director, PR group coordinator, senior consultant, and managing director.

All interviews were conducted online via Zoom, a video conferencing program, between June and August 2020. The interviews lasted on average about 70 minutes, ranging from minimum 60 to maximum 90 minutes. Each participant was informed about the topic and the general procedure before the start of the interview, and they were asked if they consent to participate in the research. Upon agreement to participate in the study, all interviews were recorded and confidentiality was guaranteed. The interviews were transcribed in full. The transcriptions were made in Turkish, then they were translated into English.

An interview guide including 17 open-ended questions was followed during the interviews. Each question was clustered based on the research questions and was extracted from the related literature. Since the semi-structured interview method allows researchers to adjust the questions (Scott and Garner, 2013), some probing questions were added in some of the interviews.

After the data collection process, interviews were subjected to a thematic analysis. The analysis focused on the research questions. The interviews were evaluated and divided into sections based on the research questions. Then, the researchers discovered themes following Vaismoradi et al.'s (2016) thematic analysis: "initialization," "construction," "rectification," and "finalization."

Findings

The findings of in-depth interviews revealed themes that are presented based on the research questions. Meaning is condensed in the presentation of findings (see Kvale and Brinkmann, 2009).

Responses to RQ1: How do Turkish PR practitioners who work in public relations and consultancy firms approach social media in terms of its threats and opportunities?

The first seven questions in the interview guidebook were about social media's advantages and disadvantages in the eyes of Turkish PR consultants, and practitioners. The answers to these questions brought out five threat-related themes (lack of control, misuse of social media, malevolence, empowered social movements, and social, or political sensitivities) (see Tab. 1) and three-opportunity related themes (engagement, monitoring, content creation and dissemination) (see Tab. 2).

The analyses suggest that all participants agree that social media increases the risk of crises. According to most of the interviewees, risks vary based on sectors. Especially some sectors like fast-moving consumer goods, banking, and telecommunication were conceived as more vulnerable than others. Another consensus was on the riskiest platform, Twitter. This is because retweeting increases the speed of spread, it is sometimes impossible to identify the source, and stakeholders can easily follow and participate in issues related to crises via hashtags.

Tab. 1: Threat-Related Themes

Themes	Categories
Lack of control	Viral effect UGC / Citizen journalism Inadequacy of regulations Influencer marketing related risks

Themes	Categories
Misuse of social media	Misuse of corporate SM accounts Misuse of personal SM accounts by corporate executives Untrained/inexperienced digital content producers
Malevolence	Trolls Fake news Rumor
Empowered social movements	Activists
Social/political sensitivities	Political dividedness Cultural intolerance

From the interviews it is learned that Turkish PR practitioners see social media as a platform with lack of control. The first threat-related theme of the findings emerged from this idea. All participants emphasized the speed on social media. They stated that all kinds of negative content including fake news, and rumors can pose a crisis due to the virality effect on social media which creates a significant control difficulty. Participant 20 refers to the disadvantage of the speed on developing the response strategy: "The speed at which negative content spreads creates a serious panic for the organizations. Since this panic environment increases the pressure, there are difficulties in formulating the correct response strategy" (Participant 20).

The fact that social media allows user-generated content and citizen journalism was also considered a risk area. One of the participants explained: "People behave as a hero or a detective on social media even sometimes they search for mistakes to become popular among their followers" (Participant 2). Six PR practitioners pointed out complaints that spread virally. Participant 4 illustrated this situation as follows: "People have discovered the power of social media; rather than reaching out to customer service departments, they prefer posting on social media to solve noteless problems." In addition, it was emphasized that the ability to remain anonymous, the difficulty of tracking on social media, inadequacy of legal regulations, and sanctions increase the risks with the multiplier effect. Regarding lack of control, eight of the participants referred to influencer marketing as a risky space. It was a general view that scandals they got involved in also create control problems for the organizations/brands they work with.

The second theme that emerged from the answers of the respondents was "misuse of social media." The participants stated that misuse of official social media accounts of companies, and brands is an important risk area. Sharing incorrect information from official accounts, using inappropriate language, and sharing disturbing content and images were frequently mentioned as misuse examples. It was also stated that the personal social media accounts of executives should be managed carefully. The content shared on personal accounts of the C-suite is generally attributed to the organization; therefore, if they share strong opinions, or be a party to certain issues, the crisis risks increase highly for the organization. The participants also stated that social media campaigns or content prepared by digital communication agencies or creative agencies have been a crisis trigger in recent years and created a risk area. Participant 10 explained this in the following way:

> There are very young, and enthusiastic but also inexperienced digital content producers in the agencies. They produce content without considering the risks due to the desire to be creative. We are trying to be involved in the process as much as possible because they are not as sensitive as PR practitioners about social, political, and cultural matters, and they don't have a solid grasp of controversial issues as much as PR people (Participant 10).

The second theme revealed by interviews was malevolence. Importantly, all PR professionals noted how fake news, and rumors are serious threats. They stated that they ever-increasingly manage the risks, and crises that emerged due to fake news and rumors. One of the participants came up with an interesting metaphor while defining social media related risks:

> Fake news has always been an issue, but social media is now the homeland of fake news and rumor followed by it. Media literacy is low in Turkey. When people are exposed to fake news that was shared by majority, they think that it is true. They usually don't verify the news and contribute to circulation of fake news (Participant 4).

Trolling was another frequently mentioned malevolence on social media. Participants added that trolls work up the generation and spread fake news and rumors. Activism as a movement that cannot be dissociated from social media in the last decade was a significant threat according to Turkish PR practitioners. Participants concurred on the view that they feel under pressure more often compared to the pre-social media period. Twelve participants stated that women's rights, murders of women, child marriage, and children's rights are the subjects that attract the attention of activists. If companies do not behave expectedly when they are hot topics, negative comments on social media pose crisis risks. An example from Participant 6 depicts the situation:

> Turkish social media users are not very active in activist organizations as in Western countries. However, if the issue is women's or children's rights, they can badmouth

> companies and pose a serious crisis threat. For example, when a famous actor who played in a popular bank commercial committed violence against her famous singer girlfriend, the bank became a trending topic on Twitter within minutes. The bank was late to respond and there were many customers who broke off with the bank (Participant 6).

Half of the participants see social and political sensitivities as a considerable risk on social media. According to them, social media users are increasingly labeling companies because of their political stance. This situation triggers crises that can be risky for stakeholder relations and reputation. An interesting example about one of the well-known biscuits and confectionary producers in Turkey demonstrates this risk adequately:

> Ulker prepared a video for April Fools' Day in 2017 which led to massive reactions in society. The instant that video was shown off, thousands of tweets per minute were shared. According to social media users, Ulker was one of the forces behind the coup attempt that took place a year ago in Turkey. It was argued that the broadcasted video was actually a signal of the next coup attempt and also the joke in the video was sending a message to the relevant parties to detonate the place where the President lived and worked. It became one of the biggest corporate crises in Turkey (Participant 9).

Six participants discussed that there is a culture of intolerance reflected on social media that ostracizes or marginalizes others. Organizations feel heavy pressure whether they engage or not in discussions related to different ethnicities, religious groups, and gender. The number of boycotts or opposite movements about this subject is considerable.

Besides threats emerged thanks to social media, participants discussed opportunities that contribute to the crisis communication process. When there is a controversial issue that may pose a crisis risk, social media allows PR practitioners to create and spread the appropriate content which may shape public opinion in favor of the organization. Participant 11 addressed this subject in the following way:

> In recent years we have benefited from social media to correct misconceptions about palm oil to prevent issues turn into a crisis. We have succeeded in pre-crisis communication by telling our stakeholders that palm oil does not pose a health risk as long as it does not reach a certain temperature (Participant 11).

Tab. 2: Opportunity-Related Themes

Themes	**Categories**
Engagement	Molding public opinion Community building Two-way communication
Monitoring	Issue tracking Risk detection Real time monitoring Learning from others
Content creation and dissemination	Owned media Speed Media / channel diversity

Participants stated that social media provides advantages in developing stakeholder relations by facilitating two-way and symmetrical communication and positioning organizations as sincere. Therefore, there is a huge opportunity to engage with stakeholders. On the other hand, they argued that social media platforms, typically, are not different than bulletin boards in most cases. Participant 17 elaborated:

> The experts in the field emphasize the importance of using social media as a tool that you can talk with stakeholders rather than telling something. However, it is not applied in the same way in the sector due to workload of organizations and consultancy companies (Participant 17).

The subjects that all participants reached a consensus on the advantages of social media in crisis communication were issue tracking, risk detection, and real-time marketing which were collected under the monitoring theme. For example, Participant 8 noted the following: "Monitoring has become easier. We can follow the sectoral, local, and global risks and issues for 24 hours by following the hashtags or trending issues on social media." Most participants stated that due to the features of social media that facilitate monitoring, organizational learning is easier than ever. It is possible to use the information that is obtained through monitoring while planning or deciding response strategy.

The interviews lastly revealed the theme of content creation and dissemination. The PR professionals recognized the importance of social media in terms of owned media. Participant 20 exemplified: "We do not have to wait for newspapers to publish an information the organization wants to convey about the crisis. Our social media accounts are like our own newspapers." In addition, they highlighted how they enrich their content with technical opportunities provided by social media for preventing or responding to crises. "We can support crisis statements with videos. Studies show that most of Turkish people are not influenced from what they read but from what they watch. In this sense, social media offers a prominent advantage" (Participant 7). The participants also stated that the speed of spread, which is one of the riskiest issues of social media, also provides an advantage in terms of disseminating crisis messages in minutes.

Responses to RQ2: How is social media affecting practice of crisis consulting?

The answers related to the second research question revealed three themes: consulting in the pre-crisis period, during the crisis period, and in the post-crisis period (see Tab. 3).

Tab. 3: Crisis Consulting-Related Themes

Themes	**Categories**
Consulting in the pre-crisis period	Organizational system in the agency Crisis communication planning (contact list updates, scenario, simulations, defining spokesperson) Monitoring issues/conversations Providing training for employees of the clients, and other agencies Including influencers in risk management
Consulting during the crisis period	Time pressure Response strategies New dimensions for crises
Consulting in the post-crisis period	Tracking post-crisis impacts and conversations

Regarding the pre-crisis consulting, all participants stressed that the need for crisis communication consultancy has increased due to the risks created by social media. In addition, the interviews revealed the increased importance of crisis communication consultancy as evident from the rise in the number of demands of the clients. Several participants stated that the changing eco-system caused them to make some changes in their agency structures. Some of them reformed their crisis communication teams, while others employed personnel who are experts in social media. Another noteworthy change in the working system was about highly increased workload. Due to the never-breaking risks on social media, agency staff has started to be 7 days and 24 hours available. Moreover, all participants noted the extended range of services that PR consultants provide regarding social media in the pre-crisis period. Tracking the dynamics of online communities and inoculating on social media are some of recently added crisis consulting services. Most participants stated that, if needed, they engage in conversations or make third parties engaged to prevent the issue from turning into a crisis. "We deeply analyze conversations and try to understand certain thought patterns to deal with potential crises. In my opinion, it has a huge impact on crisis prevention" (Participant 8).

Eight of the participants claimed that they provide a consulting service to organizations to develop a social media policy to minimize corporate risks. For four participants, providing training for the use of personal social media accounts of senior executives has become a part of crisis communication consultancy services. The fact that PR agencies are seeking for new approaches to enhance the risk sensitivity of other agencies (event, marketing communication agencies, advertising, and digital communication agencies, etc.) with which companies work was another key point. All participants agreed that developing scenarios and doing simulations about social media risks has become more important, but they also acknowledged that it has been harder to do so because it is getting increasingly difficult to make predictions in this new world.

Eleven participants viewed influencer marketing as a crucial component of social media within the crisis communication services and stated that they must evaluate the risks associated with influencers about their personal lives, political opinions, or attitudes towards social issues on social media. It was mentioned that routine influencer checks are carried out as a new but crucial part of the crisis counseling process.

In the scope of the second theme which is related to the crisis phase, all the participants agreed that speed is social media's greatest impact on the crisis period. They stated that when a crisis begins, all PR professionals are in a race against time, which puts a lot of pressure on agencies. Participant 7 explained: "Crisis communication was already a stressful field, but with social media, providing consultancy services has started to become overwhelming due to never-ending time pressure." The final subcategory of "consultation during a crisis period" focuses on the new crisis dimensions that social media has brought forth. Six participants presented an opinion about the recent crisis dimensions. There are recent criteria like critical propagation factors, and conversation rate to define crisis response strategy. As Participant 1 explained:

> We have a system of damage assessment and it depends on the content and context of the crisis. If the damage is below 50% on the scale, we deliver a crisis-related message through corporate social media channels. When the damage is between 50%-80%, the board of directors makes statements both personally and as company representatives. The third level is the top level, where the board chairman comes into play (Participant 1).

Due to its two-way communication and engagement features, social media is seen by Turkish PR professionals as a new breath to crisis communication, according to the last category under RQ2. They all claimed that using social media gives them the chance to track the crisis progress. Additionally, they can directly reach people who still have questions about the crisis situation.

Responses to RQ3: What do Turkish PR practitioners recommend to crisis managers to use social media more effectively in crisis communication?

The third research question aimed to take recommendations of Turkish PR practitioners in terms of using social media in times of crisis. The themes emerged as recommendations for pre-crisis, crisis, and post-crisis phases.

Pre-crisis recommendations were in line with threats that were pointed out within RQ1 (see Tab. 4). All the participants agreed on the significance of issue tracking. Participant 9 recommended a committee that is proficient in issue tracking and risk analysis. Participant 14 underlined the value of different pools for monitoring issues related to media, competitors, and the general public to get information more effortlessly. Seven participants suggested a guide, and regulation for the control of personal and corporate social media accounts. Half of the participants claimed that there should be better integration between PR agencies and other agencies. Also, the content that is created by other agencies should be checked. According to twelve participants, online reputation and organizational positioning should be enhanced to be ready for crises.

Tab. 4: Recommendation-Related Themes

Themes	**Categories**
Recommendations for pre-crisis phase	Developing integration between agencies Policy developing Issue tracking Online reputation building

Themes	Categories
Recommendations for crisis phase	Avoiding censorship Avoiding over communication Avoiding personal discussions Relationship building
Recommendations for post-crisis phase	Keeping tracking up Answering questions of stakeholders

Regarding the crisis phase, most participants provided advice to avoid censorship such as deleting or turning off comments on social media. They also highlighted the importance of avoiding over-communication that can create clutter in the crisis communication process. According to nine PR practitioners, social media should not be a place to go into personal discussions, because it can jeopardize an organization's position. All the professionals advised using social media not only as a tool to deliver a crisis message but also as an opportunity to build a relationship with stakeholders.

Finally, the post-crisis theme includes advice on how to keep track of issues to avoid crises in the future or how to learn from past crises. Most of the respondents shared similar views on how to respond to stakeholder questions following a crisis. They believe that ignoring their questions, or expectations is a big mistake.

Discussion and Conclusion

Using 20 in-depth interviews with PR professionals, this study deepens the understanding of social media in terms of crisis communication. According to the analyses, the PR professionals agree on the idea that social media has a profound impact on crisis communication. Although they mentioned several opportunities, they focused on the threats brought by social media within the scope of RQ1. In this sense, it is concluded that they regard social media mostly as a curse rather than a gift for the crisis communication process.

The most frequent risk areas were the speed of negative content dissemination and the difficulty of controlling social media which is consistent with the related literature (e.g. Woo, 2020). The findings revealed that PR practitioners see Twitter as the riskiest social media platform in terms of initiating a crisis, and spreading it rapidly which is in line with studies that refer to Twitter as uncontrollable (e.g., Acar and Muraki, 2011). Interestingly, they did not mention other social media platforms such as LinkedIn and YouTube while discussing the risks contrary to previous research (e.g., Sandlin and Gracyalny, 2018; Thelwall, 2017; Yang et al., 2010).

As our findings suggest, Turkish PR professionals are concerned about three topics that are relatively under-examined in the literature on crisis communication. The first of these risks was the inexperience of the digital content agencies in sensing the risks that may cause the crisis. Another severe risk was related to the context of Turkey. As mentioned, there are opposing parties on social media created by the serious polarization in Turkey. These groups are likely to put organizations in a dangerous position at any moment. This finding supports research that questions political polarization on social media (Farrell and Drezner, 2008; Hong and Kim, 2016). Thirdly, the participants highlighted the need for PR consultants to pay close attention to social media influencers to prevent any possible crises (see Martínez-López, 2020). The most emphasized opportunity of social media in the crisis communication process was monitoring. Turkish PR professionals believe they do not successfully utilize interaction and two-way communication on social media, despite the fact that they value it. This underutilization might be due to a lack of resources to reply to all messages (Veil et al., 2011), or fear of worsening the crisis (Stenger, 2014).

In the scope of RQ2, the effects of social media on crisis communication consulting services were evaluated. All participants believed that the increased risks associated with social media increase the demand for crisis communication consulting. Another notable conclusion was that social media considerably increased the workload, and range of services offered in crisis communication consulting, which raised the stress level of PR professionals (e.g., Gilkerson et al., 2018). For the pre-crisis period, online monitoring and strengthening relations with online stakeholders were the most emphasized services. There was an agreement among PR practitioners that crisis response strategies are situational. When it comes to the post-crisis period, it was shown that the priorities of PR practitioners were to continue monitoring to prevent a second-wave crisis and to strengthen the damaged reputation.

This study provided recommendations that crisis consultants can apply when they need to communicate during a crisis. Avoiding censorship, and over-communication were points acknowledged by all PR practitioners. This is consistent with a study by Quesenberry (2019) that examines the serious repercussions of removing negative comments on social media. In addition, the need to accord all content created by different agencies was urgent for most participants. Monitoring before, during, and after the crisis was a focal point of all participants while giving recommendations.

In conclusion, this study proposed a comprehensive basis for the crisis consulting field in Turkey and presented practical implications. There were several limitations in the present study. Firstly, only PR agencies that are members of TUHID and IDA were included in the study. Future studies could incorporate other PR agencies to widen the scope of the research. Secondly, this study only discussed consulting services; further studies could examine the organizational part of crisis communication to compare both sides.

References

Acar, A., & Muraki, Y. (2011). Twitter for crisis communication: lessons learned from Japan's tsunami disaster. *International Journal of Web Based Communities*, *7*(3): 392–402. DOI: 10.1504/IJWBC.2011.041206.

Apuke, O. D., & Tunca, E. A. (2018). Social media and crisis management: A review and analysis of existing studies. *LAÜ Sosyal Bilimler Dergisi*, *9*(2): 199–215.

Argenti, P. A., & Barnes, C. M. (2009). *Digital strategies for powerful corporate communications.* New York: McGraw Hill.

Avery, E. J. (2017). Public information officers' social media monitoring during the Zika virus crisis, a global health threat surrounded by public uncertainty. *Public Relations Review*, *43*(3): 468–476. DOI: 10.1016/j.pubrev.2017.02.018.

Barton, L. (2001). *Crisis in organizations II.* (Second edition). Cincinnati, OH: College Divisions South-Western.

Baumard, P., & Starbuck, W. H. (2005). Learning from failures: Why it may not happen. *Long Range Planning*, *38*(3): 281–298. DOI: 10.1016/j.lrp.2005.03.004.

Beck, U. (2009). World at risks (C. Cronin, Trans.). Cambridge: Polity Press. German Edition.

Benoit, W. L. (1997). Image repair discourse and crisis communication. *Public relations Review*, *23*(2): 177–186. DOI: 10.1016/S0363-8111(97)90023-0.

Bundy, J. (2017). Crises and crisis management: Integration, interpretation, and research development. *Journal of Management, 43*(6): 1661–1692. DOI: 10.1177/0149206316680030.

Bussey, C. (2011). *Brilliant PR: Create a PR sensation, whatever your budget, whatever your business*. Harlow: Pearson.

Cheng, Y. (2016). How social media is changing crisis communication strategies: Evidence from the updated literature. *Journal of Contingencies and Crisis Management, 26*(1): 58–68. DOI: 10.1111/1468-5973.12130.

Cheng, Y. (2020). The social-mediated crisis communication research: Revisiting dialogue between organizations and publics in crises of China, *Public Relations Review*, *46*(1). DOI: 10.1016/j.pubrev.2019.04.003.

Cheng, Y., & Cameron G. (2018). The status of social-mediated crisis communication (SMCC) research: An analysis of published articles in 2002-2014. In L. Austin & Y. Jin (Ed.), *Social media and crisis communication* (pp. 9–20). New York: Routledge.

Chermack, T. J., & Lynham, S. A. (2002). Definitions and outcome variables of scenario planning. *Human Resource Development Review*, *1*(3): 366–383. DOI: 10.1177/1534484302013006.

Clayton, S., Koehn, A., & Grover, E. (2013). Making sense of the senseless: Identity, justice, and the framing of environmental crises. *Social Justice Research*, *26*(3): 301–319. DOI: 10.1007/s11211-013-0185-z.

Coombs, W. T. (1999). *Ongoing crisis communication: Planning, managing, and responding. Thousand Oaks*, CA: Sage Publications.

Coombs, W. T. (2007). Protecting organization reputations during a crisis: The development and application of situational crisis communication theory. *Corporate Reputation Review*, *10*(3): 163–176. DOI: 10.1057/palgrave.crr.1550049.

Coombs, W. T. (2010). Parameters for crisis communication. In W. T. Coombs & S. J. Holladay (Eds.), *The handbook of crisis communication* (pp. 17–53). West Sussex: Wiley-Blackwell.

Coombs, W. T., & Holladay, S. J. (2002). Helping crisis managers protect reputational assets: Initial tests of the situational crisis communication theory. *Management Communication Quarterly*, *16*(2): 165–186. DOI: 10.1177/089331802237233.

Coombs, W. T. (2014). *Applied crisis communication and crisis management: Cases and exercises*. California: Sage Publications.

Corbin, J., & Strauss, A. (2014). *Basics of qualitative research: Techniques and procedures for developing grounded theory* (Forth edition). Thousand Oaks, CA: Sage Publications.

Cornelissen, J. (2017). *Corporate communication*. Thousand Oaks, CA: Sage Publications.

Crandall, W., Parnell, J., & Spillan, J. (2014). *Crisis management in the new strategy landscape* (Second edition). Thousand Oaks, Los Angeles, CA: Sage Publications.

Denzin, N. K., & Lincoln, Y. S. (Eds.). (2011). *The Sage handbook of qualitative research*. (Fifth edition). Sage Publications.

Devlin, E. S. (2006). *Crisis management planning and execution*. New York: Auerbach Publications.

Duhe, S., & Wright, D. K. (2013). Symmetry, social Media, and the enduring imperative of two-way communication. In K. Sriramesh, A. Zerfass, & J-N. Kim (Eds.), *Public relations and communication management: Current trends and emerging topics*. New York: Routledge.

Fan, D., Geddes, D., & Flory, F. (2013). The Toyota recall crisis: Media impact on Toyota's corporate brand reputation. *Corporate Reputation Review*, *16*(2): 99–117. DOI: 10.1057/crr.2013.6.

Farrell, H., & Drezner, D. (2008). The power and politics of blogs. *Public Choice*, *134*(1):15–30. DOI: 10.1007/s11127-007-9198-1.

Fearn-Banks, K. (2016). *Crisis communications: A casebook approach* (Fifth ed.). New Jersey: Lawrence Erlbaum Associates.

Gao, H., Barbier, G., & Goolsby, R. (2011). Harnessing the crowdsourcing power of social media for disaster relief. *IEEE Intelligent Systems*, *26*(3): 10–14. DOI: 10.1109/MIS.2011.52.

Gilkerson, N., Anderson, B., & Swenson, R. (2018). Work-life balance 2.0? An examination of social media management practice and agency employee coping strategies in a 24/7 social world. *Public Relations Journal*, *12*(2).

Griffin, A. (2014). *Crisis, issues and reputation management*. London: Kogan Page Limited.

Guarte, J. M., & Barrios, E. B. (2006). Estimation under purposive sampling. *Communications in Statistics-Simulation and Computation*, *35*(2): 277–284. DOI: 10.1080/03610910600591610.

Guidry, J. P., Jin, Y., Orr, C. A., Messner, M., & Meganck, S. (2017). Ebola on Instagram and Twitter: How health organizations address the health crisis in their social media engagement. *Public Relations Review*, *43*(3): 477–486. DOI: 10.1016/j.pubrev.2017.04.009.

Heath, R. L. (1997). *Strategic issues management: Organizations and public policy challenges*. Thousand Oaks, CA: Sage Publications.

Holloman, C. (2014). *The social media MBA guide to ROI: How to measure and improve your return on investment*. West Sussex: Wiley.

Honisch, S. V., & Manchón, L. M. (2019). The effects of paracrisis origin and response strategy on Facebook audience's perceived organisational reputation and behavioural intentions. *Corporate Reputation Review*, 1–12. DOI: 10.1057/s41299-019-00070-4.

Howe, J. (2008). *Crowdsourcing: Why the power of the crowd is driving the future of business*. New York: Crown Business.

Huffman, E., & Prentice, S. (2008). Social media's new role in emergency management: Emergency management and robotics for hazardous environments. Idaho Fall, ID: Idaho National Laboratory. Retrieved from https://inldigitallibrary.inl.gov/sites/sti/sti/3931947.pdf [Accessed on Sept., 2. 2022].

Jaques, T. (2010). Embedding issue management as a strategic element of crisis prevention. *Disaster Prevention and Management: An International Journal, 19*(4): 469–482. DOI: 10.1108/09653561011070385.

Jiang, H., Luo, Y., & Kulemeka, O. (2016). Social media engagement as an evaluation barometer: Insights from communication executives. *Public Relations Review, 42*(4), 679–691.

Jugo, D. (2017). Reactive crisis strategies application of the corporate sector in Croatia. *Journal of Communication Management, 21*(2): 201–214. DOI: 10.1108/JCOM-11-2016-0088.

Kim, Y., & Park, H. (2017). Is there still a PR problem online? Exploring the effects of different sources and crisis response strategies in online crisis communication via social media. *Corporate Reputation Review, 20*(1): 76–104. DOI: 10.1057/s41299-017-0016-5.

Kvale, S., & Brinkmann, S. (2009). *Interviews: Learning the craft of qualitative research interviewing*. London: Sage Publications.

Lachlan, K. A., Spence, P. R., & Eith, C. A. (2014). Risk, crisis, and emergency communication in developing countries: Identifying the needs of urban populations. In C. Okigbo (Ed.), *Strategic urban health communication* (pp. 65–76). New York: Springer.

Lee, S. Y. (2020). Stealing thunder as a crisis communication strategy in the digital age. *Business Horizons*. DOI: 10.1016/j.bushor.2020.07.006.

Lovejoy, K., Waters, R. D., & Saxton, G. D. (2012). Engaging stakeholders through Twitter: How nonprofit organizations are getting more out of 140 characters or less. *Public Relations Review, 38*(2): 313–318. DOI: 10.1016/j.pubrev.2012.01.005.

Luttrell, R., (2015). *Social media: How to engage, share and connect.* London: Rowman & Littlefield Publishers.

Martínez-López, F. J., Anaya-Sánchez, R., Fernández Giordano, M., & Lopez-Lopez, D. (2020). Behind influencer marketing: key marketing decisions and their effects on followers' responses. *Journal of Marketing Management, 36*(7–8): 579–607. DOI: 10.1080/0267257X.2020.1738525.

McLean, H., & Power, M. (2009). *Crisis command: Strategies for managing corporate crises.* London: Ark Group.

Mitroff, I. I. (1988). Crisis management: Cutting through the confusion. *Sloan Management Review, 29*(2): 15–20.

Mitroff, I. I., Shrivastava, T. C., & Udwadia, F. E. (1987). Effective crisis management. *Academy of Management Executive, 1*(3): 283–292. DOI: 10.5465/ame.1987.4275639.

Morris, T., & Goldworthy, S. (2012). Crisis management. In T. Morris & S. Goldsworthy (Eds.), *PR today: The authoritative guide to public relations* (pp. 287–300). London: Macmillan International Higher Education.

Murray, A. (2005). *PR: Teach yourself- general.* London: Hodder Arnold Publication.

Ndlela, M. N. (2019). *Crisis communication: A stakeholder approach.* Cham: Palgrave Macmillan.

Ott, L., & Theunissen, P. (2015). Reputations at risk: Engagement during social media crises. *Public Relations Review, 41*(1): 97–102. DOI: 10.1016/j.pubrev.2014.10.015.

Pang, A., Hassan, N. B. B. A., & Chong, A. C. Y. (2014). Negotiating crisis in the social media environment: Evolution of crises online, gaining credibility offline. *Corporate Communications: An International Journal, 19*(1): 96–118. DOI: 10.1108/CCIJ-09-2012-0064.

Pavlik, J. V. (2007). Mapping the consequences of technology on public relations. Institute for Public Relations. Retrieved from http://citeseerx.ist.psu.edu/viewdoc/download?doi=10.1.1.129.6285&rep=rep1&type= pdf [Accessed on Sept. 3. 2022].

Pearson, C. M., & Clair, J. A. (1998). Reframing crisis management. *The Academy of Management Review, 23*(1): 59-7. DOI: 10.5465/amr.1998.192960.

Pearson, C. M., & Mitroff, I. I. (1993). From crisis prone to crisis prepared: A framework for crisis management. *Academy of Management Perspectives, 7*(1): 48–59.

Podolak, A. (2002). Crisis management series: Creating crisis management teams, *Risk Management, 49*(9): 54–57.

Richardson, N., & Laville, L. (2010). *Develop your PR skills.* London: Kogan Page Publishers.

Roux-Dufort, C. (2007). Is crisis management (only) a management of exceptions?. *Journal of Contingencies and Crisis Management, 15*(2): 105–114. DOI: 10.1111/j.1468-5973.2007.00507.x.

Safko, L. (2009). *The social media bible: Tactics, tools, and strategies for business success.* Hoboken, NJ: Wiley.

Sandlin, J. K., & Gracyalny, M. L. (2018), Seeking sincerity, finding forgiveness: YouTube apologies as image repair. *Public Relations Review, 44*(3): 393–406. DOI: 10.1016/j.pubrev.2018.04.007.

Saroj, A., & Pal, S. (2020). Use of social media in crisis management: A survey. *International Journal of Disaster Risk Reduction, 48*: 101584. DOI: 10.1016/j.ijdrr.2020.101584.

Scott, G. M., & Garner, R. (2013). *Doing qualitative research: Designs, methods, and techniques*. Boston: Pearson Education.

Sellnow, T. L., & Seeger, M. W. (2013). *Theorizing crisis communication* (Fifth edition). John West Sussex: Wiley & Sons, Inc.

Stenger, T. (2014). Social media and online reputation management as practice: first steps towards social CRM?. *International Journal of Technology and Human Interaction, 10*(4): 49–64.

Stern, E. (1997). Crisis and learning: A conceptual balance sheet. *Journal of Contingencies and Crisis Management, 5*(2): 69–86.

Sturges, D. L. (1994). Communicating through crisis: A strategy for organizational survival. *Management Communication Quarterly, 7*(3): 297–316.

Swann, P. (2018). From bashtags to geobombing: Modern-day digital guerrilla tactics. In L. Austin & Y. Jin (Eds), *Social media and crisis communication* (pp. 335–350). New York: Routledge.

Taylor, M., & Kent, M. L. (2007). Taxonomy of mediated crisis responses. *Public Relations Review, 33*(2): 140–146. DOI: 10.1016/j.pubrev.2006.11.017.

Tench, R., & Yeomans, L. (2006). *Exploring public relations*. Harlow: Pearson Education.

Thelwall, M. (2017). Social media analytics for YouTube comments: Potential and limitations, International *Journal of Social Research Methodology, 21*(3): 1–14. DOI: 10.1080/13645579.2017.1381821.

Sriramesh, K., Zerfass, A., & Kim, J. N. (Eds.). *Public relations and communication management: Current trends and emerging topics*. New York: Routledge.

Vaismoradi, M., Jones, J., Turunen, H., & Snelgrove, S. (2016). Theme development in qualitative content analysis and thematic analysis. *Journal of Nursing Education and Practice, 6*(5): 100–110. DOI: 10.5430/jnep.v6n5p100.

Veil, S.R., Buehner, T., & Palenchar, M. J. (2011). A work-in-process literature review: Incorporating social media in risk and crisis communication. *Journal of Contingencies and Crisis Management, 19*(2): 110–122. DOI: 10.1111/j.1468-5973.2011.00639.x.

Walker, B. (2014). *Crisis communications in the 24/7 social media world: A Guidebook for CEOs and public relations professionals*. Ithaca, NY: Paramount

Woo, C. W., Brigham, M. P., & Gulotta, M. (2020). Twitter talk and Twitter sharing in times of crisis: Exploring rhetorical motive and agenda-setting in the Ray Rice scandal. *Communication Studies*, *71*(1): 40–58. DOI: 10.1080/10510974.2019.1661866.

Wright, D. K., & Hinson, M. (2009). An updated look at the impact of social media on public relations practices. *Public Relations Journal*, *3*(2): 1–27.

Xu, S. (2018). Discourse of renewal: Developing multiple-item measurement and analyzing effects on relationships. *Public Relations Review*, *44*(1): 108–119. DOI: 10.1016/j.pubrev.2017.09.005.

Yang, S.-U., Kang, M., & Johnson, P. (2010). Effects of narratives, openness to dialogic communication, and credibility on engagement in crisis communication through organizational blogs. *Communication Research*, *37*(4): 473–497. DOI: 10.1177/0093650210362682.

Zoonen, W. V., & Meer, T. V. D. (2015). The importance of source and credibility perception in times of crisis: Crisis communication in a socially mediated era. *Journal of Public Relations Research*, *27*(5): 371–388. DOI: 10.1080/1062726X.2015.1062382.

Ömer Vatanartıran

Artists or Influencers? Digital Self-Presentation Issues in Arts

Abstract: The notion of the presentation of the self-questions the way impressions are managed in any communicative action. Accordingly, social interactions are the representations of a dramaturgy created by the communicators in order to control the perception of the other in a desired direction (Goffmann, 1956). They do not happen by themselves but the goals of the actor involved in this process lead the way it develops. In relation with this, social media accounts function as the scenes of such dramaturgy where users present themselves in accordance with their priorities, interests and emotional needs. In return, the broad visibility and quick diffusion of any action offer dangers as well. Any post conflicting with the values of the audience and/or politically correct ideas may harm the dramaturgy. In other words, the strong feedback mechanism poses challenges to the presentation of the self on digital media. Artists, in specific, usually encounter crisis while using social media. They get lynched on twitter, cancelled on digital streaming platforms and/or face hate speech on Instagram due to their "offensive" posts. Moreover, their commercial ties with brands limit their personal freedom as well. While promoting the services and products of their "clients," they become the representations of the brand's values and strategies rather than their own artistic identity. Again, the digital presence designed by the artist gets disrupted. Thus, the dramaturgy planned by the artist experiences discord. In this chapter, the challenges artists face on social media in their journey of digital self-presentation will be reviewed. The situations favoring being an influencer rather than a free artist will be analyzed. Issues, such as artistic freedom, political correctness, market demands of the influencers, will be discussed in order to develop an insight on the way the artist's self is presented on digital media.

Keywords: Artistic Freedom, Influencer, Digital Self-Presentation, Digital Communication, Social Media

Introduction

The emergence of Web 2.0 in the early 2000s sparked controversies over the role of the digital media in societies' journey towards the democracy. This "new communication realm" (Castells, 2007, p. 248) differed from the traditional or early digital media by enabling users to give their feedback and create their own content. As emphasized strongly then by scholars such as Van Dijk (2009), Rheingold (2008) and Dahlgreen (2005), the capacity of content generation, interaction, and many-to-many communication with a never-seen-before feedback mechanism raised the hopes for the world democracy. In particular, the idea of "public sphere" developed by Habermas (1996, p. 360) encouraged media scholars to reveal this brand new medium in the light of free speech and independent exchange of ideas which would regenerate the Ancient Greek agoras on digital media. However, issues such as state intervention, commercialization (Kellner, 2000, p. 8), digital divide (Jenkins, Thorburn, and Seawell, 2003, p. 8) and manipulative algorithms (Caplan and Boyd, 2016, p. 3) discouraged pro-digital public sphere scholars due to the constraints for high-quality and high-frequency digital participation among global citizens.

The advent of Web 2.0 offered new opportunities to the art scene as well. In addition to archiving digital versions of numerous traditional art pieces and making them available for a broader global audience, it has also reshaped creative artistic processes (Lughi, 2014, p. 44). The limitless interaction, spatial and temporal boundlessness, and accessibleness redefined the relationship between the artists and their audience. Moreover, the bypass of traditional filter mechanisms in culture industry such as managers, galleries, event organizers, recording companies, art catalogues, etc. offered the possibility of direct communication which was unimaginable before the digital age. Artists gained the freedom of expressing their ideas and sharing their work without the approval of such mediators and agents. Audience engagement became a concern of the artists' personal use of social media rather than marketing professionals and this corresponded to the two-way symmetrical PR model of Grunig (2001, p. 15) with its participative and collaborative nature. Furthermore, they were categorized as influencers by PR professionals due to their vast number of followers and use their own sphere as a medium of commercials, testimonials, and even political opinions.

The tension between the emancipating nature of the digital media and some techno-political pressures over its use is multidimensional. Despite the barrier-free distribution of artistic work, this individualism has also developed its own threats. Artists are estimated as influencer celebrities and their marks on any social, artistic and cultural issue have the potential to incite crisis such as hate speech or cancel culture. Moreover, the digital personality presented by the artist suffer from such interaction. The digital presence which seeks for more "likes," retweets, reposts, citations, popularity in general, becomes a continuous test of coping with social pressures. Thus, their self-presentation becomes as prominent as their artistic work circulating online. In this chapter, the online presentation of the artistic self will be questioned in the light of issues such as cancel culture and influencership.

Digital Public Sphere

Compared to traditional media, digital media have many advantages in terms of functioning as a public sphere. First of all, it is based on many-to-many communication (Castells, 2008, p. 90) whereas traditional media is only capable of generating one-to-many communication. Regardless of the background, time and location of the users, it enables endless interaction in a chosen network and generates decentralization (Poster, 1997, p. 205). As Thompson states (1995, p. 245), these networks are "non-localized, non-dialogical, open-ended space of the visible in which mediated symbolic forms can be expressed and received by the plurality of non-present others." Instead of central political or economic regulators, these networks mostly set their own codes and norms, users actively define the nature of the transactions happening in that network. Moreover, they do not face gatekeepers as they used to on print or analogous media. Decision-makers such as editors, agents, producers, directors are replaced by the users who became "prosumers" according to Van Dijk (2009, p. 41). In other words, digital media allowed users to design their own content, share it on social media, and create their own story as a member of a large social network.

This technological infrastructure empowered the audience to take a more active and participative role in communication systems (Jenkins, 2006, p. 167). In fact, this plural and global society on interaction removed the former borders set by the technology or the owners of these technologies. This "mass self-communication" Castells (2008, p. 249) leading to a global public sphere changed the "asymmetric relationship between broadcaster and audience" (Rheingold, 2008, p. 100) in favor of the users. Certainly, the free exchange of ideas without the control of the state or the capital is suggestive of Habermas' concept of public sphere. Accordingly, media has the potential to function as an Agora in Ancient Greek or cafes where intellectuals used to meet during the Enlightenment Age (Calhoun, 1992, p. 4). However, the subordination of the traditional media to the political and economic elites along the 20th century had failed to fulfill the expectations of such scholars. In return, digital media emerged as a more promising public sphere where rational actors can freely discuss their political opinions or share their artistic work in the name of human progress.

Habermas' public sphere theory is based on the assumption that the actors of this online agora would act rationally and prioritize public issues to be discussed (Papacharissi, 2009, p. 232). In fact, his early analysis did not take into account the irrationality of the users but mostly drew attention to the danger of state and capital manipulation. However, more and more scholars, including Habermas himself later, defended the idea that online universe is not the exact equivalent of the ideal public sphere. Ideas such as the out-of-control circulation of opinions and the discontinuity of communication in an over-stimulated environment (Poster, 1997), its conflict-favoring nature (Dean, 2003, p. 108); and the digital divide (Van Dijk, 2006, p. 222) and many more contributed to such counterarguments.

Digital Media as Public Spheres of Art

The "decentralizing, globalizing, harmonizing, and empowering" (Negroponte, 1995, p. 229) qualities of digital media have had their own effects on art. The way art is produced, shared, consumed and evaluated online has transformed as digital media evolved. First of all, art became more available. Instead of physical visits to art galleries, museums or institutionalized art spaces, users gained the advantage of remotely watching, reading, listening and experiencing artistic work (Blais and Ippolito, 2006, p. 8). Secondly, artists obtained the chance to share their work without any filters. Unlike an Adornian culture industry model which emphasizes the role of the producers encouraging standardized, repetitive and predictable works in accordance with the market demands, or cultural imperialist point of view (Hesmondalgh, 2007, p. 214) stressing the dominance of Western societies over global culture industry; digital media allowed each and every artist to be present on a chosen network. Moreover, it has not been limited to their individual work. Instead, a globally more cooperating, collaborative and collective form of art became possible since physical and economic constraints were minimized by online facilities. For example, digital visual arts witnessed the "user shapes the work of art and becomes the main source of aesthetic experience" (Lughi, 2014, p. 45). Furthermore, the possibility of interaction through an artistic work increases both the quantity and quality of communication between the artist and the audience, the fans and naysayers, corporate entities and many other publics. In other words, it is an artistic medium where the discourse can evolve over time with the feedback of the followers, the interpretations during its distribution by them and reactions of the artist who produced it.

Art has the ability to speak for itself (Dewey, 1934). It is able to transcend the borders, social and cultural barriers, language and educational differences. In this sense, it is a kind of communicative action, an aestheticized version of rationality and an attempt to define human feelings (Habermas, 1979, p. 91). Digital media, in this sense, enrich artistic communicative action by providing an endless interaction between the artist, the consumer, and all kind of actors involved in this process. Art, in other words, becomes an instrument of public discourse and sphere. Its function of representing conflicting ideas, ideologies, cultural structures and subjective meanings (Williams, 1986, p. 20) flourishes as the artist and audience communicate around the artistic work. The subjectivity of the artist connects to the subjectivities of the followers and this process redefines the value of the artistic work. The consensus around its value, negative or positive, is continuously formed through their communication on this public sphere (Habermas, 1979, p. 91). Similar to the idea that the meaning of any media content is negotiated between the sender and the receiver (Stuart Hall, 1981, p. 128), art is evaluated, defined and interpreted by a larger community than only the artist and art experts. Its quality, motivation, purpose, effects are constantly questioned on social media, even retrospectively, art is laid on the table. Thus, negotiation over its meaning continues in a more inclusive, dynamic and open way.

Digital Self Presentation

Artists' presence online puts the issue of ethos forward. According to Aristo's definition of rhetoric (Mccormack, 2014, p. 131), any persuasive message consists of three elements: Ethos- Pathos and Logos. While pathos refers to the emotional tone and arguments, logos signifies its rationality, the calculable and analytic side of the message. Ethos, on the other hand, is concerned with the personality of the sender of the message. The more impressively the background of him/her is given, the more reliability and credibility the message gains. Thus, any artistic work shared online by the artist becomes more ethos-dependent than its presentation offline. Due to the limited information about the artist's personal life, artistic work used to be evaluated more independently from the personal context before social media. However, artists now deliberately share their journey of creation, production and performance online as well as the motivations and stories behind; they even comment on public issues coinciding to such periods. Therefore, the morality, worldview, political attitudes, level of experience, education, know-how, endorsements from earlier collaborations become as important as the most recent message itself.

According to Goffman (1956), everyday interactions do not flow authentically but social actors present themselves as the actors do in theater. Here, he distinguishes the backstage, which is the "natural" way of living, and the front stage where a performance occurs according to the needs and desires of the audience and the actor. In this social setting, behaviors are staged with the goal of minimum harm and maximum benefit. Through that performance, the actor reproduces his/her identity and is confirmed by the audience. Similarly, social media is the social setting where the performance takes place. Secondly, the artist's posts composed of texts, images, videos, memes, GIFs, audio material, etc. on Twitter, Instagram, TikTok, etc. function as the tools on the stage and become the instruments of artistic identity. Once it is shared, the performance of the self-starts, the impression of the initial post transforms as likes, answers, tags, hashtags, reactions, citations, reposts, and discussions arise in response. Moreover, the consistency of the artist is constantly tested through the comparison between the earlier and recent posts. Therefore, the dynamic between the ethos and the artistic work affect the artist's digital self.

Presentation of the self can either be assertive or defensive (Lee et al., 1999, p. 701). While the former refers to the active control in the creation process of the desired impression, the latter signifies the tactics used against the threats to ruin the image presented to the audience. Digital media offers both opportunities and threats for such performances. Although it is easier to behave out-of-the-real-character and design his/her own dramaturgy online, it is also extremely context dependent and exposed to other users' immediate, direct and game-changing interventions (Fox and Rooney, 2015, p. 162). Still, social media sites provide numerous facilities to create a certain "self," control its image, and "target specific audiences" (Hernandez-Serrano, Jones, Rene-Arellano, and Ortuno, 2022, p. 49). In this sense, artists follow a dramaturgical strategy which supports the effect of their work, at the same time, they defend themselves against attacks coming from the art critiques, fans, offended communities, target or non-target audiences. The digital self improves, gets damaged, recovers, fails, develops; in short, constantly negotiates with followers and interacting communities. In Belk's terms (2013, p. 478), the artist's self becomes digitally extended, an avatar version of the real artist is re-embodied and an online identity is co-constructed through narratives, likes, shares, interactions, emojis, reactions, reproductions, etc.

Challenges

Digital public sphere multiplies the identity of the users (Castells, 2014) as well as the artists. While artists used to have a more homogeneous public image as a result of their artistic work, events, interviews, PR campaigns, etc; social media represent many different aspects of the artist in various channels. There can be official, anonymous, fake or restricted accounts as well as the accounts of closer professional or social circles constantly sharing content about the artist. Thus, managing the impression of this online persona becomes harder. In addition to this multiplication as a challenge, the artist's past may pose problems since anything came up online never gets deleted technically. Moreover, the commercial potential of the artist's number and quality of the audience presents its own challenges. While being an influencer increases the commercial potential, it may restrict the artistic freedom.

Cancel Culture

Many of the early 20th century scholars took attention to the tension between the media freedom and state and/or market pressures. On the one hand, certain criticized the state regulated media in terms of its pressure on free speech, tendency to become a propaganda machine and loss of reliability and accuracy in the public eye. On the other hand, the opportunism of the economic elite at the risk of responsible citizenry and public goodie a free marketplace was also underlined (Muntenau, 2010, p. 7). After the spread of social media especially in the 2010's, this long-time dilemma turned its focal point to something different than the libertarian fears of government control or social responsibility issues within a profit-oriented market. Cancel culture as a new fashionable concept became a bigger question mark in freedom of speech.

Although the term has been barely in use for a decade, cancel culture is not something new, from John Stuart Mill to Alexis de Tocqueville, the threat of forcing people to speak and act in a certain way and silence them according to a certain agenda have been widely discussed among scholars after the Enlightenment Age (Strossen, 2020, p. 2). Such debates encouraged maximal participation of citizens in public debates in order to maximize the quality of democracy (Ogbebor, 2020, p. 56). Until the rise of the state interventions or business interest-oriented algorithms, digital media promised solutions to this conflict between the media owners and the users about equal participation, fair representation and free expression. However, even that golden age witnessed issues such as the violation of political correctness, use of offensive discourse towards certain political, racial, ethnic or gender identities, and misrepresentation of minorities. Actually, stereotyping or deliberate/accidental harming of disadvantaged groups had already led to the rise of political correctness in the 1980s in the States which would eventually become a vital issue in normative media discussions. Accordingly, political correctness is an attempt of "sanitizing the language by suppressing some of its uglier prejudicial features, thereby undoing some past injustices with the hope of improving social relations" (Hughes, 2011, p. 1). Since individual users with no corporate codes and control mechanisms hardly adopt politically correct language, cancel culture emerged as a public reaction.

Cancelling artists because of their posts covering political attitude, strong language, offensive expressions, politically incorrect arguments, etc. has spread along the last decade. Artists' controversial posts sometimes spark protests and trigger harsh reactions including pushing political entities and artist's professional affiliations for sanctions. From cancelling the distribution and/or representation of the artist's works to his & her appearance on media, events and sponsorships, this ruins the artistic career. Before it incites huge corporate reactions, cancelling operates as public shaming among digital communities. Followers and offended communities provoke others for an online lynching and thus delegitimize the artist's persona, work, eventually ethos. In other words, it disrupts the digital self-constructed and presented by the artist until then. Through social media mobilizing instruments such as hashtags, reposts, trending topics, tags, GIF's, memes, disclosure of past controversial issues, engagement of other celebrities, bombardment of the entities involved; the artist's ethos is ruined and the act of the digital self-deviates from the dramaturgy. As a result, the artist becomes an instrument of an online polarization (Hands, 2014, p. 243), confronting defenders with adverse communities. From then on, the artist's digital self cannot be decontextualized from this incident. Here, social media's ability to immediately diffuse and multiply such incidents without any conventional filter mechanism functions as a double-edged sword: While it empowers participants for a public debate, set their own norms and put forward their own agenda, it may also silence the artist. Users' initial motivation of raising awareness of discriminations, offensive acts, ignorance of changing norms, turning a blind eye to the dynamics of progressive societies sometimes turn into a collective act of trolling which is "an online subculture primarily interested in upsetting and alienating as many people as possible" (Aspray, 2019, p. 155). Moreover, doxing as an another subculture which means the leak of personal data including any kind of contact info, location of work or residence, financial transactions, details of private life point artists as a target. Finally, artists develop their own censorship which impoverish their creative skills and limit intellectual boundaries. In short, although cancel culture functions as a public pressure mechanism in favor of inclusion, respect and political correctness, it sometimes disrupts originality, authenticity and sincerity of the artists.

Influencership

Influencer marketing, which "dates back to the 1760's, with the pioneer being Josiah Wedgwood who produced ceramics for the British Royal Family" (Wielki, 2020, p. 3), benefits from the dynamics of opinion leadership. Those with both quantitative and qualitative potential to influence certain communities share their ideas and experiences, thus affect the consumer behaviors. The emergence of social media "has dramatically changed the ways in which consumers communicate and create bonds, both among themselves and with brands" (Wielki, 2020, p. 3) thanks to the facilitation of endless interaction. Here, popularity has a key role in attracting the brands or other clients corporate into their campaigns, products and services.

Artists as popular public figures have always been seen as impactful influencers by the brands. Their ability to influence the audience's perception of reality even shapes the norms and values of their era. In fact, social media can be seen as a stage for "communicative capitalism" (Dean, 2003, p. 95) which glorifies the commercial interests of the participants rather than free exchange of ideas. To put it differently, audience turns into a client instead of an equal participant of the process while the artist becomes a promoter of the capital's interests. Once the priority is set as the sales and marketing of goods and services through artists hired as influencers, the authenticity of the digital self is disrupted. The artist reproduces the reality of the brand advertised and his & her account loses its effect as a free public sphere. Instead, it becomes an instrument of market dynamics which restrain artist's free expression in case it conflicts with the brand's interests. Similar to the mass media which omits the counter-arguments against business elites funding them (Negt, Kluge, and Labanyi, 1988, p. 61), artists' discourse is shaped by their clients. They become an ambassador of the consumer culture according to which only certain issues are highlighted or kept silent.

Censorship inevitably arises as the artist becomes an influencer. Corporate agreements in terms of what is to be shared and what is not limit their expression. Moreover, they become a tool of personalized direct marketing and targeted advertising through algorithms. Social media is constantly planned, calculated and filtered according to the priorities of those who design both the hardware and the software in addition to the sponsorships of certain content. Therefore, what is more visible or willingly muted is managed by a more complex mechanism including "automation and bots," "clickbait journalism," and "search engine optimization- SEO" (Caplan and Boyd, 2016, p. 5). Once the artist is positioned as an influencer, such dynamics transform the process of the dissemination of art on digital public sphere. The diversity of the ideas, inclusion of the underrepresented, presentation of the marginal become possible only if it serves to the commercial interests of the partner.

Influencership does not only defy artistic expression but it also attempts to redefine art. In addition to the artists who have proved themselves in conventional art such as theater, literature, cinema, music, etc. going online; less experienced individuals with questionable talents but large audience compete with them on digital sphere. It is a kind of "social recognition of amateurs" (Flichy, 2010, p. 53), as the number of followers and interaction increase, their capacity of doing art becomes more and more acceptable. These amateurs form the popular culture, make their own contributions, push the audience to discuss their performance or content, they even gain importance in conventional art spheres. YouTubers acting on award-winning movies or theater shows, singers with viral videos offered to take the stage of megastars or make their own albums; as a consequence, a wide array of art scene witnesses the entrance of such "artists." According to Keen (2007, p. 27), this is blurring the lines between established values, know-how and criteria of art and deficiencies of amateur production. However, algorithms put those amateurs with high number of followers forward in order to increase commercial opportunities, hence the audience recognizes their ethos, performance and content as art.

Conclusion

Digital media offers both opportunities and threats to artists. While it encourages more and more artists to find their own audience, create in collaboration with other artists, involve other enthusiasts to their artistic work, bypass traditional gatekeepers of representation, distribution, and even state and market pressures to a certain degree; it also poses problems to their freedom of expression and presentation of the digital self. Especially, cancel culture and influencership might affect the authenticity of their ethos and work of art. Further research on the psychology of being an artist in a such environment and the outcomes of this hard-to-control interaction would be valuable in order to gain a deeper insight on artistic creation in this digital age.

References

Aspray, B. (2019). On trolling as comedic method. *Journalism of Cinema and Media Studies, 58*(3): 154–160.

Belk, R. (2013). Extended self in a digital world. *Journal of Consumer Research, 40*(3): 477–500.

Blais, J., & Ippolito, J. (2006). *At the edge of art*. London: Thames & Hudson.

Caplan, R., & Boyd, D. (2016). Who controls the public sphere in an era of algorithms? *Data & Society*. Retrieved from https://datasociety.net/pubs/ap/MediationAutomationPower_2016.pdf [Accessed on Sept., 14. 2022].

Calhoun, C. (1992). Introduction: Habermas and the public sphere. In C. Calhoun (Ed.), *Habermas and the public sphere* (pp. 1–51). Cambridge: MIT Press.

Castells, M. (2014). The impact of the Internet on society: A global perspective. *Open Mind: BBVA*. Retrieved from www.bbvaopenmind.com/en/article/

the-impact-of-the-internet-on- society-a-global-perspective [Accessed on Sept., 1. 2022].

Castells, M. (2008). The new public sphere: Global civil society, communication networks, and global governance, *Annals, AAPSS*, 616: 78–93.

Castells, M. (2007). Communication, power and counter-power in the network society, *International Journal of Communication*, 1: 238–266.

Chalaby, J. (2007). Beyond national-centrism: Thinking international communication from a cosmopolitan perspective. *Studies in Communication Sciences*, *7*(1): 61–83.

Dahlgreen, P. (2005). The internet, public spheres, and political communication: Dispersion and deliberation. *Political Communication*, *22*(2): 147–162.

Dean, J. (2003). Why the Net is not a public sphere, *Constellations*, *10*(1): 95–112.

Dewey, J. (1934). *Art as experience*. New York: Capricorn Books.

Flichy, P. (2010). *Le Sacre de l'amateur, Sociologie des Passions ordinaires à l'ère numérique*. [The sanctification of the amateur, Sociology of the ordinary passions in Digital Era]. Paris: Seuil.

Fox, J., & Rooney, M. C. (2015). The dark triad and trait self-objectification as predictors of men's use and self-presentation behaviors on social networking sites. *Personality and Individual Differences*, 76: 161–165.

Goffman, E. (1956). The *presentation of self in everyday life*. Edinburgh: University of Edinburgh Research Centre.

Grunig, J. E. (2001). Two-way symmetrical public relations: Past, present and future, *Handbook of Public Relations*, 11–30.

Habermas, J. (1996). Bet*ween facts and norms: Contributions to a discourse theory of law and democracy*. Cambridge: Polity Press.

Habermas, J. (1979). *Communication and the evolution of society* (T. McCarthy, Trans.). London: Heinemann.

Hall, S. (1981). Encoding / decoding. In S. Hall, D. Hobson, A. Lowe, & P. Willis (Eds.), *Culture, media, language: Working papers in cultural studies, 1972-79* (pp. 128–138). London: Hutchinson.

Hands, J. (2014). General intellect or collective idiocy? Digital mobs and social media mobilization. *Popular Communication*, 12: 237–250.

Hernandez-Serrano, M. J., Jones, B., Renes-Arellano, P., & Ortuno, C. R. A. (2022). Analysis of digital self presentation practices and profiles of Spanish adolescents on Instagram and TikTok. *Journal of New Approaches in Educational Research*, *11*(1): 49–63.

Hesmondalgh, D. (2007). *Internationalization, globalization, and cultural imperialism: The cultural industries*. London: Sage Publications.

Hughes, G. (2011). *Political correctness: A history of semantics and culture*. New Jersey: Wiley & Blackwell.

Jenkins, H. (2006). *Convergence culture: Where old and new media collide*. New York: NYU Press.

Jenkins, H., Thorburn, D., & Seawell, B. (2003). *Democracy and new media*. Cambridge: MIT Press.

Keen, A. (2007). *The cult of the amateur: How today's internet is killing our culture and assaulting our economy*. London: Nicholas Brealey Publishing.

Kellner, D. (2000). Globalisation and unequalisation: What can be learned from value chain analysis?. *Problems of Economic Transition*, 47: 74–115.

Lee, S. J., Quigley, B. M., Nesler, M. S., Corbett, A. B., & Tedeschi, J. T. (1999). Development of a self-presentation tactics scale. *Personality and Individual Differences*, *26*(4): 701–722.

Lughi, G. (2014). Digital media and contemporary art. *Mimesis Journal*, 686: 43–52.

McCormack, K. C. (2014). Ethos, pathos, and logos: The benefits of Aristotelian rhetoric in the courtroom. *Washington University Jurisprudence Review*, *7*(1):131–155.

Muntenau, M. (2010). *Media in crisis: Should the state intervene?*. Reuters Institute Fellowship Paper, UK: University of Oxford.

Negroponte, N. (1995). *Being digital*. Michigan: Knopf.

Negt, O., Kluge, A., & Labanyi, P. (1988). The public sphere and experience: *Selections*. *October*, 46: 60–82.

Ogbebor, B. (2020). *Media policy, democracy and theories of the press in British media coverage of the press reform debate: Journalists report journalism*. London: Palgrave Macmillan.

Papacharissi, Z. (2009). The virtual sphere 2.0: The Internet, the public sphere and beyond. In A. Chadwick & P. Howard (Eds.), *Routledge handbook of internet politics*. London: Routledge.

Poster, M. (1997). Cyberdemocracy: Internet and the public sphere. In D. Poster (Ed.), *Internet culture* (pp. 201–217) New York: Routledge.

Rheingold, H. (2008). Using participatory media and public voice to encourage civic engagement. In L. W. Bennett (Ed.), *Civic life online: Learning how digital media can engage youth* (pp. 97–118). Cambridge: MIT Press.

Strossen, N. (2020). *Resisting cancel culture, promoting dialogue, debate, and free speech in the college classroom: Perspectives on higher education*. Washington: American Council of Trustees and Alumni.

Van Dijk, J. (2009). Users like you: Theorizing agency in user generated content. *Media, Culture and Society*, 31: 41–58.

Van Dijk, J. (2006). Digital divide research: Achievement and shortcomings. *Poetics*, 34: 221–235.

Wielki, J. (2020). Analysis of the role of digital influencers and their impact on the functioning of the contemporary online promotional system and its sustainable development. *Sustainability*, *12*(7138): 1–20.

Williams, R. (1986). The uses of cultural theory. *New Left Review*, 158: 19–31.

Bülent Sezgin

Digi-Theatricality: Transformation of Theatricality from Live Performance to Digitalized Stage

Abstract: Theatre has developed as an art form based on live performance since ancient times. The dynamic structure of the theater in front of the audience creates classical theatrical forms. Theater art, which has undergone avant-garde, post-avant-garde, post-modern and para-theatrical transformations in the 21st century, is also undergoing a digital metamorphosis today. The meeting of digital arts with the art of theater leads to the development of new expression possibilities on the stage. In this chapter, the relationship between theatricality and digitality will be examined in depth in terms of theoretical and aesthetic rhetoric. Based on the important references to the digitalization of theater in the world, the performance analysis of selected digital-theatrical applications will also be examined as a model. It will be an innovative approach to combine the digi-theatrical artistic products used in all genres of performing arts with performance analysis, which tools they use, and how they transform the stage.

Keywords: Digi-Theatricality, Digitalization of Art, Performance Theory, Theatre

Introduction

The art of theater has developed as an art form based on live performance with the principle of "being here and now" since Ancient Greece. Although the development of technology through centuries has transformed the effects of theater art on the audience, the innovative effect of digitalization is quite different. Digital theater, questioning the existential state of classical theater based on live performance, has been one of the most discussed concepts of the post-pandemic period in the field of art. The literature on digital theater is quite limited, especially in the field of performing arts and social sciences; however, some researchers define digital arts as the new avant-garde.

The fact that digitally in theater is a fairly new concept compared to the classical form of this art poses some challenges to the researcher keen on understanding its rise. For example, Blake draws attention to the dynamic nature of the relationship between theater and digitality and the difficulties of defining the relationship:

> The digital cyberspace, information webs, social media, computational process, electronic representation, and so on is nearly perfect for his purpose. Live interaction, genuine intimacy, real presence, and bodily expression are all exactly what the digital lacks, and indeed often seem to suggest we could just as well do without. The opposition between theatre and the digital, in this formulation, is neither new nor unexpected (Blake, 2014).

Although the relationship between theater and technology had been discussed along the 20th century, the inevitable use of digitality during and after the pandemic from 2019 made it even more crucial. The necessity for a certain time for theater artists who ensure their visibility on the stage through digital tools gave the issue a bigger prominence. Along with the pandemic, actors, directors, directors, and dramaturgists have started experimental searches to establish an alternative aesthetic language by trying to understand and explore digital theater.

To discuss this issue, Masura (2020) in her doctoral research, asked some basic questions regarding the definition of digital theater and the analysis of the relationship between digitality and theater:

> Digital Theatre is live theatre that incorporates digital technology into the production in an essential way that fundamentally shifts our understanding of the principles of theatre, and potentially the world we inhabit. There are four necessary conditions to distinguish Digital Theatre from the broader worlds of digital performance and traditional theatre.
> 1. Limited interactivity of message.
> 2. The presence of verbal communication.
> 3. A co-present audience and actor.
> 4. The existence of digital technology in the central creation of the performance (not as an archival tool). (Masura, 2020)

In this part of this book, to interpret the main debates on the digitalization of theater, the main sources will be examined as a literature review and an analysis will be made on the axis of the theatricality and digital-theatrical concepts. The historically changing position of theater in the face of digitalization will be examined with examples from the world and Turkey including its theory and practice.

Transformation of Theater Art with Technology and Multi-Media Tools in the Historical Process

Throughout history, theater has been an aesthetic art branch that transforms the imagination and images of the audience, showing and listening to the reality and images in the empty spaces created on the stage. Theater as a creative form is like a prototype of computer visualization and has integrated the technology of its age as an aesthetic form (Masura, 2020). Considering the theater and computers as virtual reality machines, Reaney states:

> Theatre is the original virtual reality machine. Accessing it, audiences visit imaginary worlds which are interactive and immersive. Noting that thespians used theatre to create virtual worlds when the most powerful CPU was an abacus does not disqualify it; it simply makes the comparison more remarkable. Theatre and computers functioning as virtual reality generators have remarkable similarities. Both offer fleeting, metaphysical experiences. Both create fictive worlds in which intangible concepts can be given perceptible form. (Reaney, 1995)

There are different opinions about how theater emerged. According to the most accepted theory of ritualism, Anthropologist James Frazer claimed that theater emerged as a spectacle art with the evolution of primitive rituals (Brockett, 1982). After its rise from rituals, it was used as a governmental instrument in Ancient Greek city-states to control the citizens. The art of theater then faced a shift towards a structure focused on catharsis and identification, around the principles laid out by Aristotle in his Poetics. Amphitheaters, which are large open-air halls built on a scenic hillside in the ancient Greek city-states, were used as playgrounds. Mass performances started to take place over such stages in the form of tragedy, comedy, and satyr plays with very effective sound acoustics. At that time, there was no need for any microphone other than the natural human voice; moreover, sunlight was used as the light source. In some plays, when the chaos in the plot could not be resolved naturally, instruments called "Deux-ex-Machine" were lowered onto the stage with the help of a crane. Thanks to these tools, which symbolized supernatural and mythological powers such as Gods and angels, the final scene of the play could be artificially staged.

Looking at these technical details, we can say that the theater used minimal technology in the beginning. A story-oriented theater style that attaches importance to the communication of the actor and the audience, found its place in the imperial show culture during the Roman period. Yet, other popular forms of entertainment such as gladiator-ship, boxing, and horse races in the Roman period reduced theater's popularity. However, the design and use of the decor on the stage advanced technically. In the Middle Ages, when scholastic thought was dominant, the theater was seen inappropriate for the religious way of life and it was banned. Only after the rise of utilitarian approaches in order to popularize the religion and teach language, it was started to be used again. In the forms of miracle, mystery and morality play, new forms of religious teachings have emerged. The theater companies on the tour technically made the theater popular by using wheeled cars with a stage on them. During the Renaissance, the theater was reborn from its ashes, and the development of Baroque architecture experienced its golden age with the texts of powerful playwrights such as Jean Baptiste Moliere and William Shakespeare. The tradition of perspective, which emerged technically in the art of painting, has created today's red-curtained Italian stage architecture and 3D decors have been used in the plays.

From a technical point of view, gas lamps and candlelight were used. After the invention of electricity during the industrial revolution and Edison's invention of the light bulb in 1879, stage lighting became a brand new profession and matter of aesthetics in theater. After the 1900s, thanks to scientific and technological developments, cinematic tools such as light, projection and film machines were also included in the laboratory work of the theatre. Emphasizing the importance that theater attaches to technology as an integrative multimedia art, Steve Dixon (2007) states that we should seek the roots of digitalization in the history of performance:

> Theatre has always used the cutting-edge technology of the time to enhance the "spectacle" of productions. From the early Deus ex machine to the guild-produced Medieval pageant wagons, to the innovation of perspective painting and mechanical devices on Italian 16th Century stage sets, to the introduction of gas, and later electric, lighting effects, to the modern use of computers to control lighting, sound and set changes, technology has been used in ways that have created incredible visual and auditory effects. (Dixon, 2007)

The avant-garde artists' idea that theater should not only be based on the text also led to the development of new forms of expression that encourage the use of technology on stage. Historical avant-garde and later formalist post-avant-garde artists, who wanted to discover the reality behind the visible, used the technology of their period as a mean of the expression of the invisible. This approach also facilitated many interdisciplinary collaborations. For example, Dixon (2007) likens the development of Wagnerian opera and total art to the meta-medium of today's computers:

> Wagner's conception is central to the lineage of digital performance both in its advocacy for grand theatrical spectacle and in the paradigm of "convergence" that unites the Gesamtkunstwerk with contemporary understandings of the modern computer as a "meta-medium" that unifies all media (text, image, sound, video, and so on) within a single interface. (Dixon, 2007)

The space experiments of Bauhaus architects and the adaptation of the technology of the period to the stage by directors, such as Max Reinhardt, Meyerhold, and Erwin Piscator, are pioneering attempts. Ballet, opera, musical theatre, revue shows, circuses, the development of the art of cinema, and the technological devices on the stage and the screen have entered the service of the stage in line with the periodic political perspectives. For example, Dixon, who defines the period between 1911 and 1959 as multimedia theater, emphasizes that the elements of cinema in musical, cabaret, and opera genres are the technological tool of mise-en-scene in the theatre. Radio theater trials during the war years in Europe and the USA also led to audio live performances.

After the World War II, literature of destruction led to the emergence of absurd and post-absurd theater movements. Although the technological devices brought by modernity are questioned by certain artists from time to time, technological tools have always become an important language of expression in modern show business. After the 1970s, it was widely used for transformative purposes in intercultural theatre, post-dramatic and post-modern theater experiments. After the 2000s, digital revolution virtualized daily life globally, and digital platforms such as Facebook, Instagram, Twitter, YouTube, TikTok, Vimeo, and Daily Motion, have started to compete with television, cinema and theater. In the post-pandemic period, a new phase of artistic production has entered the world, in which digital technologies play a central role.

Although digital artistic productions were seen as a "threat" or "temporal necessity" at the beginning, aesthetic advantages began to be discovered with synchronous, asynchronous and hybrid forms over time. At a time when theaters were closed around the world due to public measures and financial difficulties, some popular theaters began to share the recordings of their shows with the audience for free. However, the prolongation of the pandemic deepening global economic crisis particularly experienced by the freelance artists paved the way for digital productions after a while. For example, famous production companies in England produced their musical projects in parody style based on live digital screenings and started to sell tickets for these shows (live-streamed theater) broadcast on the internet (Charlesworth, 2022).

In the so-called new normal, where thousands of theaters were closed for weeks and there were serious economic losses, theater artists experimented with three types of new performance forms in the digital field to maintain their creative existence:

> The UK Government's "Boundless Creativity Report" (2021), reaches the same conclusion, arguing that: [a]s a consequence, [of lockdown restrictions] digital content production boomed during the pandemic as traditionally physical modes of production shifted in response to restrictions. Digital content production can broadly be categorized into three types:

> • Pre-recorded content being streamed, either through bespoke platforms or existing streaming services;
> • Live intra-media performances making use of new popular technology like Zoom and occasionally including interactive elements;
> • Live streaming entirely new content, either free to view or to paying audiences. (Chatzichristodoulou, Brown, Hunt, Kuling, and Sant, 2022)

In his doctoral dissertation research on digital dramaturgy, Kouratoras (2022) talks about approaches that link interactive video games and theater with the terminology of Aristotle, Antonin Artaud, Jean-Paul Sartre and Augusto Boal. He especially emphasizes the similarity of the cyborg theater concept, which is a post-phenomenological and hybrid concept, to the immersive structure in interactive fictional video games.

Digital Theater Trials and Approaches in the World

With the development of information and internet technology, after the 1980s, we can easily see that new computer and information technology devices are used on the stage in different types of performance arts. Directors in Europe and the USA started to use webcams, computer games, images manipulated by LED televisions, motion capture techniques, animation films, algorithmic light shows, internet-based virtual reality shows, and three-dimensional sets, on the stage (Dixon, 2007). Defining digital theater within the broad set of digital performances, Dixon emphasizes (2007, p. 3) that:

> We define the term "digital performance" broadly to include all performance works where computer technologies play a *key* role rather than a subsidiary one in content, techniques, aesthetics, or delivery forms. This includes live theater, dance, and performance art that incorporates projections that have been digitally created or manipulated; robotic and virtual reality performances; installations and theatrical works that use computer sensing/ activating equipment or telematic techniques; and performative works and activities that are accessed through the computer screen, including cyber theatre events, MUDs, MOOs, and virtual worlds, computer games, CD-ROMs, and performative net.art works. (Dixon, 2007, p. 3)

Masura (2020) emphasizes that digital technologies add imaginative meaning to objects by making elements such as stage design, costumes, decor, lighting and acting fantastic using 3-D technology. She also emphasizes that decor transitions have become easier and more impressive thanks to digital technologies. For example, the head of the Institute for the Exploration of Virtual Realities at the University of Kansas, Prof. Mark Reaney (2010) in his speech; he states that the production of *Kansas' The Magic Flute*, is very experimental in the communication of the actors with digital landscapes on stage. In this show, digital images were created by using seven digital intervention methods (independently moving details, video inserts, instantaneous scene shifts, rotating multiple views of the set, emotive scenery, camera point of view and interactive elements) of the scene design.

In 2003, in the show *Alladeen*[29] directed by Marianne Weems, the space was separated into rooms digitally. At another show named *Wings*[30] audience's use of virtual reality googles, the famous Canadian theater director Robert Lepage's digital multimedia staging of Richard Wagner's Siegfried is important example of the digital theater after the 2000s (Masura, 2020).

It is the synchronicity in the spatial environment of the theater that provides live communication between the audience and the actors on the stage. Digital facilities, simultaneous video-video conversations, and telematic facilities enabled synchronous performance even between players from different countries. Costumes, masks, puppets, robots and the positioning of the actors on the stage are used to create different layers of meaning through digital possibilities. All these digital innovations expand the limits of reality perceived by the audience in the theater building. Masura (2020, p. 43) states that digital theater products have four types of effects on the theater space:

1. **Portability**: Mobile theatre and tools which allow a troupe to perform in a wide variety of buildings and locations;
2. **Site-Specific Performances**: Performances created about and around a specific location, generally not a theater building;
3. **Extended Playing Space**: Multi-site performance which composite two or more geographic locations;
4. **Intelligent Spaces:** Interactive playing spaces which utilize integrated digital technology to partner directly with the actor, giving them agency (Masura, 2020, p. 43)

In a special research conducted by Pascale Aebischer and Rachel Nicolas (2020); the transformation of the digital theater has been comprehensively examined and remarkable outcomes have been presented. The report provides practical examples of the transformation experienced by theater producers in the UK in terms of sectoral, organizational and production style. About digital theater transformation, the report highlights:

- Digital transformation of creative work was facilitated by Creation Theatre's prior experience of site-specific immersive modes of working and the adaptability of the creative team.

- Digital theatre is related to live film and live gaming, with a palette of genres it can draw on and combine, involving various levels of audience participation.
- Digital theatre is much faster to produce than physical theatre and requires fewer core members of backstage creative staff. (Aebischer and Nicolas, 2020)

The steps taken toward the digitalization of the theater gained momentum after the pandemic worldwide. The new tools of the digital scene have brought new possibilities and new creative production forms to the agenda for the artists. However, there is a worldwide debate about transforming both audience habits and the way artists produce.

Digital Theater Trials and Approaches in Turkey

The advent of practical and theoretical innovations in Turkey happened relatively later than western countries. Despite a history of approximately 150 years of practicing Western modern theater, the products of European modernization are experienced by artists with a delay. However, globalization on the base of digital communication offered artists in Turkey the possibility to follow innovations in Europe and the USA more quickly. Particularly, the pandemic period enabled them to take steps similar to foreign examples which are widely revealed as the issue of "forced digitalization."

In this section, I would like to explain the concrete developments experienced in the production of digital theater in Turkey after 2019 from my perspective. In the pre-pandemic period, some of the private and corporate theaters in Turkey could use multimedia tools and some digital tools on stage. Directors of digital theater, who usually are open to innovative experimental works, were inspired by the examples they watched abroad; performances were presented to the audience in new formats.

- In some performances in the "New Text New Theater" project of Galata Perform, which was established in 2003.
- In some performances prepared by the young director Berkun Oya.
- In experimental theater projects in alternative theater venues.
- In the political theater performance of Bosphorus Performing Arts Ensemble (BGST) staging the new version and combination of The Good Soldier of Sveyk and King Ubu, *Historical Encounter of* Sveyk and Ubu.
- In some performances at the İstanbul State Theatre.
- Digitization and the use of multi-media have been applied in the works of artists who have international connections and know languages, such as Kerem Kurdoğlu and Zişan Uğurlu.

However, these attempts, which were made due to both technological inadequacies and audience habits, appealed to very limited audience. Due to the high costs; private, state and municipality theaters have shown reluctance in adopting digital technologies in Turkey (Şeyben, 2016).

In the post-pandemic period, theater artists in Turkey tried to adapt quickly by following some examples in the world regarding the transition to the inevitable digital theater. According to my observation, three types of theatrical performances were produced.

(a) A-synchronous theater as digital recording.
(b) Theater where live performance is watched online simultaneously: Broadcast from the stage.
(c) Synchronous or a-synchronous online theater produced with programs such as Zoom.

After the March 2020, the pandemic severely affected artists economically and psychologically. Most of the actors were temporarily unemployed or without a project because of the closed theaters and performance venues. During the days when there was a curfew in Turkey due to the epidemic, the fact that some famous theaters in Europe exhibited their shows online free of charge created excitement among theater enthusiasts in Turkey. Dozens of shows, which could not be watched due to high ticket prices, were opened to art lovers for a short time. While digital artistic resources were free, it was a positive situation for the audience, while it caused copyright and loss of income problems for art producers.

As the pandemic progressed, the Ministry of Culture and General Directorate of Fine Arts started the Digital Theater Library project and paid royalties to private theaters, albeit in low numbers. Turkey's first private theater TV[31] has become popular. Some important theater festivals, such as the İstanbul Culture Art Foundation (İKSV) Theater Festival, started to include online digital recording plays within the festival.

The display of theatrical productions as videos on online platforms brought up the issues of digital recording quality and lack of technological equipment. The necessity of a good camera, microphone – sound system and light system has emerged to record the live performance in a qualified way. Some private theaters that wanted to increase their competitiveness had to make investments in this regard. In addition, there was a need for a production team who knew editing, editing and camera acting. It turned out that the bond between cinema and theater needed to be strengthened. For example, to close this gap, Google-supported projects were developed. Recording the live screening is also an important task, as Yeşim Özsoy, one of the project team, emphasized below[32]:

> Yeşim Özsoy, the founder of Galata Perform and the vice chairman of the board of directors of the Theater Cooperative, also talked about her experiences of the pandemic and how digital technology has infiltrated our lives. Özsoy said, we actually filmed our own theatre plays for the archive and transferred them to digital over time. But they were for archival and not quality footage that we could offer the audience. Of course, we didn't know exactly how to do it, and we understood that there was a serious need to learn this. (Kolukısa, as interviewer, 2021, Özsoy, as interviewee, 2021)

Those who believe that theater should be presented to the audience with a live performance rather than a recorded image, emphasizing the principle of being here and now, implemented the project of "*Broadcast from The Stage.*" The project transferred from the stage took place at Moda Sahnesi [Theatre], one of the famous alternative theaters in Istanbul. The performances, which were performed live by theater groups at the Moda Sahnesi, but watched online simultaneously by the audience, quickly attracted great interest. While the capacity of the hall was 100 people under normal conditions, hundreds of people watched the online simultaneous live shows by purchasing tickets. However, because the audience was not on the stage in the idea of "Broadcast from The Stage" actors and directors were also in a dilemma as to whether they were making a movie or a theater. For many actors, it was not customary to play without an audience in the theater.

Domestic violence, women's rights, economic crisis, gender and pandemic problems were the main themes of the theater projects in the form of reading theatre, podcasts and short plays produced with Zoom, and WhatsApp programs. Thanks to the chat feature of Zoom or WhatsApp programs, attempts were made to enable the audience's active participation into play. *A Case for Every Day*[33] the project produced by BGST Theater, one of the alternative theater group, on the other hand, *The Voice of K*[34], which deals with the effects of the pandemic in Turkey through seven female characters and is designed as a pod-cast theater, can be shown as qualified examples advocating the equality of different genders. *Ayşegül is at Quarantina*, produced by Cihangir Academy: Quarantina 2020 Video Performance Series[35] is a remarkable project of experimental director Şule Ateş. Also produced by Platform Theater as an international collaboration, directed by Mark Levitas *Map to Utopia*[36] project is an example of innovative digital theater that personally involves the audience in the play thanks to the programs added to the smartphones (Aydoğan and Aydoğan, 2021). Bringing together the art of painting and storytelling in the digital *Painttelling*[37] the project also seems to be a new project where theatre, music and painting arts meet interdisciplinary.

As a result, it is possible to say that digital theater studies, which are avoided due to financial difficulties and lack of information about digital theater in Turkey, gained momentum after the pandemic. Theater actors have made digital experiments to fulfill their economic and artistic needs. However, it should be said that after the decline of the pandemic, the classical face-to-face production method quickly returned. The most important achievement of the process is the partial reduction of time loss and financial losses thanks to digitality.

Conclusion

When the digital theatre is examined with its historical roots, it can be evaluated as an art form that puts digital technologies at its center. Digital technologies are accessible around the world due to the affordable access causes artists to use digitality more as a means of expression on the stage. In the unavoidable digitalization process that came with the pandemic, digitality has increased its impact. Experimental studies have been carried out around the world on how theater as a mimetic art branch based on live performance and active audience communication, can be reproduced with digital tools. In this regard, the pandemic process has been quite instructive for theater artists in the world and Turkey.

From this point of view, the idea of digital theatricality has been formed by the hybrid combination of forms of classical theatricality. A classical theatricality is a story-driven form based on a live performance between the actor and the audience who share a common space. Theatricality, which emerges as a result of a dynamic relationship between the beholder and the beholder, transforms the reality of everyday life with the forms of fictional aesthetics. Digi-theatricality is a new form that transforms the body, space, time and interactivity with digital tools (Dixon, 2007). In the Digi-theatrical process, some digital tools (such as media images, videos, animations, avatars, robots and artificial intelligence) that are alternatives to living players and an interactive association have been formed between the player. However, for these interactions to continue, equal access to technology by creative artists and active participation in digital tools and context are necessary to understand the world (Masura, 2020). When the researches in the field are examined, the questions waiting to be solved, especially at the point of defining digital theatricality, have been identified as follows:

- Does recording and filming of the theater damage its live performative feature?
- What are the main differences between the theater scene and the digital scene?
- How will the digital space supported by avatars, holograms and VR affect the future of theatre? (Diaconita, 2022).

- How critical performativity and design thinking affects the democratizing of digitality? (MacKinze, 2017).

Discussions about the solution to the above discussed problems continue among art theorists and academicians. As it is known, every crisis period is also a period in which new opportunities arise. If digital theatricality is to truly be the avant-garde art of our age, it must have a post-humanist understanding that has a word to say in life, makes the audience interpret life and develops an aesthetic perspective from the past to the present. Digital aesthetics apparently will continue to evolve as a part of theater as long as humanity needs more insight about life with its transforming and unchanging aspects.

Notes

29 Visit: https://vimeo.com/338484922 [Accessed on Sept., 4. 2022].

30 Visit: https://www.youtube.com/watch?v=hKkHi7-noJQ [Accessed on Sept., 4. 2022].

31 Visit: https://tiyatrolar.tv [Accessed on Sept., 4. 2022].

32 Translation is mine. This interview was published at the newspaper *Cumhuriyet*. Retrieved from https://www.cumhuriyet.com.tr/kultur-sanat/dijital-sahneye-dogru-1881476 [Accessed on Sept., 4. 2022].

33 Visit: https://www.youtube.com/watch?v=lRQmqJUozWM&t=2s [Accessed on Sept., 4. 2022].

34 Visit: https://www.youtube.com/watch?v=1yUmBuwFuJw&t=6s [Accessed on Sept., 4. 2022].

35 Visit: https://www.youtube.com/watch?v=zPHDJdX6pOY&t=71s [Accessed on Sept., 4. 2022].

36 For more information, please visit the project's original website (https://maptoutopia.com/map-to-utopia-eng/)

37 Visit: https://paintelling.org/ [Accessed on Sept., 4. 2022].

References

Aebischer, P., & Nicholas R. (2020). *Digital theatre transformation: A case study and digital toolkit*. [Final report]. October. The University of Exeter. Retrieved from https://ore.exeter.ac.uk/repository/handle/10871/123464 [Accessed on Sept., 5. 2022].

Aydoğan, D., & Aydoğan, Ö. (2021). A general overview of theater and digital initiatives of private theatres in İstanbul during Pandemic. *ODU Journal of Social Sciences Research, 3*(11): 951–964.

Blake, B. (2014). *Theatre and digital*. London: Bloomsbury Publishing.

Brockett, O. (1982). *History of the theatre*. Boston: Allyn and Bacon Publishing.

Charlesworth, H. L. (2022). Nightmare time and a case study for digital theatre during the COVID-19 Pandemic. *Networking Knowledge, 15*(1), YouTube and Online Video in Lockdown Special Issue.

Chatzichristodoulou, M., Brown, K., Hunt, N., Kuling, P., & Sant, T. (2022). Covid-19: Theatre goes digital – provocations. *International Journal of Performance Arts and Digital Media, 18*(1): 1-6.

Diaconita, A. (2022). On the verge of a new fusion: Theatre space – digital space. *Theatrical Colloquıa*. DOI: 10.35218/tco.2022.12.1.20.

Dixon, S. (2007). *Digital performance: A history of new media in theater, dance, performance art, and installation*. Cambridge: The MIT Press.

Kolukısa, E. (2021). (Interviewer). Özsoy, Y. (Interviewee). Dijital sahneye doğru. [Towards the digital stage]. *Cumhuriyet*. Retrieved from https://www.cumhuriyet.com.tr/kultur-sanat/dijital-sahneye-dogru-1881476 [Accessed on Sept., 5. 2022].

Kouratoras, M. (2022). *Digital dramaturgy – interactive fiction video games as cyborg theatre of cruelty and ethical choice-making*. Aalto University publication series Dissertations. Helsinki. Retrieved from http://urn.fi/URN:ISBN:978-952-64-0705-0 [Accessed on Sept., 3. 2022].

MacKinze, J. (2017). Performance and democratizing digitality: StudioLab as critical design pedagogy. In M. Leeker, I. Schipper, & T. Beyes (Eds.), *Performing the digital performativity and performance studies in digital cultures* (p. 247). Verlag, Bielefeld: Transcript.

Masura, N. (2020). *Digital theatre: The making and meaning of live mediated performance, US & UK 1990-2020*. London: Palgrave MacMillan.

Reaney, M. (1995). Virtual reality on stage. Appeared in *VR World*, May/June 3: 28–31.

Reaney, M. (2010). Virtual reality and the theatre: Immersion in virtual worlds. *Digital Creativity, 10*(3): 183–188.

Şeyben, B. Y. (2016). *Tiyatro ve multimedya*. [Theatre *and multimedia*]. İstanbul: Habitus Publishing.

İsmet Aydın

A Meta Independent of Time and Space: New Music Trends in Digitized World

Abstract: Thinking of music only as a sound element means ignoring many aspects of the cultural dimension of human life. The evolution of music as a phenomenon in terms of a human communication form reached a tipping point in the 20th and 21st centuries. As a result of new outcomes emerging from its interaction with society, music, which is gradually becoming a form independent of time and space, can present new practices to the history of humanity that we cannot anticipate in the next century. The music phenomenon with all of its humane and artificial aspects which evolved from the hybrid use of analog and digital sound combinations is moving to the future way of musical expressions. Thinking of this phenomenon regarding its commodification through mass and now digital media offers new question marks for researchers and enthusiasts from different backgrounds. In this chapter, the breaking points of the Turkish music ecosystem within changing musical cultures shaped by different technological eras are examined. By following a discourse analysis, arising music trends are examined in relation to changing practices offered by digital technologies.

Keywords: New Music Trends, Digitized World, Music Ecosystem, Time and Space

Recording Audio: Initial Changes in Time and Space

A journey towards music history would present Thomas Edison's phonograph as a milestone since it offered the ability to record and listen remotely in 1877. According to Attali (2014), music, like all other human activities, was strongly attached to religious practices as a sensitive and ambiguous art form throughout history. While the music was initially performed in the context of social activities, its composition and consumption had been a part of the inner world of the individual listening to it. As Pierre Schafer's statement that "music is the definition of man in the language of objects" shows, this has been an essential issue for many philosophers throughout the history. In other words, music is more than the parts of which it is composed, it is embedded in any human activity, individually or socially.

With the invention of the gramophone, music, which was normally performed to a limited audience in a fixed venue or concert hall, gained the opportunity to meet larger audience. It would not be wrong to assume that humans as social beings are keen on consuming music as an experience of social interaction, sharing its rational and emotional effects with the community consuming in the same place and time as in the concerts. However, the effect of music listened to on any digital platform on the same person is quite independent and different compared to those consumed in a concert hall. This difference is worth to understand in order to gain an insight on the complex structure of human mind.

Changes in the concepts of time and space have gone through various breaking processes throughout history. The perception of time and space shifted away from God and toward man from the Middle Ages to the Renaissance (Şeyben, 2009, p. 100). This process is closely linked to the shift of perspective in painting. The enlightenment age deepened the questioning of time and space thanks to scientific developments and technology. In the 20th century, art passed through individualistic experiences of the artist rather than following approved methods (Cage, 2012, p. 85). In other words, science and art created a shift from a homogeneous way of understanding time and space towards a customized version of it. According to Jameson (1994), spatial categories began to dominate time categories on the one hand, but they change so rapidly that it is impossible to keep up with. Indeed, the pandemic emphasized the inevitability of this shift in favor of space and its facilitation through technology.

The beginnings of the professional concert tradition in history are known as the events organized in London in 1672 by the English composer and violinist John Banister, and date back to the late 17th and early 18th centuries (Cesur, 2021, p. 298) The evolution of performing music in changing spatial atmospheres and capacities was followed by the recording industry which gave the audience the chance to listen to it at any time and space. As a situation that could not be imagined before, it presented today's musical re-culturation phenomenon in a unique way. This way of consuming music encountered the old and the new, and multiple musical styles, which are subject to great changes in the context of time and space, and which are shaped in parallel with the spirit of different periods of society. According to Ersoy (2021, p. 318), there is a close relationship between music and space, and they are "symbiotic" which means "the vital dependence of two elements on each other for their existence." Music's interaction with space has changed, but it may still be impossible to imagine music that is completely independent of space. The relationship of music to time is an ontological debate in and of itself. Music's independence from time can be defined as its freedom in the time zone in terms of the timing of its production and consumption.

The concept of justification (*Rechtfertigung*) is one of the most important concepts developed by the Frankfurt school (Dellaloğlu, 2014, p. 43). Frankfurt School thinkers argue that all established discourses of truth are not absolute, but rather justified. The motion of a bouncing ball in a moving train is observed differently by two different people, one inside the train and one outside the train, according to Einstein's theory of relativity. This is due to the fact that these two observers are in different coordinates. As a result, this theory has primarily been applied to social fields. When all of the behaviors revealed by music in this process of change and transformation are evaluated objectively from this perspective, accurate process analysis is possible. Examining a dynamic phenomenon like music from a variety of perspectives may result in more accurate results. According to Einstein, the evaluation of concepts based on different dynamics emerges as a fact of relativity.

According to Dellaloğlu (2014), art's autonomy is disrupted by the development of capitalism as it commodified art in marketplaces. Accordingly, music's plays a commercial role in social life; and its value is its market value. This mighty reification, which established music as an art in the first place has today taken music out of people's hands and left only its consumed appearance (Adorno, 2019, pp. 48–49). Moreover, the music phenomenon has lost many of its functional properties and meaning at the point it has reached today. However, it is hard to evaluate its gains or losses in the light of the romantic theory of the artwork which focuses on its form (Benjamin, quoted from Dellaloğlu, 2013). The early romantics equated the limiting nature of form with the limits of all reflection, and they determined the concept of the work of art on the basis of their worldview within this framework. The rapid changes stemming from technological developments today faces with such prejudices and defy to such perceptions of music as an art.

Music Commodified in the Consumer Society

According to Herbert Marcuse (1997), consumer society and culture create false needs that force people to buy consumption-based lifestyles. Marcuse contends that the happier the modern individual is, the more resolutely he/she supports the power of the established socioeconomic system (Coşgun, 2012, p. 846). Music is a part of such ideologies not only in Western capitalist systems but also Islamic culture as well with all its mobilizing power as well as the aesthetic-artistic satisfaction it offers to individuals (Tatar and Aydın, 2017, p. 5). These commercial and ideological instrumentalization of music reached its peak after the recording technologies. For example, a folk song composed in a rural life may transcend its authentic time and place and become an instrument of the masses to experience their realities. This situation makes it essential to reconsider the ontological meanings of music. According to Attali (2014), innovations like the gramophone announced that humans would be replaced by machines and that everything would be copied in series; recording technology was the forerunner of consumer society. In his book, "*From Noise to Music*," Attali (2014) discusses the relationship between music and power throughout history in a critical and interpretive manner, from the beginning of time to the present.

Music has formed an open market in the 19th century. Even as a minor component of capitalism, it has exemplified today's information economy and entertainment society with its profit-oriented market structure. Since then, it has taken the attention of many economic theorists who are curious about how music generates value (Attali, 2014, p. 79). This transformation of music has resulted in changes in performance practices and production styles. According to Adorno (2019), the ability of music to be separate and independent from social reality is under threat every day. If non-market-oriented music today is not music that most can comprehend and enjoy, it would be wrong to claim that this type of music is objectively reactionary. Music, like theory, should be able to aim beyond the masses' existing levels of consciousness (Jay, 1989, p. 264)

The Conflict of Music Cultures and Technology in Turkey: First Records

Between 1887 and 1889, the gramophone and music records were commercially released and well-received by the Turkish audience especially based in Istanbul. From the early 1900s to the early 1960s, companies based in the United States and Europe dominated the Turkish music market. These companies are Odeon, founded in Germany in 1904 and active in Turkey since 1906; His Master's Voice, founded in England in 1897 and active in Turkey since 1924; Columbia, founded in the United States in 1890; and Pathe14, founded in France in 1894. They have sometimes established a market monopoly (Ünlü, 2004, p. 49).

Tanburi Cemil Bey, one of the most impactful musicians in Turkish music history, is one of the early-owners of such record companies in Turkey. (Karabey, 1999, p. 169) Still, he complains that recording music destroys the performance and its uniqueness. There are interviews showing that Tanburi Cemil Bey was not happy with the widespread use of his records sold in the market, and after a while, he stopped recording music despite very appealing offers (Akçura, 1990). Cemil Bey's approach exemplifies how the traditional perception of music conflicted with the market demand for commodified music and changing way of its consumption. Given that the first music genres recorded in Turkey were canto, fantasy, ghazal, songs, and even religious music, it is reasonable to believe that the music industry invests in genres that are expected to be commercially successful or whose success is desired to be measured. All of these developments and innovations, music genres that are performed in local areas and thus enable the common acculturation of a limited audience, have nearly rebuilt the ecosystem that interacts with time and space by listening to wider audiences, other cultures, or regions other than its geography.

American Cultural Hegemony: Fusion Music Trends in Turkey in the 1950s and After

Concerts and music programs were generally held in concert halls, casinos, schools, restaurants, coffee shops, squares, and parks, as well as mansions and houses, during the early years of the Republic in the 1920s. However, the origin of regular broadcasts of Istanbul Radio on May 6, 1927 provided this limited audience with access to all types of music programs such as Alaturka (classical Turkish music), Alafranga (Western music), folk music, and jazz throughout the country (Deniz, 2019, p. 813). It is possible that radio has started a transformation in the concept of time and space. After the start of radio broadcasts in Turkey, jazz or classical music can be heard all over Anatolia, while a black sea song can only be heard in an Aegean village.

Following the World War II, the international economy was restructured under the leadership of the United States of America, the country with the dominating economy of Western capitalism. With its economic power, the United States actively participated in the reconstruction of their economies by providing financial aid to the war-damaged European economies. Turkey, a capitalist country, has been included in the scope of American aid (Kılıç Akoğlan, and Ruben, 2021, p. 49). Accordingly, the spread of socialism was prevented and a new international market for American products were created (Dikmen, 2015, p. 169). Thus, American cultural goods were supplied highly as the masses became more and more keen on Americanization.

In the early 1960s, when the first Turkish pop experiments were made as the "Arrangement music" (also known as the "light music with Turkish lyrics"), songs made by world-famous singers and groups such as Elvis Presley and The Beatles began to be played and sung on the stage by various Turkish bands. These songs arranged in blues, cha-cha or twist genres became and dominated for decades the music industry in Turkey. The song "*Bak Bir Varmış Bir Yokmuş*," written by Fecri Ebcioğlu and performed by İlhami Gencer has been the first example of that type of music (Erdoğan, 2019, p. 26). It is possible to argue that this cultural interaction has offered the possibility to mix different time and space belonging to a different culture by the use of technology without experiencing the same historical and political processes which gave birth to this genre in the West.

The 1960s has been the scene of many global social movements. This decade witnessed years of struggles for civil rights, racial equality, social justice and the impact of all of these events on music (Herzhaft, 2005, p. 100). These social upheavals have affected music production and consumption in Turkey as well in terms of cultural originality. Traditional music used new recording technologies as a utilitarian-industrial response to that global context with a tendency to glorify current local culture. Thus, the pursuit of originality with the search of new sound, content and material aimed to reach more audience through a common music culture (Aydın, 2018, p. 69). Such efforts point to situations increasing the communication between the old and the new, global and local, blurring the lines between these contrasts with the use of technological advances. In the fusion music style known as Anadolu Pop, which emerged in that decade, for example, electronic sounds and a traditional instrument can be used in the same music. It is important to remember that these now-commonplace practices were novel at the time. Bringing the old and the new together, the concepts of time and space have evolved significantly, particularly since the 1950s.

Uniformity of Music Preferences as the World of Sound Grows

Advantageous situations such as recording sound, accessibility to music, its variety, global circulation and market demand did not necessarily increase the artistic quality. Music is sold as a commodity in the market, the artistic value of music is bound to supply and demand rates in the economy. Composer, whose knowledge of the world of sound and music culture he has expanded, does not necessarily have easy access to large audiences when he makes new experiments or productions with artistic concerns that are not common or easily consumed. As a result, can it be argued that technological advancements and the digital world have a greater impact on music consumption than on music production? And can it be said that this consumption has not spread to a musical culture as diverse as the diversity of the sound world, which the digital world makes accessible?

Aside from that, the contribution of current developments, particularly information technologies, to the music production and creation phases continues to expand. For example, he created approximately 11.000 recombined compositions with the software he named EMI, which was the result of algorithmic work on Bach's chorales by American composer David Cope in 1983. Cope claims that, in addition to the techniques used by the composer to imitate EMI, such as fugue and counterpoint, the composer also used key figures that reminded him of himself (Sağıroğlu and Türkmen, 2017, p. 63). It is well known that such works can be applied to a wide range of musical styles whose algorithms are derived through style analysis. However, despite the fact that artificial intelligence-based musical productions can create many technical layers of music by mastering information such as stylistic knowledge and structural features of music, debates about whether it is a work of art continue.

There is a long history of examples of converting given information about the structural features of music into production through chance-based re-editing. For example, the game introduced in the book "*The Dice Game*" published in 1757 by Johann Kirnberger, a student of Johann Sebastian Bach, was also very popular during the Classical Period (Sağıroğlu and Türkmen, 2017, p. 68). The game is basically defined as the use of the next indicator among the previously determined melodic measures as a result of rolling one or two dice, as in random music practice.

Consumption of Music in the Digital World

Neil Postman (2013) emphasizes the importance of technology in people's daily lives, he also highlights that after the introduction of a technology into a culture, it plays its own role and fulfills the needs of that specific era while also transforming it. From a similar lense, music creation and consumption has changed with the technology of the new age (Oğuz, 2016, p. 45).

According to Oğuz's (2016) research, 150 (75%) of participants prefer to consume digital music "While Traveling Outside" on digital platforms. This study is significant since it shows the tendency for a fast, mobile and dynamic life of the youth. The fast access and role of complimenting the experienced background have pushed the fast consumption as well. Here, the state of reculturation, which is formed by the continuity of musical styles as an outcome of the articulation of some musical cultures over the years, gained importance (Aydın, 2022). In other words, music becomes the medium o the interaction of the past, present and the future through digital technologies. For example, in Turkey, the transformation of arabesque music can be seen as the emergence of new interpretations and performances by distinguishing some sensory features within other music styles such as pop, rock, and so on. This situation could be interpreted as the result of a strategy of remarketing commercially successful music styles within the market with different appearances or innovations.

Discussion and Conclusion

Several research has shown that the concepts of time and space have evolved significantly since the Renaissance. Comparability of scenarios related to the concepts of time and space with the past has become exceptionally hard, particularly in the digital age. The transformation of the music towards rapid access, VST instruments, production with artificial intelligence, increase in quantity and quality in different aspects through digitalization brought about such hardships. Both authentic hybrid fusion versions of popular songs are attracting a lot of attention today and this can be seen as an incline to revive the traditional music in the form of modern times, thus the transcending temporal barriers in a digital age. As a result of the blurriness of the distinction between the old and the new, classical music produced earlier in time may be perceived as modern by the consumer, whereas a folk song composed more recently may be perceived as older music. Therefore, with digitalization, can it be assumed that the phenomenon of music has become a commodity independent of time and space? How would it be a correct approach to attribute all of this effect to digitalization in this study, in which we also emphasize the standardization of the quality or artistic characteristics of music, whose production and consumption are accelerated? Although digital technologies still in progress draw attention to such questions, their effects of today's consumption culture cannot be denied. Its challenges to artistic depth, authenticity and originality due to commodification are worth to discuss in the light of future technological developments.

References

Adorno, W. T. (2019). *Müzik yazıları* [*Music articles*]. (Ş. Öztürk, Trans.). İstanbul: YKY Publishing.

Akçura, G. (1990). Gramofon çağı [Gramophone age]. *Güneş* Newspaper. August, 1990.

Attali, J. (2014). *Gürültüden müziğe* [*From noise to music*]. (G. Türkmen, Trans.). İstanbul: Ayrıntı Publishing.

Aydın, İ. (2018). *Türkiye'deki caz müziği pratiklerinde folklorik öğeler: Geleneksel Anadolu müzik kültürlerinden devşirilenlerden konvansiyonel stratejiler ekseninde icat edilenlere yerellikler ve temsiliyetler* [*Folkloreic element in jazz music practices in Turkey: Localities and representations of inventions gathered from traditional Anatolian music culture within conventional strategies*]. Master Thesis. Bahçeşehir University. İstanbul.

Aydın, İ. (2022). Reculturation in music ecosystem: Digital music villages in Turkey. In T. Tetik, B. Sezgin, & Ö. Vatanartıran (Eds.), *Transformation of the industry in a brand new normal: Media, music, and performing arts*. (pp. 141–160). Berlin: Peter Lang.

Cage, J. (2012). *Seçme yazılar* [*Featured articles*]. (S. Fırıncıoğlu, Trans.). İstanbul: Pan Publishing.

Çavdaroğlu, S. Z. (2009). *Türkiye'nin ses kayıt tarihine bir bakış* [*A look at Turkey's audio recording history*]. Retrieved from http://www.musikidergisi.net/?p=859 [Accessed on Sept., 15. 2022].

Cesur, Ö. (2021). Konser geleneğinde yeni boyut: Dijital konserlerde mekan ve seyirci [A new dimension in concert tradition: Space and audience in digital concerts]. *Afyon Kocatepe University Journal of Academic Music Research*, *7*(14): 298–315.

Coşgun, M. (2012). Popüler kültür ve tüketim toplumu [Popular culture and consumer society]. *Batman University Journal of Life Sciences*, *1*(1): 837–850.

Dellaloğlu, B. F. (2013). *Benjamin*. İstanbul: Say Publishing.

Dellaloğlu, B. F. (2014). *Frankfurt Okulu'nda sanat ve toplum* [*Art and society at Frankfurt School*]. İstanbul: Say Publishing.

Deniz, Ü. (2019). Konser salonlarindan radyo stüdyosuna (1927): Cumhuriyet döneminin ilk Türk Musikisi radyo sanatçıları ve ilk radyo konserleri [From concert halls to radio studio (1927): The first Turkish music radio artists of the Republican period and the first radio concerts]. *Motif Academy Journal of Folklore*, *12*(27): 813–832.

Dikmen, A. A. (2015). *Makine, iş, kapitalizm ve insan* [*Machine, work, capitalism, and man*]. (Third edition). Ankara: Nota Bene Publishing.

Erdoğan, G. (2019). Türk popüler müzik tarihinde Bariş Mançoʼnun yeri ve önemi (1960-1980) [The place and importance of Barış Manço in the history of Turkish popular music (1960-1980)]. *Ağrı İbrahim Çeçen University Journal of Social Sciences Institute*, *5*(1): 105–116.

Ersoy, İ. (2021). Simbiyotik bir ilişki: Kültürel bir alan olarak mekan ve müzik [A symbiotic relationship: Space and music as a cultural space]. *Alternatif Politika*, *13*(1): 318–350.

Herzhaft, G. (2005). *Blues* (First edition). (İ. Yerguz, Trans.). İstanbul: Dost Bookstore Publications.

Jameson, F. (1994). *Postmodernizm* [*Postmodernism*]. (N. Plümer, Trans.). İstanbul: YKY Publishing.

Karabey, M. M. (1999). *Müzik piyasasının yüz yılı: Cumhuriyet'in sesleri* [*One hundred years of the music market: Voices of the Republic*]. N: 69. İstanbul: History Foundation Publications.

Kılıç Akoğlan, N., & Ruben, E. (2021). Amerikan hegemonyasının Türkiye'de modernleşme ve kalkınma söylemlerine yansımaları: 1945-1960 [Reflections of American hegemony on modernization and development discourses in Turkey: 1924-1960]. *Journal of Management, Economics, Literature, Islamic and Political Sciences*, *6*(1): 49–73.

Marcuse, H. (1997). *Tek boyutlu insan* [*One dimensional human*]. (A. Yardımlı, Trans.). İstanbul: İdea Publishing.

Jay, M. (1989) *Diyalektik imgelem*. [*Dialectical imagination*]. (Ü. Oskay, Trans.). İstanbul: Ara Publishing.

Oğuz, T. (2016). Dijital müzik tüketim alışkanlıkları [Digital music consumption habits]. *Kurgu*, *24*(1): 44–62.

Postman, N. (2013). *Teknopoli: Kültürün teknolojiye teslim oluşu*. [*Technopoli: The surrender of culture to technology*]. (M. E. Yılmaz, Trans.). Ankara: Sentez Publishing.

Sağıroğlu, T., & Türkmen, E. H. (2017). *Teknolojik gelişmeler bağlamında müzik yaratım süreci ve yapay zeka kullanimi: David Cope örneği* [*Music creation process and use of artificial intelligence in the context of technological developments: The case of David Cope*]. In 8th International Hisarlı Ahmet Symposium. May, 12-14. Kütahya, Turkey.

Şeyben, B. Y. (2009). Görsel sanatta zaman ve mekan parametreleri ve sitüasyonist estetik [Time and space parameters in visual art and situationist aesthetics]. *Akdeniz Sanat*, *2*(4): 0–0.

Tatar, B., & Aydın, S. (2017). Müzik ve iktidar ilişkisi: Kuramsal ve tarihsel bir analiz [The relationship between music and power: A theoretical and historical analysis]. *Journal of On Dokuz Mayıs University Faculty of Theology*, 43:5–30.

Ünlü, C. (2004). Gel zaman git zaman [*Come time, go time*]. İstanbul: Pan Publishing.

Özgecan Karadağlı Kuntz

Comforting the Unfamiliar: Audience Development and Digital Transformation in Classical Music

Abstract: In dialogue with Pierre Boulez in "*Contemporary Music and the Public*," Michel Foucault said that "I have the impression that many of the elements that are supposed to provide access to music actually impoverish our relationship with it" (Foucault and Boulez, 1985, p. 8). In this regard, the current period of digital transformations presents many questions around technology's applications to and integrations with music. It is not that technology as an entity is new; what are new are the mediums and the effects. Does the technology help to attract and increase new audiences and how? What do we lose and gain? Is it worth it? We assume that the new generations need and desire classical music to be in some sense "upgraded" and made more palatable, more approachable through including other digital arts-but do they? Does it possibly reinforce the stereotypes of music and thus limit the hearing? In seeking to address these questions, this chapter offers that while digital transformation engagement with music may widen and/or deepen the audience for classical music, attempts at *audience development* may also, as Foucault states, "impoverish" us in some ways. Considering aspects of comfort, familiarity, and accessibility, we reflect on whether in trying to make classical music an event to attract new audiences we are in fact altering and cheapening the experience.

Keywords: Classical Music, Audience Development, Culture Industry, Comfort, Digital Transformation

Introduction

Technology in music is not something novel; in fact, music, maybe more than most areas, has engaged technology quickly in almost every possible aspect: development, design, and advancement of the instruments, such as the ancient bone flutes to the modern flute, the lyre to the harp, the harpsichord to the piano; performing, staging, or changing tuning systems, recording from phonograph to digital, dissemination, from oral to manuscripts to published sheet music to streaming. It is almost impossible to eliminate technology from music. Today, there are many different uses of digital technology. For instance, using iPads instead of sheet music, and with the help of a Bluetooth foot pedal for page turner, musicians do not need to worry about taping their sheet music together anymore, projectors are used for the opera sets and backdrops.

Such contemporary life dynamics are, obviously, quite different than a century ago, so are our relationships with music, and different genres of music, and our expectations of it. In the last few decades, classical music in particular has faced certain criticism that its audience, according to Kramer (1995, pp. 3–4), is "shrinking, greying, and overly palefaced....it squanders its capacities for self-renewal by clinging to an exceptionally static core repertoire." Kramer is not the only one who expresses these sentiments. Such observations and complaints highlight the concern about the decreasing numbers in the classical music audience. To map the issue, in 1986 The Arts Council of Great Britain conducted a survey, which echoes Kramer's statement, concluding the audience is mostly white middle aged, middle class (Maitland, 2000).

In order to address this concern and secure the future of classical music institutions, the art managers have made several attempts to attract a new generation of professionals who are digitally native, the millennials. The main "theoretical discourse" on the issue is *Audience Development*. This concept is a marketing approach aiming to grow (and keep them from dying) the business in a variety of, particularly old technology, sectors. However, with Michel Foucault we might ask whether "elements that are supposed to provide access to music actually impoverish our relationship with it" (Foucault and Boulez, 1985, p. 8). In this regard, the current period of digital transformations presents many questions around technology's applications to and integrations with music. Does the technology help to attract and increase new audiences and how? What do we lose and gain? We assume that the new generations need and desire classical music to be in some sense "upgraded" and made more palatable, more approachable through including other digital arts -but do they? In seeking to address these questions, this chapter offers that while digital transformations engagement with music may widen and/or deepen the audience for classical music, attempts at audience development and the tangential effects may also, as Foucault states (Foucault and Boulez, 1985, p. 8), "impoverish" us in some ways. Considering aspects of comfort and familiarity, we reflect on whether in trying to make classical music an event to attract new audiences we are in fact altering and cheapening the experience.

Audience Development and Comfort

According to the main advocate/theorist of the *Audience Development* concept, Heather Maitland, in her central source text titled *A Guide to Audience Development*, this is a "planned process which involves building a relationship between an individual and the arts" (Maitland, 2000, p. 6). This "process" requires a goal-oriented strategy and long term organizational planning. She suggests, "projects only work if they are part of a long term strategy for audience development which is developed jointly by the artistic, education and marketing functions of an organization" (ibid.). Because the process of "audience development.... enhances and broadens specific individuals' experience of the arts" (Maitland, 2000, p. 5), individuals' experiences become one of the focal points, since the concerts offer an experience rather than a product.

The model suggests the subjects who participate in these art organizations or events, such as concerts, are the consumers or the customers (or the potential consumers who have no interest, or for some reason have never experienced any live classical music concert before) and as such demand that these events be made more "comfortable," "inclusive," and "accessible" (Sigurjonsson, 2010, p. 266). These key words are important for the audience developers and marketers, but because both being inclusive and accessible are somewhat self-explanatory, I would like to focus on the idea of comfort. According to Maitland (2000, p. 10), because the arts institutions want to "improve" the experience for both the regulars and completely new attenders, we should change the conventions of these art forms so "more people...feel comfortable." Another important contribution on the topic was Tim Baker's *Stop Re-Inventing the Wheel* (2000), where Baker discusses the main reasons why people do not want to attend live classical music concerts; he suggests there are many people who do not attend such concerts even though they are interested in classical music. But if they are interested in the genre of the music, then why are they not attending? He argues that high cost is not the reason why people are not going but "the 'value' of concerts" as the potential audience does not want to "'risk' in investing in scarce sources...especially time" (2000, p. 49).

In this setting, the concept of supposed comfort is little tricky to define. If we look at the standard dictionary definition, comfort is being in a state of absence of pain and/or after experience something sad, or worried, feeling better (Oxford Languages and Google). In this case, obviously the second case is more relevant and another concept plays a role: familiarity. An audience member's degree of familiarity with all aspects of the experience-the physical nature of the concert setting, what to do during the concert, what to expect, and how to react-leads to comfort or discomfort. The familiar and familiarity are important aspects of our comfort, even at the subconscious level. Even our ancient gods resembled us in some way-they were familiar. Later on, our God created us in his own image; thus, we can argue that the familiar has its roots in the divine(s).

But even the divine has a dark side and there is always a possibility of being punished. The punishment of over familiarity is the sacrifice of the unfamiliar;

in our context, thus, an even stronger commitment to the familiar mass culture products is created. Foucault argues that familiarity with music produces mere marginality; and he warns us of the "everydayness of this relationship." Because it can create a "paradoxical effect of rigidifying tradition," and Boulez emphasizes the effect of the unfamiliarity on the new listeners as: "all novelty bruises the sensibilities of those unaccustomed to it" (Foucault and Boulez, 1985, pp. 9–10). Nevertheless, Adorno (2001), as one might expect, has some strong criticism on musical familiarity and rejection of the unfamiliar:

> [N]eurotic mechanism of stupidity in listening too, the arrogantly ignorant rejection of everything unfamiliar is its sure sign. Regressive listeners behave like children. Again and again and with stubborn malice, they demand the one dish they have once been served…the infantile hearing always demands the most comfortable and fluent resolutions. (Adorno, p. 51)

Because of the mechanisms of the culture industry, we could argue that most familiarity is forced on people because of the constant exposure. One of the problems of over familiarity is, according to Katz (2010, p. 30), that it could solidify a particular interpretation "even mistakes" and the possibility of the perception of *the interpretation* as the "work itself." On the other hand, one should accept that familiarity has a reassuring element. Maybe it makes sense that the generation of the existing classical music audience was familiarized to most popular classical tunes from the old generation of cartoons, from Looney Tunes to the Pink Panther, almost a warm memory from childhood.

Digital Transformations / Applications in Classical Music

Even though different marketers and Developers offer slightly different approaches, the above mentioned concepts—"comfortable," "inclusive," and "accessible"—are the core ideas for almost all efforts. The concept of comfort, or discomfort more likely, as frequently argued, comes sometimes from unexpected factors of a concert, such as the formal rituals of classical music. Because classical music concerts have established etiquette, outsiders may feel uncomfortable. Such dis-comforting factors might include wearing a tie, clapping only during certain parts of the performance, or even the "fancy" design of the concert halls. As a solution, and to provide *comfort*, Kotler and Scheff offered programs for the Sacramento Symphony such as "Jeans and Beer," a low ticket price event that took place in an old movie theatre, with artists and listeners wearing blue jeans, the availability of non-disturbing snacks, and complimentary beer with the orchestra members after the concert (p. 515; Sigurjonsson, 2010, p. 267; Frantz,

2015, p. 11). Another similar (series of) event(s) was "Mocha and Mozart," with a coffee company sponsoring the event providing free coffee, with the added "accessibility" features of casual clothing, "unceremonious lecture(s)," low ticket prices, and free children's tickets during the Sunday afternoon for subscribers (p. 515; Sigurjonsson, 2010, p. 267). The idea of free children tickets seems a strong future investment approach as there is the possibility to create a future habit or familiarity of attending classical music concerts, similar to reading books to your child from a very early age generating positive association. There is always the possibility that when they hit puberty, children may reject this family activity; but there is also the possibility they will eventually find their way (back) to the realm of the familiar.

In their marketing management book titled "*Standing Room Only? Strategies for Marketing the Performing Arts*," Phillip Kotler and Joanne Scheff (1997, p. 514) argued that the musicians (of the Sacramento Symphony) had learned that they needed professional management and a "popular new music director;" "a great performance" of a great composer (Beethoven symphony, for instance) is not sufficient anymore to attract an audience. The authors show how the idea of new programming helped the "rebirth" of the Sacramento Symphony (ibid.). The new approach included being more "inclusive" as their new mission involved being in the service of the whole community (ibid.), so they developed programs celebrating diverse ethnic backgrounds, such as the World-View Music Festival. The festival was a success, but it could be argued that they sold tickets to *ethnic music* concerts and did not succeed in making more people appreciate classical music; it was familiar music with unfamiliar instrumentation/orchestration maybe.

Almost all of these ideas and approaches require "organizational change" from small to big (Kotler and Scheff, 1997, p. 537; Sigurjonsson, 2010, p. 268). The main idea suggests that the traditional settings and norms of the classical music concerts should change: "Arts organizations must continually change to retain their effectiveness. They must change their internal structures, their way of doing business, sometimes even their mission" (Kotler and Scheff, 1997, p. 537). From the fancy concert venue to being required to be silent, to the dress code, and obviously to the repertoire, everything should change under this new regime.

To fulfill the desire of nostalgia (and also financial goals) of the good old days of the classical music and to attract our first digitally native generation, the millennials, the managers, and the orchestra administrators assumed that a digital revolution in classical music might provide an attractive feature. As the millennials are strongly attached to their smart phones and fully engaged with social media, to not be *connected* during a concert might cause a major discomfort for some. When we add the anxiety of what to expect or what to listen to during the concert to the equation, providing variety of digital tools during a concert seems a no-brainer. Even though the prototypes were developed in the early 2000s, some digital devices were developed and been used during the last 10–15 years. The app "Concert Companion" ("CoCo") was sponsored by the Kansas City Symphony and provided the program notes during the concerts to the app users in real time (Frantz, 2015). It delivered a constant flow of information every 30 seconds to the PDA (personal digital assistant) devices. The flow started before the concert and continued even after and let the newcomers know what to listen to (Child, 2003). As a result, the possible barrier of not having the relevant knowledge and the anxiety because of that is mitigated.

In order to understand the potential of the *Concert Companion*, Fred Child, a classical music radio host and musician, had the experience to test-drive one of these PDAs of the Concert Companion during Beethoven's Fifth Symphony in the summer Aspen Music Festival in 2003. Along with general information of the music and the composer, Child states that the device received texts such as "with the unlikely combination of cellos doubled by violas, a songful, long-breathed melody unfolds over plucked string basses" (Child, 2003). The creator of the Concert Companion and the former executive director of the Kansas City Symphony Roland Valliere stated that the device was like a museum audio guide and the main goal is "to attract new listeners to come and attend concerts" (Child, 2003). I do not know how helpful and successful was this *innovation*; using technology and providing this *extra help*, in theory, to make music a little more approachable, provides the vague notion of *comfort*, and even maybe it makes people feel more part of the community as they know something about the piece like a seasoned listener. The digital aspect of comfort was the aim of these tools. This so-called comfort is provided by information, even though sometimes this information does not mean much without a basic music education, it still delivers the promised comfort.

The museum audio guide analogy is well-loved among the authors and directors because of its convenience, but its analogic value has questionable applicability here, as museums mostly do not offer exhibitions of temporal arts[38], and the specific criteria of a temporal art does not and cannot be ascribed to most artefacts: music is intrinsically one of the purest temporal or time arts. As Levinson put it, "objects of the art form require time in presentation, that is, they require performance or exposition of some sort over an interval of time; the parts of the artwork are not all available at any one moment, but only consecutively" (Levinson, 2015, p. 159). It is fair to ask why we should consider about the temporality of music. We do so not only to highlight the problematic nature of the PDAs analogy but also to show why it is problematic to use such technology during temporal, linear, and unidirectional art forms. Since it is not possible to re-experience the live music, as the person who uses the PDAs is distracted every 30 seconds for the sake of feeling comfortable, s/he cannot even fully experience a live concert. We are sacrificing the aesthetic value of the music, for the sake of assumed so called comfort.

Even though the new listeners might not fully put their finger on what the problem is of getting all the information simultaneously with the music, one of the issues is they are switching auditory modes back and forth. While they continue to hear the music when they receive an info text, unfortunately they will not be able to *listen* to the music. This constant interruption creates a paradox. Using this constant "feeding information source" regularly interrupts the process (of listening). The brain choses written stimulus over aural because it is slower in processing time (Kemp, 1973). The music the arts directors are trying to market and increase the audience for, drops immediately to the level of background music. Because of the intrinsic nature of classical music, it requires your full attention, particularly when you are not familiar with the genre and the pieces.

A similar application/attempt was the "tweet-cert," a part of attracting a greater audience, organized by the Pacific Symphony during their outdoor concert. The listeners were encouraged to use their smartphones and their Tweeter accounts to receive tweets from the orchestra members before and after the concerts (so people would know what is going on backstage) and the audience discussed the performance during the concerts (Berger, 2011). As the audience becomes the consumers/customers under such applications, they have been given the power of hierarchical observation. It is an almost *Foucaultesque* gaze or a digital *Panopticon*[39] gaze that allows the audience to observe the orchestra members not only during the concert but before and after the event as well.

One effect of this "tweet-cert" gazing is suggested by a tweet offering a description of Saint-Saens' *Carnival of the Animals*: "The 'kangaroo-hopping' effect you hear is accomplished musically via the use of grace notes: small quick notes added just before each beat" and another one out of 300 total tweets was "enjoying the moon rising behind the amphitheater… What a beautiful night!" The 29-year-old tweeter user who wrote the latter tweet stated that "for me personally it was kind of distracting because even though the music was really good, I just wanted to see what other people had written…Every 15 minutes I was checking to see who had posted what" (Berger, 2011). Millennials are particularly attached to their smartphones and social media, but we assume they want to engage even more and while the music directors are trying to attract them they are unintentionally depriving them of having an aesthetic experience. You do not have to be a purist to wonder if all millennials want to do is be connected and tweeting all evening long, why on earth would they do it in such a confined and stiff environment where there is still the possibility a baby boomer or Gen Xer might shush or chide them? It almost weirdly feels like telling them to "*pay the price of the ticket and do whatever you want to do, play on your phone or something, we don't care.*" And, of course, developers and the managers seem unconcerned that a glowing phone screen might cause any distraction to the musicians; they will have to deal with it—it is *audience development* in progress. Another use of the now ubiquitous mobile phone was the creation of an orchestra and music making. There was a repertoire-based orchestra called *The Mobile Phone Orchestra* (MoPhO) that literally only uses mobile phones as their "primary musical instrument" (Wang, Essl, and Pentinnen, 2014, p. 453) The group rationalizes the use of phones, stating that "like traditional acoustic instruments, mobile phones are intimate sound producing devices" (ibid.). Similar to the new generation version of the laptop orchestra that was established in 2009, MoPhO was founded in 2007 at Stanford University's Center for Computer Research in Music and Acoustics (CCRMA) and had more than a dozen players and phones. As the first ensemble, they were the model for similar ensembles in Berlin, Helsinki, and at the University of Michigan. The group has an impressive performance history in Genoa, Belfast, Helsinki, San Francisco, and Berlin. The group wanted to show the music making possibilities of mobile phones. The programmers and the composers of the group were hoping this initiative would open doors to an alternative pedagogy and aesthetics. Even though neither MoPhO players nor their programmers claimed that they were making a new generation of *classical music*, the ensemble idea is based on the concept of a chamber orchestra with a conductor and hierarchy of a chamber group structure. We might even claim that they are not making regular contemporary art music but very niche academic digital music.

Of course the digital use in classical music is not limited to these applications and devices, some of which are already forgotten like using google glasses with an app provides the audience the supertitles or PDAs. But there are other uses of digitalization helping classical music to widen its audience, with the most important one probably being the dissemination of classical music digitally. Even the most hard-core purists could not resist using it. Composer Pierre Boulez in his dialogue with Michael Foucault warned us against being acquainted with music "through recordings," because, on the contrary to the belief that the recordings could and would open new musical horizons to people, actually they rigidify both the listeners and the performers, as in over familiarization (p. 7). In a similar vein, Walter Benjamin talks about the loss of the "aura" of an art form, which resonates on the recordings of music: "even the most perfect reproduction of a work of art is lacking in one element: its presence in time and space, its unique existence at the place where it happens to be" (Benjamin, 1985, p. 222). Even though there is a great truth in that, the technology of recording music has already completely changed not only the music but our relationship to it. Currently, it is almost impossible to not digest the majority of our musical experiences through either physical recordings or their digital substitutes. Katz has a great observation on the issue, with his words "music is now a technologically mediated experience" (2010, p. 31). Such technology has altered our modalities of listening in ways that were unimaginable even 50 years ago—just visualize listening to your favorite Spotify playlist from your iPhone while taking a subway or jogging.

One can ask why we are discussing already obsolete technology. Are there not any newer applications? Of course there are, but these are the recurring ideas and were important as they were labeled as the promising progressive initiatives; it is also important to understand why they were destined to fail. All these innovations functioned as quick fixes and did not integrate because any of these fixes developed spontaneously. Just because we spoon fed people with these ideas, it does not necessarily make them miraculously start listening to or liking classical music. Maybe people unconsciously feel the turning wheels of the "culture industry" as it "fuses the old familiar into a new quality" and "manipulated for reasons of marketability" (Adorno, 2001, pp. 35–98). Surprisingly, here, *the old familiar* is not the music but the new technology people have been using.

But technology has been affecting the ways we listen to music since the invention of the phonograph; capturing and being able to record music altered also the relationship between people and music. Particularly with the digital recording culture, a once communal activity turned into a private and isolated experience. A great example of the communal nature of music is provided by Katz quoting novelist Orlo Williams, who wonders what might be the result if one would be caught while listening to music by oneself:

> You would think it odd, would you not? You would endeavor to dissemble your surprise: you would look twice to see whether some other person were not hidden in some corner of the room, and if you found no such one would be painfully blush, as if you had discovered your friend sniffing cocaine, emptying a bottle of whiskey, or plaiting straws in his hair. People, we think, should not do things "to themselves," however much they may enjoy doing them in company: they may not even talk to themselves with our incurring grave suspicion. And I fear that if I were discovered listening to [Beethoven's] Fifth Symphony without a chaperon to guarantee me sanity, my friends would fall away with grievous shaking of the head. (Williams, 1923 in Katz, 2010, p. 20)

It is fascinating to read Williams' account on the possibility and to think about how our thousands of years' relationship with music has dramatically changed within a couple of generations. Now, people listening to their music with headphones, separating them from the rest of the world, is a normal scene.

Because of this transformation, the modes of listening and the relationship between temporality and space have been immensely altered, permanently, for the new generations. Because of this shift, today the majority of the music audience prefers digitalized music, in an almost analogous fashion to those who prefer the shadows on the cave wall to the real thing in Plato's Cave analogy. Rather than listening to live acoustical music, they desire the shadows created by digitization. It is not only negative though, sometimes the solitary listening allows us not to get distracted by the idiosyncratic ticks or behaviors of the performer.

As the recording technology has such a significant impact on our relationship with music, it requires brief consideration. Since we have been able to capture the musical sound and keep it in an object, the most significant features became its tangibility, portability, and repeatability[40] (Katz, 2010, p. 13). As music through recordings became objects, one can even carry a big symphonic orchestra in your pocket and replay the desired part of the music over and over. As part of the "rigidifying" effect, Katz explains the "phonograph effect" as "observable manifestations of recording's influence," where the standardized music did not facilitate the hoped "diversification" (2010, pp. 2–16). Even though the new generation of digitized music became less tangible, it affected our relationship with music as this property made music also a tactile experience and resulted in the "stockpiling of music" (Attali, 1985, p. 101), and made us collectors of cassettes, LPs, or CDs. This kind of "love" towards the collected object caused some to have quite negative feelings towards the small MP3 players, even though they had a huge storage potential, as it limited the relationship with music to almost only a sonic one. The repeatability comes with both good and bad properties: while it caused the standardization of many musics, a *phonograph effect*, it also allowed musicians to observe their own performances and enabled them to develop themselves.

Arguably, using digital platforms to disseminate classical music, probably unexpectedly, is more successful than trying to desperately integrate most apps and social media in a live classical music concert; needless to say, I am totally excluding the administrative aspects of digital technologies such as buying online tickets and finding season concert schedules. Today these technologies are a must for art institutions. Finding a way to convince the targeted generation to *buy* the experience of a live classical music instead of listening to a recording of popular music is a real challenge and probably we are not going to able to do it without the help of one form or another of digital technology, whether old CDs or steaming music. We hope, eventually, they will appreciate the differences between recorded and live music.

One recent attempt brings together these aspects of digital platforms and the tensions and possibilities of bridging recorded and live music. During the worst days of the COVID pandemic in Turkey, a senior internationally acclaimed pianist, Gülsin Onay, decided to share her music through social media: she organized her own digital concert in the middle of a shut-down. She managed to reach tens of thousands of people; some of the audience were from rural and remote areas and had never had a chance to even be in a city where a concert was taking place. As a consequence of having a social media concert in the manner she chose, Onay's endeavors, whether financially beneficial or not, were a good investment as she widened her audience. Now, people (young musicians/teenagers) are flocking to her summer festival and masterclasses, suggesting that overall it was not for nothing. Regardless of Boulez's warning, the digital dissemination in being able to reach masses and using the power of social media helps classical music in these anxious times.

Unfortunately, aside all the discussions on how digitization affects the music, our relationship with music, and its aesthetics, there is still the problem of the perceived value of classical music. That is why, instead of having any considerations on developing aesthetics, the Developers and the arts institutions' managers focus on the brand development and increasing the economic value of classical music (Baker, 2000; Sigurjonsson, 2010; Foucault and Boulez, 1985). Although Boulez reminds us, regardless who is paying attention, "there are musics which bring in money and exist for commercial profit; there are musics that cost something, whose very concept has nothing to do with profit" (p. 8). All of the expectations of the "exchange value" of classical music commodifies it and changes its function as Adorno points out, therefore we are losing the "use value" (p. 39).

Conclusion

Eventually all these attempts are going to change the artistic landscape. Classical music, unlike popular genres, is not as profitable for the producers; the majority of the repertoire has changed very little, with only interpretations by different conductors and orchestras. If we really believe that music carries the spirit of the time, we should not be so worried about the fact that the new generation does not want to listen to classical music and prefer Beyoncé to Brahms. That is why I question whether the whole "let's listen to Beethoven with jeans and beer" type of events can "save" classical music. Even with the help of all the digital apps and other technology, if classical music can reach the level of expected commercial success this approach seems to almost humiliate the millennials and their expectations are reduced to the level of a young child's expectations, where the main concerns when they are going out anywhere is if they can eat something and querying what it might be. One really wonders if millennials have no aesthetic expectations or concerns. If only dressing casually and snacking during the concerts would solve the issue, let's do all of it and get it over with.

During the conversation and debates over how we can help classical music and attract more audience members, the focus is usually solely on the numbers or it discusses the issue of identity politics but insistently ignores the musical aesthetics or aesthetic philosophy. On the one hand, it is true that contemporary cultural environment forces some orchestras to file for bankruptcy; on the other hand, thousands of young students still attend the auditions of the music departments and conservatories and want to pursue music as their future career.

Regardless, digitization has and will change the situation of classical music, both recorded and live. The nostalgia that classical music can be perceived, listened to, produced, and consumed as in the good old days (whenever they were for you and however you define them) while understandable harkens down the wrong path. We might better ask the following: How is aging going to change the millennials' aesthetic expectations or temporality, space, and comfort? One hopes that mere entertainment will no longer satisfy them. As we tend to cycle everything, perhaps one-day classical music will become desirable, not in an elitist way but more in an expressive way and almost like a *retro-new* soundscape providing its audience comfort. What we do with technology, and technology itself, is not always linear. Who knows if, similar to the popularity of the LP technology generations after its replacement, there can be a classical music revival and cycling back to the real cutting edge technology of the acoustics and acoustical sound, something that is familiar in its unfamiliar newness, attracts a growing audience, (maybe even pays for itself) and ultimately offers the comfort and challenge at the core of music itself.

Notes

38 According to Levinson, very few indoor installations could be temporal.
39 The idea of the Panopticon belongs to Jeremy Bentham.
40 Katz adds to the list: (in)visibility, temporality, receptivity, manipulability.

References

Adorno, T. W. (2001). *The culture industry: Selected essays on mass culture*. (J. M. Bernstein, Ed., & J. M. Bernstein, Trans.). London and New York: Routledge.

Attali, J. (1985). *Noise: The political economy of music*. (B. Massumi, Trans.) Minneapolis: University of Minnesota Press.

Baker, T. (2000). *Stop re-inventing the wheel: A guide to what we already know about developing audiences for classical music*. London: Association of British Orchestras.

Benjamin, W. (1985). The work of art in the age of mechanical reproduction. In W. Benjamin & H. Arendt (Eds.). *Illuminations*. (H. Zohn, Trans., pp. 217–252). New York: Harcourt Brace Jovanovich, Inc.

Berger, K. (2011). Classical music waltzes with digital media. *Los Angeles Times*. Retrieved from https://www.latimes.com/entertainment/music/la-xpm-2011-aug-07-la-ca-classical-technology-20110807-story.html [Accessed on Sept., 15. 2022].

Child, F. (2003, September 30). A digital companion for concert fans. *NPR*. Retrieved from https://www.npr.org/2003/09/30/1434167/a-digital-companion-for-concert-fans [Accessed on Sept., 15. 2022].

Foucault, M., & Boulez, P. (1985). Contemporary music and the public. *Perspectives of New Music*, *24*(Fall): 6–12.

Frantz, E. L. (2015). *Is technology the way forward for classical music? Exploring audience engagement in the digital era*. [B. A. Thesis]. Ohio: The Ohio State University.

Johnson, J. (2002). *Who needs classical music?: Cultural choice and musical value*. Oxford and New York: Oxford University Press.

Katz, M. (2010). *Capturing sound: How technology has changed music*. Berkeley: University of California Press.

Kemp, B. J. (1973). Reaction time of young and elderly subjects in relation to perceptual deprivation and signal-on versus signal-off condition. *Developmental Psychology*, *8*(2): 268–272.

Kolb, B. M. (2001). The effect of generational change on classical music concert attendance and orchestras' responses in the UK and US. *Cultural Trends*, *11*(41): 1–35.

Kotler, P., & Scheff, J. (1997). *Standing room only? Strategies for marketing the performing arts*. Boston: Harvard Business School Press.

Levinson, J. (2015). *Musical concerns: Essays in philosophy of music*. Oxford: Oxford University Press.

Maitland, H. (2000). A *guide to audience development.* London: Arts Council of England.

Oxford Languages and Google. (n.d.). Oxford University Press. Retrieved from https://www.google.com/search?q=define+comfort&rlz=1C1GCEA_enTR978TR979&oq=define+comfo&aqs=chrome.1.69i57j0i512j0i10l2j0i512l3j0i10j0i512l2.8247j1j7&sourceid=chrome&ie=UTF-8 [Accessed on Sept., 15. 2022].

Sigurjonsson, N. (2010). Orchestra audience development and the aesthetics of "customer comfort." *The Journal of Arts Management, Law, and Society*, 40: 266–278.

Wang, G., Essl, G., & Pentinnen, H. (2014). The mobile phone orchestra. In S. Gopinath & J. Stanyek (Eds.), *Oxford handbook of mobile music studies* (Second edition, pp. 453–469). Online Edn: Oxford University Press.

Williams, O. (1923). Times and seasons. *Gramaphone I*, 38–39.

List of Tables

List of Figures

Biographies of the Authors

(In Alphabetical Order)

Bülent Sezgin received his doctoral degree from the Ankara State University theatre program. He is an associate professor in the Faculty of Conservatory at Bahçeşehir University. He has directed theatre plays and wrote original texts that are related to alternative theatre projects. His research interests are game-based learning, drama in education, the Stanislavski system, alternative theatre, curriculum development, and art education. He is currently teaching several courses on theatre theory and history, drama in education, and art education.

Çisil Sohodol (Ph.D.) has been working as a professor for 16 years in Public Relations Department in the Faculty of Communication at Bahçeşehir University. She received her bachelor's, master's, and Ph.D. degrees on Public Relations at Ege University. Her research focuses on crisis communication, CSR, sustainability and ESG. Sohodol is also an editor and translator of several books, and sectoral reports in the field of communication. She is director of the Centre for Social Impact and Responsibility at Bahçeşehir University.

Ece Arıhan (Ph.D.) is a lecturer in the Faculty of Communication at Bahçeşehir University. She earned her doctoral degree at Bahçeşehir University in Cinema and Media Research. She has written and directed her own short animation film called '*Never After*,' which has won international awards. In addition, she has animated shots for various short animation films which have been screened at international animation festivals and have won awards. Her interests include animated films, games, women's studies, gender, and feminist film theory.

Dilay Özgüven Tetik earned her doctoral degree at Bahçeşehir University, Cinema and Media Research Ph.D. program with her thesis titled "*The Uniqueness of Müge Anlı ile Tatlı Sert in Turkish Crime-Based Reality Programs: The Analysis of the Format's Evolution*." Özgüven Tetik has work experience in painting, illustration, video, and photography. She received her M.A. degree at Sabancı University and has experience in movies as the first assistant director. Her research interests are reality television, crime, memory studies, and game theory.

Hakan Erkılıç completed his undergraduate study at Anadolu University Film and TV Department in 1994. He got his master's degree from Anadolu University in 1997. He performed his competence in art in Mimar Sinan University Film-TV field in 2003. He became an assistant professor in 2004 and an associate professor in 2018. He has been working in Mersin University since 2004. His field of study involves Turkish cinema, cinema and ideology, mode of production/economic structure of cinema, digital cinema and documentary. He has articles and papers about these subjects in various journals and books. He is the General Director of Atıf Yılmaz Short Film Festival (Mersin/Turkey). He conducted a project titled "COVID-19 Pandemic and Crises of Turkish Film Industry," which was founded by TUBITAK (The Scientific and Technological Research Council of Turkey). He is currently working on a project titled "Film Festivals in Turkey: Structure, Economy, Organization and Audience Profile (Case Study of the Film Festivals of Antalya, Adana, İstanbul, and Ankara)," which is founded by TUBITAK.

Hasan Kemal Suher is a professor in the Advertising Department and the Dean of the Faculty of Communication at Bahçeşehir University. He received his Ph.D. in Advertising and Public Relations from Anadolu University. He is currently teaching several undergraduate courses on media planning, research in advertising, advertising campaign, and graduate courses on historical and social research, mass communication theories and research. He has edited many inter/national books. His research interests include creative industries, new trends in communication education, and data analysis with SPSS. He continues his researches at national and international levels.

Hüseyin Kutay Tinç, Ph.D., started his academic career in 2005 in the Industrial Engineering department of İstanbul Technical University. After mainly focusing on mathematical modelling and game theory subjects, he started teaching in Game and Interaction Technologies master's program in 2019. He's currently teaching game design, probability and game theory courses and researching game balance optimization.

İdil Karademirlidağ Suher (Ph.D.) is a professor and head of the Public Relations Department at Bahçeşehir University since 2006. She received her bachelor's, master's, and Ph.D. degrees in public relations and communication from Anadolu University. Suher teaches both graduate and undergraduate courses on public relations management and strategy, and internal communication. She gives seminars about persuasive communication. Besides her academic studies, she has contributed to the field by being involved in several sectoral research projects. Suher is a board member of Turkish Football Federation.

İsmet Aydın is a lecturer in Bahçeşehir University Conservatory. He is Ph.D.(c) in the Music and Performing Arts Program at Yıldız Technical University. His interest in traditional Anatolian music started at an early age. He took his undergraduate degree in vocal & opera studies at İstanbul University State Conservatory and his master's degree in jazz theory and composition at Bahçeşehir University. As the solo singer of the world music band MESEL, he performed on the world's major stages, like the Royal Albert Hall, and participated in international music festivals. He participated in various musical projects by bringing an up-to-date approach to the traditional Anatolian vocal performance with his influential interpretation of Turkish folk songs and his aesthetic approach to the use of folkloric material.

Murat Durusoy is an İstanbul-based artist, photographer, and academic. He has a B. A. degree in Manufacturing Systems Engineering and M.A. in Visual Arts/Visual Communication Design from Sabancı University, Turkey. He is currently pursuing a Ph.D. degree in Cinema and Media Research at Bahçeşehir University. He is currently Deputy Head of the Visual Communications Department at Bahçeşehir University. His research interest revolves around virtual photography, lens-based imagery, game worlds, virtual worlds, and media art studies.

Nilüfer Geysi (Ph.D.) has been working in the Faculty of Communication at Bahçeşehir University since 2016. She has completed her undergraduate degree in Public Relations and Advertising, and her master's degree in Marketing Communication and Public Relations at İzmir University of Economics. She has a Ph.D. in Advertising and Public Relations program at Bahçeşehir University. Geysi's academic interests include corporate culture, digital media, sustainability, and climate change communication.

Nisa Yıldırım had B.A. degree in Computer Science and M.A. degree in New Media from Kadir Has University. She began her professional career as a CGI artist in post-production, continued as a producer in television and executive editor in leading Turkish cinema websites. She had Ph.D. degree in Cinema and Media Research from Bahçeşehir University, with her thesis on 'post-television era in Turkey.' Currently, she works as an assistant professor in Radio, Television and Cinema Department at İstanbul Gelişim University. She continues to write research articles -mostly based on 'the evolution of fictional narratives in the digital era,' besides novels and screenplays.

Ömer Vatanartıran has a B.A. in Communication and a Ph.D. in Organization Studies. He is an assistant professor of the Faculty of Communication as well as the Conservatory at Bahçeşehir University. He is a multi-dimensional communicator: TV Presenter; university lecturer in theater, ethics, media and communications; experienced voice-over artist, specialized in commercials, movies and animations; and theater actor with international experience.

Özgecan Karadağlı Kuntz, receiving her Ph.D. in Music from the University of Alberta, is an interdisciplinary researcher, specializing in music and nationalism, Western art music during the nineteenth-century Ottoman Empire and the early Republic of Turkey in the construction of a national identity and of cultural politics. She has taught Aural and Keyboard Skills and Music Theory at the University of Alberta and is currently teaching as an assistant professor at Bahçeşehir University Conservatory in İstanbul.

Servet Can Dönmez was born in Adana in 1985. After graduating from Adana Communication Vocational High School in 2003 and Atatürk University Communication Faculty, Radio, TV and Cinema Department in 2008, he started to work as a research assistant at Mersin University Faculty of Communication in 2013. In 2016, he completed his master's degree from Mersin University Social Sciences Institute, Radio, Cinema and Television department. He is still continuing his doctorate education at Mersin University Institute of Social Sciences, Radio, Cinema and Television department. His study topics include virtual reality, augmented reality, digital narrative, digital cinema, new media titles.

Sırrı Serhat Serter received his doctoral degree with his dissertation titled "*Style in Film: The Cinema of Lütfi Ömer Akad*" at Anadolu University, Cinema and Television program, and has been working as an associate professor at the same department since 2017. He teaches scrip-writing, history of film, film style, TV production, mythology as bachelor's degree and Turkish cinema & modern cinema as graduate degree. He has been the festival director of Eskişehir International Film Festival since the beginning (1998). He directed two short documentary films screened at several international film festivals in 2016. Besides, he published two books as an editor about Contemporary Turkish Cinema and Star Wars Movies in 2016. In addition, the second & expanded edition of his book about Star Wars Movies was published in January 2018.

Şafak Şahin graduated from Anadolu University, Public Relations and Advertising Department. Şahin has completed his master's program in Advertising Brand Management at Bahçeşehir University. He completed his Ph.D. thesis titled "*Personality Features, Creative Thinking Processes and Advertising Creativity Relation*" at Bahçeşehir University, Department of Advertising and Public Relations. He was a sales manager at Boyner Holding. He is an assistant professor and lectures on advertising, text writing, and creative communication in the Advertising Department. He is the director of Bahçeşehir University, Center of Creative Industries, BAUKEM.

Tolga Ovatman completed his undergraduate education in Hacettepe University Computer Engineering Department in 2003 and moved to İstanbul to continue his graduate education at İstanbul Technical University department of Computer Engineering. After receiving his MSc degree, he continued his Ph.D. education in the same department and started working on model-based software parallelization for multicore systems under supervision of Dr. Feza Buzluca. During his PhD study he has worked on formal methods and model checking as a visiting researcher at Denmark Technical University and studied parallelizing class diagrams at U.S. Missouri University of Science and Technology. In 2011, he has delivered his dissertation and started working as a lecturer in İTÜ Faculty of Computer and Informatics. He was later recruited as an assistant professor in the same faculty on April 2012. He was awarded with associate professor degree by YÖK [CHE] on December 2017.

Tuna Tetik is an assistant professor in the Film and Television Department and the Vice Dean of the Faculty of Communication at Bahçeşehir University. He received his doctoral degree at Bahçeşehir University, Cinema and Media Research Ph.D. program, and directed short films and a documentary that received international awards. His research interests are superheroes and comics, transmedia, film genres, video-on-demand services, and video games. He has five books, including *Multidisciplinary Perspectives on Narrative Aesthetics in Video Games* (2021, Co-Editor), *New Communication in the Post-Pandemic Era* (2021, Co-Editor), *Transformation of the Industry in a Brand New Normal* (2022, Co-Editor), *Marvelous Rise of Superheroes in Cinema* (2022, Author), and *Turkish Cinema and Television Industry in the Digital Streaming Era* (2022, Co-Editor). Tetik is currently teaching several undergraduate courses on digital editing and film production, and graduate courses on screenwriting.

Volkan Hacıtahiroğulları got his Bachelor's Degree in Computer Engineering. He continued on to get his Master's Degree in Game and Interaction Technologies at İstanbul Technical University. Throughout his education he was a part of multiple engineering student clubs' administrative boards (inc: IEEE) and was the president of İTU Game Design and Development Club for a year, where he was previously in charge of the management of the clubs' educational workshops. During his master's education, he worked as a game designer for Nowhere Studios in the indie game project Circadian City, as well as giving game design and documentation workshops. He has been a research assistant for the Digital Game Design Department of Bahçeşehir University since February 2020. Research topics include; game design, role playing games, player engagement, game mechanic design, flow.

www.ingramcontent.com/pod-product-compliance
Ingram Content Group UK Ltd.
Pitfield, Milton Keynes, MK11 3LW, UK
UKHW020710041026
15590UKWH00002B/582

9 783631 888490